A PLAIN
SAILORMAN IN CHINA

A PLAIN
SAILORMAN IN CHINA

The Life and Times of Cdr. I. V. Gillis, USN • 1875–1948

Bruce Swanson with

Vance H. Morrison, Don H. McDowell, and Nancy N. Tomasko

Naval Institute Press
Annapolis, Maryland

Naval Institute Press
291 Wood Road
Annapolis, MD 21402

Library of Congress Cataloging-in-Publication Data
Swanson, Bruce, 1937–
  A plain sailorman in China the life and times of Cdr. I. V. Gillis, USN, 1875–1948 / Bruce Swanson ; with Vance H. Morrison, Don H. McDowell, and Nancy Norton Tomasko.
    p. cm.
  Includes bibliographical references and index.
  ISBN 978-1-61251-105-4 (hbk. : alk. paper) 1. Gillis, I. V. (Irvin Van Gorder), 1875–1948. 2. United States. Navy—Officers—Biography. 3. Military attachés—United States—Biography. 4. United States—Military relations—China. 5. China—Military relations—United States. I. Morrison, Vance H. II. McDowell, Don H. III. Tomasko, Nancy Norton, 1947– IV. Title.
  V63.G53S93 2012
  359.0092--dc23
  [B]

                                                                  2011051955

♾ This paper meets the requirements of ANSI/NISO z39.48-1992 (Permanence of Paper).
Printed in the United States of America.

20 19 18 17 16 15 14 13 12   9 8 7 6 5 4 3 2 1
First printing

TO THE LATE BRUCE SWANSON, HIS WIFE, ROSEANN,

AND THEIR CHILDREN,

ERIN, MEGHAN, SHANNON, AND BRUCE

CONTENTS

ILLUSTRATIONS

MAPS

PREFACE

Bruce Swanson loved working on the story of Irvin Van Gorder Gillis, and, when he visited us in Washington on several occasions while he was performing research there for the book, he was always animated and excited as he discussed Gillis and his exploits. In the late fall of 2007 Bruce fell terminally ill. Shortly before his passing he called a very surprised and saddened Vance Morrison and asked him to complete this book. Vance, a former career naval officer and U.S. naval attaché to China—as was the book's subject, I. V. Gillis—was, according to Bruce, a logical choice. Vance quickly asked Rear Admiral Don McDowell, Bruce and Vance's immediate superior in Japan in the 1960s, to assist in this endeavor.

Bruce's reasons for writing the book were best described by Bruce himself when he wrote an e-mail to a relative of I. V. Gillis, Mrs. Bonnie Gillis Waters, in January 2006. It read in part as follows:

> I come to this from a purely academic view and am not a rela-
> tive [of Gillis]. First, let me give you some background on who I
> am. I retired from the U.S. Navy in 1982 and spent much of that
> time in intelligence as a China specialist. In 1982 I had a book
> published [*Eighth Voyage of the Dragon* (Naval Institute Press)]
> that is a history of China's struggle to develop into a maritime/
> naval power. One of the most fascinating periods was that from
> 1894 to about 1930. During the course of my research I discov-
> ered that Irvin [Gillis] had been the first naval attaché to China in
> about 1907—a position he held again from 1911 to 1919 when
> he retired. While I did not treat him in a lot of detail at that
> time, I did not forget either and decided that at some point later
> I would come back and revisit his life in China. (I had to first
> work for a living and get my children raised and educated before
> I could do this). Last year I determined that the time was right
> and promptly discovered the other half of I. V.'s life—that being
> his collection of priceless Chinese books residing at Princeton

University. I visited there and found his almost 20 years of private correspondence for this period of his life.

Bruce went on in some detail about specific discoveries and missing information he sought in his initial research, but we think that this e-mail sets the stage well for his efforts.

When we began to tackle our task, Bruce's text was written entirely in hand on yellow legal pad paper because, by his own admission, he was not a typist. His widow, RoseAnn, who understandably was eager to have the book completed, had the manuscript typed. We collected that computer-generated text—with all its typographical and substantive challenges—along with much of Bruce's collected research materials and associated notes and created a draft, printable text. Bruce often had several versions of a passage, and we selected the passage we thought was best in each case, hoping it would be the one Bruce would have wanted. For the final chapter, Bruce had written virtually no text. He had assembled a substantial amount of research material, mostly of letters exchanged between Gillis and Dr. Nancy Lee Swann, some of which Bruce had already collected and some of which are located in the East Asian Library at Princeton University. We added to that with the help of Dr. Nancy Norton Tomasko, at the time the editor of the *East Asian Library Journal* at Princeton and our colleague in completing this book. We liberally used material from a published article by Dr. Martin J. Heijdra, also at the East Asian Library. The final chapter, then, is our summary of Gillis' activities in China during the 1920s, 1930s, and 1940s, until his death in 1948. We think we are close to what Bruce desired for that final chapter.

Except for the first chapter, there were no footnotes; researching those as well as preparing the final chapter have been our biggest challenges. Such footnotes and bibliography that we have assembled to the best of our ability, working essentially "backward" from the normal process, are provided, recognizing that we could not possibly have covered them all. As a result, we apologize in advance for any errors of omission that we feel certain must exist. The wording is as close to Bruce's original work as we could make it and still have a readable text, with necessary changes and transitional passages injected where needed for clarity. We also introduced some new, footnoted material as a result of performing research to develop the footnotes for the original as well as in preparing the last chapter. It has been our objective to produce a printable book about this admittedly fascinating "plain sailorman" (he was anything but!).

We want to express our appreciation for the invaluable assistance and encouragement provided by Dr. Tomasko, who worked with Bruce, edited and published the first chapter of this narrative in the autumn 2009 *East Asian Library Journal*, and provided invaluable advice, not only earlier to Bruce, but also to us in the latter stages of the book's preparation; Martin Heijdra, at Princeton University's East Asian Library, who provided valuable and unique information on I. V. Gillis' life after his Navy career; Elizabeth Bancroft, AFIO executive secretary, for her continuing technical help, advice, and constant encouragement; Dr. William Dudley, former historian of the Navy and mentor in the early stages of the publishing process; Janis Jorgensen, photo archivist at the U.S. Naval Institute, for her extensive research and assistance with ship photos and artwork; Christopher Robinson for his professional crafting of our maps; Tom Cutler, our patient, understanding, and encouraging editor at Naval Institute Press; Jim Gullickson, our extraordinary copy editor who amazingly transformed the manuscript into a book; and, especially, Irvin Gillis' relatives, including Bonnie Gillis Waters, David Murray, Carol Murray Gates, and Martha Gates Mawson, for their interest, contributions, and patience.

We also want to thank our wives, Helen McDowell and Libby Morrison, for their extraordinary indulgence, encouragement, research efforts, and editorial assistance.

Finally, this book is dedicated to the late Bruce Swanson and, as we are certain Bruce would have done, also to his wife, RoseAnn, and their children, whose love and support enabled this work to be accomplished.

Vance H. Morrison   *Don H. McDowell*

AUGUST 2011

INTRODUCTION

Among that devoted group of China scholars and research specialists who are familiar with Princeton University's Seeley G. Mudd Library, it is well known that a collection resides there of rare Chinese books totaling more than 100,000 volumes. About 42,000 items of that total have been described as "collector's pieces." Known as the Gest Collection, taken from the name of its patron and founder, Mr. Guion Gest, the compilation indeed represents a collector's library that the eminent Dr. Hu Shih, curator of the collection from 1950 to 1952, labeled as "unique, priceless and, so far, matchless among all Chinese collections outside of China and Japan."

This extraordinary assemblage of rare Chinese imperialist books was the direct result of a collaboration of three disparate individuals who, over ten years and each possessing a special genius and resourcefulness, shaped the collection into the masterpiece that it is today. Much has been written about Mr. Gest himself, the Canadian engineer who suffered terribly from debilitating glaucoma. Though not a rich man, he time and time again managed to scrape together the necessary funds required to purchase the books. Likewise, much is known about Dr. Nancy Lee Swann. A Texas native, she was the administrator of the collection from 1928 to 1948 and, perhaps, the first American woman to be awarded a PhD in Chinese history. It was through her diligence and sense of devotion that the Gest Collection took form and became cataloged, first at McGill University and then at Princeton University.

The third individual was Irvin Van Gorder Gillis, a retired U.S. Navy officer and expatriate residing in Peking. Of this triumvirate, Gillis was the most interesting, for it was he who had the most challenging role and upon whom the success of the endeavor squarely fell: It was left up to him to locate books. In the latter chapter of his biography, much of the emphasis is given to his ability to identify and then acquire the collection of rare Chinese books; verify their authenticity; arrange their purchase (very often from a prominent Chinese who was down on his luck); and, finally, arrange safe shipment under sometimes trying conditions—in the midst of a highly charged time of war and political turmoil. It was not a job for the squeamish.

Of the three principals mentioned, Gillis has remained the most enigmatic. It is the purpose and focus of this work, then, to examine more closely the enigmatic figure of Irvin Gillis. Whenever his name comes up, it gives rise to several interesting questions. First, what was in his background that gave him the skill and nerve to carry out the operation? Second, what event(s) led to his being in the right place at the right time? Third, at a time when Chinese antiquities were being threatened with wanton destruction or traded like commodities for profit, what moved Gillis to want to see them preserved? A nearly complete record of his official military files was found in U.S. naval archives. In it are his career history and correspondence that cover nearly three decades of naval service, from 1890 to 1919. It also reveals much about Gillis as a person and, largely, explains how he became the right man at the right place at the right time.

The thrust of this work has been twofold. First, I have attempted to complete the record on Commander Gillis through examination of his Navy career. It is an odyssey that keeps him at sea for more than ten years, encompassing duty on board five battleships, a cruiser, a monitor, a gunboat, and a torpedo boat. It was a period filled with adventure, challenge, and war and helps to explain more fully why he came to China and lived there for the final three decades of his life. It is an odyssey that takes him to the Far East, initially in 1900 on board a gunboat bound for the Philippines. Thereafter, he is rarely separated from the Pacific theater, ultimately serving four tours of duty as a U.S. naval attaché—three in China and one in Japan. During his final fifteen years of naval service, all but two were spent in the Far East.

The second purpose was to examine more closely the nearly three decades after Gillis settled in China. Of particular interest was his motivation in regard to the creation of the Gest Collection. Was he merely "an intriguing foreigner fishing in the muddled waters of China's misfortunes," or was he driven more by a desire to save and preserve a part of China's soul? It was not a job for an amateur. Instead, it required a man who possessed a unique blend of talents, knowledge, and nerves as well as a rare combination of social connection, business acumen, language facility, historical scholarship, and sheer nerve. Rarely does a story of bibliotheca revolve around such a singular character. For these reasons it was easy to make him the subject of a biography, and it was precisely these reasons that made me want to examine the life and times of Gillis more closely. But I quickly learned that there were two stories that required telling.

The first revolves around Gillis' career in the U.S. Navy, which spanned nearly thirty years. Of the several articles that describe his activities in China in later life, most emphasize his book collection skills and linguistic abilities, while only passing reference is made to his naval past. Despite the achievement of the Gest Collection, precious little has been published about Gillis, and most references to his life have been anecdotal. They merely refer to his once having been a naval attaché and that he may have been involved in "cloak-and-dagger" episodes at the head of an intelligence organization in China. Another aspect of his tours of duty in China had him active as an agent for the Bethlehem Steel Company, selling warships to China. In these activities he led a life that could compare to Sidney Reilly, the British "Ace of Spies."

Undoubtedly, Gillis viewed himself differently. He realized that the coincidence of his being in Peking and his acquired knowledge of China principally stemmed from his naval service. Furthermore, we learn only the barest of personal details. For example, some accounts credit him as being a "Yankee" from New England; state that he was born in 1875; and indicate that he died in 1948. Still others briefly describe his detective-like qualities and facility with the typewriter. All are correct, but only whet a desire for more information. The only detailed description is that provided in an unpublished personal remembrance written sometime in the 1950s by Gillis' lifelong friend Thomas "Tommy" Sze. All of these remembrances focus on Gillis' post-1925 book-collecting activities, however. None delve into when, where, why, and how Gillis acquired the set of distinctive qualities that made him the right person, in the right place, at the right time.

The second part of the story, of course, is fixed on Gillis' expatriate life in China after leaving the Navy. Of particular interest is what motivated him, then a man in his twilight years. Was he merely in the business of trading Chinese antiquities for profit—one of many "intriguing foreigners" who fished in the increasingly muddier waters of China's misfortunes? Or did he have more altruistic motives? For example, did he cherish his adopted home so much that he feared the destruction that modern armies could reap upon monuments and ancient texts—those things that represented the very soul of China? And if he harbored such a feeling as that, then what moved him to take the necessary steps to preserve these texts?

Gillis himself makes reference to his earlier life. In his meticulously researched etymological study, *The Characters Ch'ao and Hsi*, published in Peking in 1931, in which Gillis challenges previous assumptions made by the eminent China scholar Herbert A. Giles, Gillis refers to himself as a "plain sailor-man." It was, of course, a major understatement—one that cannot but whet one's desire for more detail. While he could discourse on the form and meaning of classical Chinese characters, his self-description hinted at another competency. The entire passage from whence the self-description appears is one in which Gillis bluntly critiques Giles' article, published ten years earlier. It also reveals Gillis' trademark style, which could be sometimes puckish and sometimes acerbic. It is from this self-characterization that I have drawn the title of this work. It is also why I have expended great energy in attempting to fill the gap in our knowledge of Gillis' earlier life experiences that caused this complex and fascinating man to be the right person, in the right place, at the right time. Gillis reported to the U.S. Naval Academy as a member of the Class of 1894. His story would end almost exactly fifty-four years later in Peking with his passing. The purpose of this work is to tell that story by first examining Commander Gillis' naval life, and then how it ultimately led him to make China his home for the final three decades of his life.

— *Bruce Swanson*

2007

CHAPTER 1

⟨—

Education, Sea Duty in the Atlantic, and Trial by Fire: 1875–1900

FATHERS AND SONS: 1875–1890

In the fall of 1890 fifteen-year-old Irvin Van Gorder Gillis entered the U.S. Naval Academy as a member of the Class of 1894. His appointment by Congressman Milton De Lano of New York had been automatic due to his first-place finish in a rigorous competition examination at the local congressional district level followed by Gillis' successful passing of the academy's tough three-day entrance test. The decision by young Irvin to pursue a naval career was largely inspired by the example of his father, Commodore James Henry Gillis (1831–1910), who had graduated from the academy in 1854 and was at the time beginning his fourth decade of naval service. During his naval career James H. Gillis endured nearly twenty-five years of sea duty while serving on twenty-one different ships, of which he commanded seven. He likely inherited his interest in the sea from his grandfather Robert Gillis (1745–1836), who spent time with young James in Ridgway, Pennsylvania. As a teenager in colonial America, Robert had been a merchant seaman on ships engaged in the coastal trade between Boston, Charleston, and New Orleans. As Irvin Gillis prepared to report to the Naval Academy in September 1890, he would, only briefly, be reunited with his father, who was expected back at the family residence in Binghamton, New York, following a three-year absence. The elder Gillis was completing yet another long tour of sea duty, this time as commander of the U.S. Navy's South Atlantic Squadron, whose home port was Buenos Aires.[1]

Nearly everything about I. V. Gillis' early life, in fact, reflected the influence of the Navy. He had been born on 1 January 1875 in the commanding officer's residence near the Navy docks in Erie, Pennsylvania, where, at the time, his father was the captain of the USS *Michigan*, a gunboat responsible for patrolling the Great Lakes.[2] As a toddler he lived in officer's quarters at the naval base at Newport News, Virginia, where James H. Gillis commanded the barracks ship *Franklin*. From the age of seven until he was ten, Irvin resided in naval housing on the edge of the sprawling Brooklyn Navy Yard. His father, then a captain, commanded the USS *Minnesota*, a training ship based at New York City, and was responsible for the recruitment and basic training of young boys who would ultimately serve as enlisted men in the U.S. fleet. The *Minnesota* did not spend much time at sea; instead, the bulk of recruit basic training was conducted at anchor off West 23rd Street in the lower Hudson River. On occasion Captain Gillis would take Irvin on board the ship, where he could see firsthand the various drills and evaluations that young seamen were expected to master.

Perhaps the most lasting impression young Gillis formed, however, was witnessing his father in uniform overseeing the daily routine of the *Minnesota*. The elder Gillis, though in his early fifties, very much epitomized the image of a senior naval officer of that period. He was a lean and handsome man whose deep-set, steely-blue eyes had an honest and open look, but also hinted of sternness. He had high cheekbones, and his sunken, Lincoln-like jowls and lips were well hidden behind a full, snow-white extended goatee and heavy, integrated mustache. His wavy gray hair was worn short, without extended sideburns. Without doubt he carried himself in a proud and dignified manner, but he also had the rolling gait of a man who had spent much of his life at sea.

During this time the Gillis family was comfortably housed in a two-story brownstone bordered by gardens and carefully manicured lawns separating it from the other similarly landscaped officer's quarters. A short distance away a fence formed the border to the Navy base proper. On walks in company with his father, Gillis saw many monuments commemorating various stirring moments in naval history. As he grew older his father probably arranged for visits to the adjacent shipbuilding facility, taking him to see the dry dock, where warships rested on chocks undergoing major overhaul or repair. Such visits would have surely included observing the foundry, the engine and machine shops, the ordnance buildings, and the forge and blacksmith shops.[3]

At some point in his adolescence, Irvin learned of his father's Civil War exploits, particularly his participation at the Battle of Spanish Fort near Mobile, Alabama, in March 1865. In that encounter James H. Gillis was commanding the monitor *Milwaukee*, which struck a torpedo (mine) and sank. After swimming ashore he volunteered to command a naval shore battery and fought bravely, ultimately assisting in the capture of the fort. For that action he was promoted for gallantry and received a special commendation from Gideon Welles, President Lincoln's secretary of the Navy.[4]

Another favorite story concerned his father's daring rescue of a group of Argentinean sailors in Montevideo

James Henry Gillis (1831–1910), Rear Admiral, U.S. Navy, I. V. Gillis' father

(Naval History and Heritage Command, Washington, D.C.)

Harbor in August 1857. The evidence of that event was prominently on display at the Gillis home; awarded by the Argentine government, it was a magnificent medal of steel and gold surmounted by a life buoy in white enamel and a setting sun of gold whose rays were set in diamonds.[5]

In the early 1880s Irvin, in company with his family, visited the U.S. Naval Academy for the first time. The reason was to see his older brother Harry (1861–1938), who was a naval cadet at Annapolis from 1879 to 1883. As Harry advanced through his four years, on occasion his parents and siblings were present to observe the respective classes march and drill accompanied by martial music. It was always a dramatic display and likely made a lasting impression on the precocious younger Gillis.

Harry's experience at the academy was a bittersweet one, however. In those days many cadets were subject to discharge upon graduation because of a backlog of naval officers. The final determination was based on class standing, and sometimes less than half of the members of a class would ultimately gain their commission. In Harry's case he ranked forty-fifth of fifty-four cadets and did not meet the threshold. Great disap-

Harry Alexander Gillis (1861–1938), Midshipman, U.S. Naval Academy, I. V. Gillis' brother

(Courtesy of Bonnie Gillis Waters, Victor, N.Y.)

pointment came in August 1883 when Harry received word that he was to be honorably discharged and given one year's salary of $1,000. As will become evident, Harry's classroom difficulties would not be lost on his younger brother, who would excel academically during his time at the academy, from 1890 to 1894.

Ironically, Harry was stymied by a ponderous, yet demanding promotion system prevailing throughout his father's career, whereby an officer could expect to be promoted about every ten years if his record was without serious blemish and if he completed the requisite amount of time at sea. Thus, as long as his health was good, he could remain on active duty until the mandatory retirement age of sixty-two. This system, coupled with a postwar no-growth policy, produced a surfeit of officers competing for positions on board relatively few, obsolete ships. As a result there was a paucity of billets open to new academy graduates like Harry.

One other prominent reminder of the family's rich tradition of service provided an example for young Irvin. It was his grandfather James Lyle Gillis' (1792–1881) cavalry sword, which had been willed to his father. Irvin's grandfather had enlisted during the War of 1812 as a volunteer from Hebron, New York, but, because of his leadership qualities, he gained a commission as a lieutenant of cavalry under General Winfield Scott. From 1812 to 1814 he participated in a number of battles, including Fort George, Chippewa, and Lundy's Lane. In the last encounter, which took the most lives of any battle in the war, Irvin's grandfather was badly wounded and taken prisoner but subsequently escaped in Montreal. He was soon recaptured and transported to a more secure fortress in Halifax, where he remained until the end of the war when he was released in a prisoner exchange. Upon his death in 1881, it was reported that James L. Gillis was one of the last surviving veterans of the War of 1812.

James L. Gillis led a most robust and colorful life. Following the War of 1812 he pioneered the Ridgway, Pennsylvania, frontier area, north of Pittsburgh, operating a tannery and sawmill. He went on to become a judge and then entered politics at the state level and was subsequently elected to the U.S. Congress for the single term 1857–1859. Prior to the Civil War, President James Buchanan appointed him Indian agent for the Pawnee Nation in Nebraska. He was a lifelong Freemason and had been arrested but later acquitted in the famous 1829 murder case of William Morgan, who had publicly revealed certain secrets surrounding Freemason rituals.[6]

James Lyle Gillis (1792–1881), I. V. Gillis' paternal grandfather

(Courtesy of Bonnie Gillis Waters, Victor, N.Y.)

I. V. Gillis' decision to embark upon a naval career, then, was hardly surprising considering that most of his early years were spent experiencing the naval milieu surrounding his father. He had also inherited a spirit of adventure and resoluteness characteristic of his other Scottish forebears, who had successfully grappled with the many challenges presented in a vibrant and often violent early America. Blessed with a lively mind and keen intelligence, he had all the "right stuff" necessary to play a prominent role in America's next challenge—the onset of the Age of Navalism and its bid to create a navy second to none.

EDUCATION AND ACHIEVEMENT: 1890–1895

On 6 September 1890 Irvin Gillis reported on board the training ship *Santee*, which was permanently assigned to the Naval Academy. He and his classmates underwent a three-week intensive indoctrination program that was intended to familiarize the cadets with shipboard life as well as break any bad habits learned in civilian life. At the end of the period the class moved back onto land and into their stark living quarters at Bancroft Hall, where they prepared to commence the academic year. The *Santee* experience had demonstrated to all that they had entered a new world in which members lived by a rigid set of rules, moved about with precise military bearing, and communicated in their own curious jargon. Floors were decks; walls, bulkheads; bathrooms, heads; and stairs were ladders. Directions were now given in standard naval argot. For example, left was port and right was starboard.[7]

Once at Bancroft Hall, another set of slang was soon mastered that was designed to make the class aware that it was now part of an exclusive fraternity peculiar only to naval cadets. For instance, a perfect academic mark was termed a "four"; to do a thing well was to "biff"; to fail was to "zip"; "sux" meant "not difficult"; and "bilge" meant "to be dismissed or dropped." If something was swell or good, it was just "doggy"; to study was to "bone"; an especially awkward cadet was called a "squid"; a cadet lieutenant or petty officer was a "buzzard"; a senior or first classman was a "firstie"; a firstie without office or rank was a "clean sleever." The chaplain was known as "Holy Joe," and anyone in the Engineer Corps was known as a "greaser."[8]

Commencement of the academic year also marked the beginning of hazing, which had always been a problem, but by the time Irvin arrived at the academy hazing had become more mental than physical. Whole paragraphs had to be memorized and recited faithfully even as the hapless plebe was braced at attention and the eyes of an upperclassman burned at him like a mad, feral animal. One such quotation had been imputed to be the words of John Paul Jones: "None other than a gentleman, as well as a seaman, both in theory and practice, is qualified to support the character of commissioned officer in the navy; nor is any man fit to command a ship of war who is not capable of communicating his ideas on paper, in language that becomes his rank."[9] Another favorite to be shouted out, perhaps at mealtime, was from Shakespeare's *Henry V*: "I am not covetous of gold, but if it be a sin to covet honor, I am the most offending soul alive."[10]

A further ritual involved the assignation of nicknames, which more often than not were unflattering. In the 1894 Naval Academy yearbook, *The Lucky Bag*, Irvin was dubbed "Splint," a variety of bituminous coal known for its dull, stony appearance. "Splint Gillis" it was then, for four years. *The Lucky Bag* also listed Gillis as being only five feet five inches tall and weighing but 125 pounds. In fact, the yearbook tells that Irvin's keenest desire at graduation was to be taller. It is also learned that Splint was apparently a teetotaler. While most of his fellow cadets listed their favorite drinks as ones containing some form of alcohol, Splint Gillis listed his as sarsaparilla.[11]

Irvin's straight-arrow qualities were also evident in the nature of his demerits over his four years at the Naval Academy. During that time he received 63 demerits, most awarded for a variety of petty infractions. The majority were for talking in formation. His biggest single infraction, however, was for 10 demerits, which he received in his third year for being disrespectful to a coxswain of a small boat. As a measure of comparison, Gillis received but 9 demerits in his final year while the worst offender in the class, Arthur Kavanaugh of Nebraska, received 172.[12]

Midshipman Irvin Van Gorder Gillis

(Naval History and Heritage Command, Washington, D.C.)

Despite his youth and diminutiveness, Gillis was an outstanding student and had no apparent difficulty with recitation, which stymied many midshipmen.[13] Three hours each day, five days a week, and one hour on Saturdays, he was required to meet with instructors and review the subject matter assigned from the previous day. For mathematics, the recitations were principally conducted at the blackboard in the development of formulas and propositions and the solving of problems. In history and English, the recitations were often oral but sometimes written, with the instructor correcting the cadet where necessary for style, grammar, punctuation, spelling, and choice of words, as well as factual mistakes. At the end of each session the instructor would award a numerical grade, with 4.0 being the highest.[14] (Gillis' courses of instruction for the four years are listed in appendix D.)

By the time Gillis became a firstie, he had achieved the rank of cadet lieutenant, being one of only eight naval cadets to be awarded that title. It meant that he had charge over a division of his fellow classmates, twelve midshipmen in all, who were divided into three four-man crews. As such, Gillis enjoyed special privileges but also had the authority to issue orders to his division that were to be considered official and obeyed. This carried over to drills and practice exercises in which his three crews might man a naval gun, form an infantry landing party, or crew a small boat.

A serious family crisis occurred in the late summer prior to Irvin's final year. On 1 August 1893 his mother, Lydia Gillis, died following a stroke. She had lingered for two weeks as family members rushed to her bedside in Alexandria, Virginia.[15] Her death, at the relatively young age of fifty-seven, came just two and a half months after Commodore Gillis retired, having been relieved by George Dewey as a member of the Lighthouse Board.[16]

Following his mother's interment at Arlington National Cemetery, Irvin returned to the Naval Academy to resume his final year. In June 1894 he graduated with honors, finishing third in his class with a four-year grade-point average that exceeded the coveted 85th percentile. Despite his

U.S. Naval Academy Class of 1894, from *The Lucky Bag* (Annapolis, Md., U.S. Naval Academy, 1894)

(Courtesy of Nimitz Library, U.S. Naval Academy, Annapolis, Md.)

mother's death and concern for his father, he managed to finish second in the annual examination given in June 1894. He finished first in four of the nine academic groups: ordnance and gunnery, navigation and surveying, navigation practice cruise, and least square/applied mechanics. He also had the distinction of finishing first in his class in mathematics three of the four years.[17]

Two more requirements remained before Irvin could gain his commission. He had to satisfactorily complete the customary two-year cruise on board a U.S. Navy warship and then pass a final examination for promotion back at Annapolis. Within days following June Week, he received his orders to report on board the armored cruiser USS *New York*, the flagship of the North Atlantic Squadron. The assignment carried a special honor. Only the top few of a class were ordered to the North Atlantic Squadron, which usually contained the newest, most modern naval ships.[18] The *New York* was but three years old and represented a faster class of heavily armored cruisers. It also carried rifled, breech-loading guns as well as torpedoes.

Once on board, Irvin and seven fellow classmates soon found themselves under the baleful eye of Captain Robley Evans, the commanding officer of the *New York*. Evans was a charismatic, somewhat bellicose officer who, in 1891–1892, had acquired the popular nickname "Fighting Bob" when he faced down a hostile Chilean government challenge in the Port of Valparaiso.[19] He also was known affectionately as "Gimpy Bob," due to a pronounced limp resulting from several Civil War gunshot wounds he received while leading Marines in the assault of Fort Fisher in December 1864. Nearly all of the officers in the fleet knew the story of how Evans had aimed his pistol at the doctor who was ready to amputate both legs, calmly informing him, "If he or any one else entered my door with anything that looked like a case of instruments, I meant to begin shooting and that [the doctor] might rest perfectly sure that I would kill six before they cut my legs off." The legs remained attached for the rest of his life, but Evans endured constant pain and had to move about with the use of a cane.[20]

His colorful past notwithstanding, Evans was also highly respected by his peers for his naval expertise and his penchant for detail. He was a "hands-on" commanding officer who, despite his handicap, frequently moved about his ship chatting with enlisted men while carefully observing various drills and shipboard evaluations. He demanded perfection and took great pride that his crew on board the *New York* could close all watertight doors within thirty seconds after the general alarm was sounded.[21] Although one might think Evans a plain old "seadog," he also moved easily in higher circles. He maintained friendships with many influential politicians, including Theodore Roosevelt, Grover Cleveland, and William McKinley. He also was well connected with international royalty as well as ranking European naval officers. And, due to a previous tour as the Navy's equipment officer, Evans had made many friends in the upper echelons of private industry.[22] As will later be evident, Gillis' exposure to Evans while a young midshipman would have lasting benefits, as their paths would frequently cross in the future.

For Gillis, the primary purpose of the so-called middie (midshipman) cruise was to observe carefully the shipboard routine as well as to participate actively as a member of the crew. One important duty was that of standing watches both in port and under way as a junior watch officer. He might also act as messenger, relaying word from the officer of the deck to the embarked admiral, Richard Meade, or to Evans himself.[23] Under way he would be allowed to use a sextant and practice celestial naviga-

USS *New York* (ACR 2)
(U.S. Naval Institute Photo Archive)

tion, comparing his results in fixing the ship's position with that of the *New York*'s navigator. Other activities involved observing gunnery exercises, which were frequent. The ship, in company with other vessels of the North Atlantic Squadron, would often steam to training areas on the East Coast, where they would also practice maneuvering drills at different courses and speeds. Much time was also spent on two new techniques: the live firing of torpedoes and flashing-light signaling.[24]

There was one major highlight for Gillis in the summer of 1895. At that time the *New York* and several sister ships were chosen to represent the United States at an international naval pageant that included observing the opening of the Kiel Canal.[25] It turned out to be a grand event, and Gillis got to see and visit the newest warships from nearly every major country in the world. On one occasion, the German emperor, Wilhelm II, paid a visit to the *New York*.[26] Besides Germany, the *New York* also visited England and Denmark before returning home in the early autumn.

In April 1896 Gillis returned to Annapolis, where he took his final examinations before commissioning. The following month, having passed easily, he was granted two months' leave. During that time he received notification of his official promotion to ensign, effective 1 July of the same year. He also received orders to report for duty on board the first U.S. battleship, the USS *Texas*, which had been in commission for less than a year.[27]

OLD HOODOO: 1896–1897

During his six "apprentice" years, Gillis was probably too preoccupied with his academic and postgraduation-cruise requirements to take full notice of the changes taking place in world naval circles. However, the visit to Germany gave him a new perspective on the growing emphasis being placed on the construction of more-heavily armored and more-lethal warships that were simultaneously becoming larger and faster. Moreover, by the time Gillis was commissioned, he, like most officers, had become familiar with the writings of Captain Alfred Thayer Mahan, who, in 1890, had introduced the world to a new vision, which posited that the combination of mercantile imperialism and naval power could make a nation prosperous and great.[28] The naval review at Kiel confirmed that the Age of Navalism had begun. (See appendix A for more about Mahan and his impact on Gillis.)

In the United States, Mahan's disciples, led by Theodore Roosevelt, had successfully lobbied for a naval-building program as well as a more expansive foreign policy. A jingoist spirit was beginning to pervade the land as speeches and newspaper editorials preached a more bellicose and aggressive patriotic message. When the British navy landed troops in British Guiana in 1895, the result of a boundary dispute with Venezuela, the United States demanded that the Monroe Doctrine be respected, and a war scare swept the country. Roosevelt was quick to declare: "Let the fight [with England] come if it must. I rather hope that the fight will come soon. The clamor of the peace faction has convinced me that this country needs a war."[29] The British eventually agreed to arbitrate, and the storm passed.

When Gillis returned to Annapolis in the spring of 1896 to be examined for promotion, the papers were also reporting that a group of hawkish congressmen and senators were already urging intervention in Cuba and the sending of a fleet there to protect American interests. For Gillis, who was eager at long last to embark upon his naval career, the future seemed to offer bright prospects for action and adventure.

The *Texas*, as the first U.S. battleship, represented a considerable technical challenge as well as an expensive item of naval hardware. To protect its investment, the Navy Department undoubtedly picked the *Texas*' officers with care. It was commanded by Captain Henry Glass, and the executive officer was Lieutenant Commander J. D. J. Kelley. Both had been ordered to the *Texas* from the new cruiser *Cincinnati*, which, under their hand, had attained a high degree of proficiency and discipline. Similarly, Gillis' selection was primarily based on his high standing at the Naval Academy as well as his high marks while on board the *New York*.

Two weeks after his commissioning on 1 July 1896, Ensign Gillis reported to the *Texas*. The *Texas* was in its final four weeks of fitting out before it, too, would be commissioned to take its place in the North Atlantic Squadron. Once on board, Gillis was assigned duties as Glass' aide and also was designated the ship's signal officer, in charge of communications and responsible for that group of enlisted men making up the ship's Signal Division. Very soon, he also became qualified to stand deck watches both under way and in port.[30] As the captain's aide, Gillis had a unique "inside look" at the day-to-day decision making that took place in the running of the ship. The position undoubtedly made him popular in the wardroom, for he most certainly was privy to the ship's schedule and operational orders. These were always important bits of information

USS *Texas* (battleship)
(U.S. Naval Institute Photo Archive)

that provided lively gossip about what to expect in the way of the ship's future ports of call.

As in the course of much of his career, Gillis would encounter officers and enlisted men who had served with his father, and his service on board the *Texas* was no exception. Lieutenant Commander Kelley, for example, had commanded the *Tallapoosa* in Rear Admiral Gillis' South Atlantic Squadron in the late 1880s.[31] Kelley, in fact, was a most unusual person and one of the earliest "activist" officers who had written articles on naval affairs as well as the need for a strong commercial-shipping industry. He was a close friend of James Gordon Bennett, the influential publisher of the *New York Herald*, and upon retirement in 1901 Kelley would become the *Herald*'s naval editor and later serve on the paper's board of directors. Like Mahan, he was a devout navalist and in the early 1900s had authorized a number of articles in support of a strong, modern navy. He likely encouraged the officers of the *Texas* to be current on all manner of naval topics.

The honeymoon on board the *Texas* was a brief one for Gillis. On 16 September 1896 she ran hard aground at Newport, Rhode Island, while still undergoing sea trials. The mishap was caused by miscommunication over engine signals from the bridge to the engine room via the *Texas*' new engine-order telegraph system. Although the ship continued to operate after being freed by tugs, the hull had been weakened, and the *Texas* subsequently went to the Brooklyn Navy Yard in early November for inspection and repair. It was soon discovered that sixty-one compartments below the waterline were confirmed to be leaking. The worst was yet to come, however. On 9 November a faulty sea-cock valve led to massive flooding belowdecks, and the ship, still moored to the dock, sank to its gun deck. The flooding created yet another serious problem. The water that rushed in was highly polluted and contained solid-waste par-

Ensign Irvin V. Gillis, USN

(Naval History and Heritage Command, Washington, D.C.)

ticles. The crew had to be evacuated ashore to avoid a typhoid epidemic, and it took a number of weeks to clean and sanitize the ship. For a brief period in late November it was believed doubtful that the *Texas* would ever again be ordered to sea.

In February 1897, however, the ship was at last ready and headed for Galveston, Texas, for a belated ceremony celebrating that it was not only the first U.S. battleship, but also the first to bear the name "Texas." Upon arrival at Galveston it once again ran aground, but the sandy bottom treated the ship more kindly than had the rocks off Newport. Though embarrassed, Captain Glass quickly freed the ship, and the banquet went on as scheduled. Upon departure from Galveston several days later, the *Texas* went to New Orleans, where it and the *Maine*, the latest U.S. battleship, represented the U.S. Navy at Mardi Gras. The *Texas* subsequently returned to the East Coast, where it commenced operations with the North Atlantic Squadron.

The gala banquets and parades notwithstanding, the atmosphere on board the *Texas* soon changed to gloom. Between the groundings and the dockside sinking, various members of the *Texas*' officer cadre became the subject of two naval courts of inquiry. When the findings were handed down, letters of censure and reprimand were issued to several officers. By now the *Texas* had a poor reputation, and Navy men in the fleet had begun calling it the "USS *Hoodoo*." Few wanted to see any duty on board what they believed to be a jinxed vessel.

Gillis was not affected by the legal inquiries, but he and two other senior lieutenants found an outlet for relieving their frustrations. Two papers survive that he sent to the New-York Historical Society in 1934 that reflect his efforts.[32] In late September 1896 the Navy Department had issued a circular letter requesting proposed changes to the fleet's tactical signal book, which, with the advent of new battleships and cruisers, had become outdated. It contained a vast set of signals to be employed during action or emergency situations as well as routine tactical maneuvering. Additionally, there were flag signals intended to acknowledge or direct speed and course changes. The signal book also listed light signals, which would be used to inform other units of a man overboard or need for assistance. Captain Glass had passed the circular letter down to the officers directly involved in the ship's communications, who obviously included Gillis. Within several weeks a detailed list of proposed changes was jointly submitted to Captain Glass by Gillis and the two other lieutenants. It was a reasoned and comprehensive report covering a variety of signaling situations principally related to the new evolving tactics requiring ships to maneuver in concert from line, column, and echelon formations. It listed thirteen changes to the signal book, including a clearer definition of engine speeds as marked on the engine room annunciator. Gillis further established himself as an improviser of solutions when he submitted precise instructions for the care and inspection of the ship's double bottom. They were intended to prevent a future accidental flooding of belowdecks spaces, such as that which had occurred in the Brooklyn Navy Yard.

By late summer of 1897 the *Texas* was once again back in dry dock undergoing extensive modifications. This time it had to have its bow and stern torpedo mounts removed as they could not be fired without risking danger to the ship. There were other problems as well. The *New York Times* reported on 30 September that twenty crew members had deserted while the ship was in dry dock.[33] The *Times* indicated that the main reason for the desertions stemmed from the ship's being "uncomfortable" because the engine room and crew's living quarters were excessively hot and impossible to cool.

The problem was greater than matters of comfort, however. The Navy's building program was already straining its ability to provide trained enlisted men to operate the increasingly complicated equipment. Many sailors were foreign born and not well educated. Moreover, the excessive amount of time spent in Navy yards for repairs and upkeep was often too much of a temptation for men who often drank to excess, and ship's logs were replete with instance of desertion or absence without leave. As a result, the ship's brig was invariably provided with a steady supply of transgressors. For young division officers like Gillis, the challenge of leadership was difficult and often discouraging. As his tour came to an end, however, Gillis had met his first test. He distinguished himself as a smart, capable young officer by receiving from Captain Glass the highest mark of "excellence" in all graded categories in his report of fitness.[34]

"NOTHING IN HIS COMPOSITION BUT NERVE": 1897–1898

Just one week prior to the desertions on the star-crossed *Texas*, Gillis had received his orders to the USS *Porter*, a torpedo boat that was in port at New York also undergoing modifications and repairs. For Gillis the duty on the *Porter* must have been an exciting prospect because he knew that on a smaller ship he would have a much broader range of responsibilities.

USS *Porter* (TB 6)
(U.S. Naval Institute Photo Archive)

In fact, he was to be the ship's second in command under Lieutenant John C. Fremont Jr., son of the famous explorer, politician, and military officer. Gillis' primary duty on the *Porter* was that of chief engineer, which was a demanding assignment because the *Porter*, like the *Texas*, was also a new, experimental class of ship. The ship had been in commission for less than a year, and several design and technological challenges were readily apparent. Heading the list were problems with the propeller shaft and blades. The high speeds for which they had supposedly been designed caused them to twist or break when the ship was put to maximum limits. Second, the ship had two steam reciprocating engines fed by three coal-fired boilers capable of developing 4,000 horsepower. At higher speeds the vibration and pounding of the reciprocators caused many pieces of auxiliary machinery to break free from their deck fasteners. The *Porter* was cramped, dirty, and noisy, with minimal space left over to provide comfort for the crew. When the *Porter* was under way, some men slept on deck, but this could often be quite hazardous as these craft were poor sea keepers in all but the calmest conditions.[35]

The main weapon system also had serious problems. The torpedoes were inaccurate and went off course at high speed. Even during stationary firing, they had a tendency to go off course when they hit a small object or if their propellers struck the tube at discharge. Eventually the torpedo problems were solved through a series of experiments with a new steering mechanism.

All of this activity had gone on throughout the summer of 1897 at Sag Harbor, New York, often under the critical eye of Theodore Roosevelt, then the assistant secretary of the Navy, who maintained his home, Sagamore, nearby. In fact, it was Roosevelt who had pushed hard for the creation of a "mosquito war-fleet," which, if successful, would spawn the creation of others to be used in defense of the coastal waters of the United States.

In January 1898 a six-month shakedown cruise for the flotilla was ordered. It was to proceed down the East Coast using the inland water-way, and then via the Gulf of Mexico it was to go up the Mississippi to St. Louis. Early on it proved to be a tiring and stressful trip, as all systems had to be tested under a variety of sea conditions. One vessel in the flotilla, the USS *Foote*, had severe problems and averaged only a slow twelve knots against its contracted speed of thirty knots. It soon became known as the *"Footless"* among the other torpedo-boat crews. The *Porter*, meanwhile, performed so well that it was recognized as the best ship from reliability and efficiency standpoints. Fremont would later give credit to Gillis in his report of fitness with the highest mark of "excellent" in all graded categories. He also added the following remark: "Ens. Gillis has shown exceptional zeal, intelligence, and resourcefulness in performing the various duties required of him during the cruise of this vessel."[36]

The ships never made it any farther than Key West. War fever was now running high in the United States over mistreatment of Cubans by Spanish colonialists. Outrage in America was fueled in no small part by the newspapers of William Randolph Hearst, Joseph Pulitzer, and James Gordon Bennett. For some months they had run stories of atrocities in Cuba, both real and imagined. As the *Porter* pulled into Key West for upkeep and repair, Fremont had orders to ready the ship for patrol duties. Toward the end of *Porter*'s upkeep period, the USS *Maine* was reported sunk in a furious explosion while it lay at anchor in Havana Harbor. An inquiry was ordered, but the headlines screaming "Remember the Maine" were an obvious call for the United States to teach Spain a lesson. On 26 April 1898 President McKinley finally declared war.

The *Porter* was quickly under way from Key West, and upon arrival at Havana, it immediately was assigned close-in patrol duties by the battle squadron commander, Admiral William Sampson, who was embarked on board the *New York*. Its first chance at action came within a few days when it intercepted and captured the Spanish schooner *Sophia*, loaded with rum and sugar. Everyone on board celebrated because there was a bounty on such ships, and the *Porter*'s crew stood to divide up a fair sum of prize money.

Less than a day had passed after the *Sophia* capture when the *Porter* became involved in a clandestine effort to gather information ashore per the direction of Admiral Sampson. Sampson had become friendly with Sylvester H. "Harry" Scovel, a reporter for Pulitzer's *New York World*. Scovel had already earned a reputation as one of the most celebrated correspondents covering the war, having been the first on the scene in Havana Harbor within minutes of the sinking of the *Maine*. His subsequent stories captured the attention of the world with his lurid descriptions of the event and suspicions that the ship had been a victim of Spanish sabotage. Scovel also had a long history of writing articles about Spanish atrocities against the Cubans and had excellent connections with General Maximo Gomez, the chief of the Cuban insurgents. Moreover, Scovel directed the efforts of a small group of other reporters ashore whose job it was to spy on Spanish activities in Havana as well as to provide Scovel with scoops over his rivals from other newspapers. None of this had escaped Admiral Sampson's attention, and he asked Scovel to provide him with badly needed intelligence ashore. It fell to the *Porter* to act as Scovel's transport for the dangerous mission.

The first story Scovel filed from the *Porter* appeared in the *World* on 28 April 1898 and featured Ensign Gillis. Apparently the *Porter* was to land a boat ashore to pick up one of Scovel's reporter-spies, operating under the pseudonym "Holmes," with the hope that Holmes could provide much-needed updates for Admiral Sampson as to the situation in Havana. Scovel's description of the event read in part:

> For hours the *Porter's* officers watched. The moon was not yet risen; coast and sky were of the same inky black. The loom of the shore a few hundred yards distant, although obscuring the coast line, did not obstruct the view seaward. The *Porter* could be seen, and any moment the near-by Cojimar field artillery might begin puncturing the thin-skinned, valuable, almost defenseless torpedo-boat.
>
> Holmes was to be waited for three hours. The officers watched longer and then reluctantly gave up.
>
> On the night of the 24th the hour set was "soon after dusk as possible."
>
> Again the swift *Porter* ran into the shaded bay. The moon enabled them to find it easily. This was the second trial.
>
> The officers, to give Holmes every chance to reach them and the admiral every chance to learn the facts about Havana's sealed interior, decided to go right to the beach.
>
> Ensign Gillis took an eighteen-foot boat, four willing jackies swept the oars and the sandy beach was almost touched.
>
> Gillis signaled. No answer.
>
> It is now known that this point was patrolled that night.
>
> The signals of the previous evening had been seen, and Holmes either could not approach the beach or had attempted it and been captured. Gillis held to the shore for an hour, then, after his return, the *Porter's* electric masthead light itself shot the white beams in proper intervals; but no Holmes.[37]

Over the next five days Scovel remained on board the *Porter* as it continued its vain attempt to contact Holmes. Admiral Sampson finally instructed the *Porter* to land Scovel at Caibarién, on Cuba's north shore. Once the mission was completed, the *Porter* received orders to link up with the flagship, the *New York*, which was in the process of organizing an expedition to San Juan, Puerto Rico, in hopes of intercepting Admiral Pascual Cervera's fleet, which was reliably reported to be heading there from the Cape Verde Islands. Battle plans were drawn up as the *Porter* ferried the commanding officers of the San Juan expedition back and forth between their ships and the *New York*. One of those passengers was Robley Evans, then the commanding officer of the battleship *Iowa*.

On 11 May the ships of Sampson's squadron commenced a bombardment of San Juan, and the *Porter* was ordered to remain close by the harbor entrance looking for any sign of Cervera and his fleet. On one occasion it came under heavy fire from shore batteries but was not hit. After three hours Sampson withdrew, disappointed not to have found Cervera. The *Porter* was ordered back to Key West for refueling and some rest for the tired crew.

Upon arrival at Key West, the *Porter*'s crew had a sobering moment when it saw the battered and broken *Winslow*, one of its sister torpedo boats. Following the declaration of war, the *Winslow* had been the war's first serious casualty when it was struck by fire from shore batteries on 11 May at Cárdenas. Its captain, Lieutenant John Bernadou, had been badly wounded, and its executive officer, Ensign Worth Bagley, and five crewmen had been killed instantly. It had taken a herculean effort by the revenue cutter *Hudson* to tow the *Winslow* to safety, all the while receiving fire from Spanish guns ashore.

Upon the *Porter*'s return to Cuba in mid-May, it took up picket duties protecting the larger force of U.S. combatants, which began to form up at Santiago, where Admiral Cervera and his fleet had finally been discovered. During this period, a near catastrophe was averted by the *Porter* and the *New York*. Gillis had the night watch, and at two o'clock in the morning on an especially dark night with rain squalls, he had spotted a large unlit ship in the gloom. He woke Fremont, and it was decided that since they were located well to the east of Havana, the ship could not possibly be one of the U.S. blockaders. The crew quietly made preparations for battle as the *Porter* began a stealthy approach from astern of the mystery ship. Within a short time the torpedo boat was able to come within yards of the unknown vessel, and Fremont later noted that "excitement on the *Porter* was at a fever heat, and the enforced silence and the nervous tension were hard to bear."[38]

Fremont decided to make sure that the ship was Spanish and turned on his signal light. This produced no answer. He tried again, and this time fired his forward gun in warning. The response was immediate, as the unknown ship showed a light signal but fired at the *Porter*. The signal, however, was the wrong one, and the *Porter* rang up full speed for a torpedo attack. At the very last moment the ship was recognized to be the *New York*, Sampson's flagship. Both ships now slowed, and via megaphone, signal officers exchanged apologetic explanations. It was later confirmed that the *New York* was the ship in error for having responded with incorrect recognition signals.[39]

A few days after the *New York* incident, the *Porter* was again involved in a situation that soon became the talk of the fleet. On 4 June, while patrolling near the mouth of Santiago Harbor, the *Porter*'s lookout spotted two (presumably Spanish) torpedoes floating dead in the water. It was decided to try to recover them in the hopes that considerable technical intelligence could be gleaned once they were thoroughly subjected to examination back in the United States. The *Porter*'s log entry of the event, written and signed by Gillis, was succinct and laconic in the extreme: "During the forenoon saw two Schwartzkopf auto-mobile torpedoes floating in the water. In attempting to pull them up one sank, but secured the other and took it on board. It had war head and nose on."[40] Lieutenant Fremont, in an article the following November, treated the incident with somewhat more detail:

> These torpedoes were still extremely dangerous. Any ship striking the forward end of one would have fared exactly as if the torpedo had run into her. It was therefore necessary either to destroy or recover these machines. Recovery was preferable, of course, but extremely dangerous in the heavy sea running, unless they could be rendered harmless by the removal of the firing pin or war-nose. There was a gallant attempt to do this by a young officer [Gillis] attached to the *Porter*, who jumped overboard and wrestled with the torpedo single-handed, while trying to unscrew the firing pin. One of these torpedoes was lost during these operations, sinking despite all efforts to recover it. The other was

taken on board the *Porter*, where it remained an object of curiosity to all until, on our arrival at New York, it was transferred to the torpedo depot at Newport.[41]

The incident quickly made the rounds among the blockading ships and following the war was retold in several books and magazines. One of these even contained a full-page artist's rendering that depicted Gillis grappling with the torpedo in heavy seas.[42] Another, in the best tradition of pulp novels of that era, provided this highly embellished description:

> Gillis clutched the rail firmly and prepared to make the jump.
> "Don't do it, Gillis; she's got her war nose on!" exclaimed the Captain, reaching for his ensign.
> "I'll fix that, sir," replied Gillis, leaping into the sea before his superior officer could restrain him. . . .

> No more daring deed has been done during the war, and Rear Admiral Gillis (retired), of the United States Navy, who is the father of the boy, and resides in Delhi, N.Y., can well be proud of the youth. He was graduated at Annapolis from New York, and went to the front to serve his country and his flag at any cost.
> Captain Fremont sums Gillis up in a few words: "He has nothing in his composition but nerve." The war is surely building up a new generation of heroes, and Ensign Irving [sic] Van Gordon [sic] Gillis stands in the front rank."[43]

Following the torpedo-recovery incident, the *Porter* was directed to an obscure bay where it participated in providing covering fire for Marines who had established a beachhead at the village of Guantánamo. It was still there when word came that Admiral Cervera was attempting to run the blockade. Fremont quickly made for Santiago but arrived too late to participate. The Spanish fleet had been intercepted by the U.S. blockading force and destroyed. The war was all but over. On July 9, after the torpedo was disarmed, the *Porter* was ordered to make best speed and return to New York. Ten days later it arrived with its trophy and once again commenced badly needed repairs at the Brooklyn Navy Yard. The *Porter* was one of the first returning ships, and the *New York Times* sent a reporter to interview Lieutenant Fremont, but he had already departed

ENSIGN GILLIS ATTEMPTING TO UNSCREW THE WAR-NOSE ON A SPANISH TORPEDO.

Drawing by Henry Reuterdahl (1871–1925), in "Torpedo Boat Service," by John C. Fremont Jr., *Harper's New Monthly Magazine*, November 1898, 836

for his home on Staten Island. Instead the interview was conducted with the *Porter's* second in command, Ensign Gillis, who eagerly provided details of the *Porter's* adventures:

> "We left Santiago," said Ensign Gillis, "on July 9, sailed from Key West northward on July 14, and from Savannah three days later, arriving here ten days out from Santiago. A torpedo boat, of course, is not as steady in the heavy seas as a battleship, but the Porter has proved herself in every emergency and in all weathers a stanch, swift, and at all times capable boat. Our water-tube boilers have given us our speed whenever wanted, but we come up here now for a little professional attention—much less, however, than might be expected when a vessel has been so long in service without docking or overhauling."[44]

Gillis' optimistic assessment notwithstanding, a closer inspection of the *Porter* revealed a need for an extreme overhaul of her engineering plant. The Brooklyn Navy Yard had higher priorities, with many of the fleet's capital ships also in need of repairs resulting from extended operations during the war. As a result, it was decided to place the *Porter* out of commission while she awaited her turn. Returning from a week's leave in early August, Ensign Gillis received orders to report once again to the USS *Texas*, which was conveniently moored at the Brooklyn Navy Yard, also having just returned from Cuba, where it had seen much action and received considerable battle damage at Santiago.

"FROM COUPLER-FLANGE TO SPINDLE-GUIDE I SEE THY HAND, O GOD": 1899

If Gillis had any doubts about returning to the *Texas*, they were quickly dispelled.[45] The ship, having acquitted itself well in the war, had, at last, shed its bad-luck image. At the same time Gillis was preparing to report back on board the *Texas*, the *New York Times* recorded the following on 2 August 1899: "The Texas looking every inch the fighting machine that she is, lay at the cob dock in the Brooklyn Navy Yard yesterday, almost over the spot where she sank in the soft mud not many months ago and brought discredit on herself. But if there were any who were ashamed of her and had called the old ship a "hoo-doo," they were not in evidence. There wasn't a man in all her crew yesterday who wasn't proud of her, proud of her sons, her bent deck plates and her grimy look."[46]

The *Texas* also no longer held status as a first-class battleship. The U.S. Navy's construction program, aided and abetted by a sympathetic Congress, had moved into high gear by the late 1890s. At the close of the Spanish-American War, the Navy listed in its inventory eight new first-class battleships that now formed the core of the first U.S. fleet. Meanwhile, many new cruisers and a miscellany of other smaller combatants had also been added. Even more ships had been approved for construction and would join the fleet in the next several years. The *Texas*, now labeled a second-class battleship, also had a new commanding officer, Captain Charles D. Sigsbee, who had graduated from the Naval Academy in 1863. Sigsbee had had the misfortune to have been the commanding officer of the *Maine* when it exploded in Havana Harbor in February 1898. Surviving the explosion, he had to endure a difficult court of inquiry following the incident that left his reputation tarnished when he was seen to have not taken adequate precautions to protect his ship.

In the immediate post–Spanish-American War period, a major deficiency within the expanding Navy was a lack of qualified officer engineers. In order to make up for the shortage, commanding officers had to assign line officers to engineering duties, a move that did not always produce the best of results. Many simply did not have the expertise to operate machinery, diagnose or troubleshoot problems, or understand how to maintain or improvise repairs of the increasingly complicated engineering systems. The *Texas* was no exception. Captain Sigsbee, taking note of Gillis' mathematical and technical talents, assigned him to stand engine-room watches.

Gillis did not seem to mind being a "greaser." He easily grasped the concept of steam propulsion and electricity and was evidently comfortable with getting his hands dirty working on the array of auxiliary machinery, boilers, condensers, and generators that were necessary to drive a ship through the water. He very much epitomized a maxim coined by Theodore Roosevelt several years earlier when he was assistant secretary of the Navy: "Every officer on a modern warship has to be a fighting engineer."[47]

Following a three-month repair and upkeep period, the *Texas* resumed its routine duty with the North Atlantic Squadron. The next nine months proved uneventful, until Gillis received orders in July 1899 to report for examination for promotion. On 1 August 1899 he received word that he had passed and was promoted to lieutenant (junior grade). He also received orders to proceed home to await reassignment. In Irvin's final report of fitness from the *Texas*, Captain Sigsbee rated Gillis "excellent" in all categories and stated that he was "a highly intelligent, well equipped and zealous officer of all round aptitude, including engineer's duties." Sigsbee also added that he was "glad to have him" under his command and that he considered Gillis "very fit" to be entrusted with hazardous and important independent duties.[48]

"AND THE *MAINE* HAS BEEN REMEMBERED IN THE GOOD OLD FASHIONED WAY": 1899

On 11 September 1899 Gillis received word that he was to become the commanding officer of the *Porter*, which was scheduled to be recommissioned the following month.[49] In the interim he was to proceed to the torpedo station at Newport, Rhode Island, for a two-week concentrated weapons-training program on the latest torpedo developments, including propulsion, guidance, and power-generation systems.

At the end of the refresher training period, the torpedo-boat flotilla, now at Newport, had been alerted to proceed to New York City on 26 September to take part in the huge naval review to honor Admiral George Dewey and the other participants of the Spanish-American War. Gillis was given the high honor of commanding the *Winslow*, which had been repaired following its distinguished action in Cárdenas Harbor in May 1898. The *New York Times* had highlighted the fact that the *Winslow* would have a venerable place in the naval review, stating on 30 August that "the gathering of representatives of the Navy will be the largest ever seen in the waters surrounding New York. Prominent among them will be the plucky little torpedo boat *Winslow*, on which the first blood shed in the Spanish-American War was spilled."[50]

On 29 September the five-boat flotilla slowly moved in column up the Hudson River alongside several dozen battleships, cruisers, and gunboats. The main attraction, however, was the hero of the Battle of Manila Bay, Admiral George Dewey, embarked on board the cruiser USS *Olympia*, which steamed proudly at the head of the column of gleaming white-and-buff vessels extending from 110th Street to 69th Street. The next day a massive parade of 35,000 soldiers and sailors from the ships marched down 5th Avenue to the site of the proposed Dewey Arch on 23rd Street. Several hundred thousand people turned out to greet the admiral, waving signs proclaiming "Dewey for President." Alongside Dewey and receiving equal adulation was Theodore Roosevelt, beaming proudly before another sea of signs and cheers that honored "Teddy the Rough Rider." Meanwhile, all of the naval officers and squadron commanders who had commanded the major warships, as well as senior Army officers who had engaged the Spanish, were driven along the parade route in a procession of more than forty horse-drawn carriages. The day soon dissolved into a round of patriotic speeches and songs constantly interrupted by loud hurrahs and applause. The pageantry, parades, and banquets continued for nearly two weeks, gratefully concluding, at least for the worn-out participants, in mid-October.

"LT. I. V. GILLIS READ HIS ORDERS AND ASSUMED COMMAND": 1899

Following the naval review, Gillis remained in New York until taking command of the *Porter* on 10 October 1899. Without doubt this was a singular achievement for the twenty-four-year-old Gillis. In the modern vernacular, he was on the Navy's "fast track" and considered to be a young officer of great promise. The ceremony was in fact a double one, for the *Porter* was also officially recommissioned at the same time. The *Porter*'s log entry, as approved by its new captain, offers an interesting contrast between the sublimity of the event and the challenge of command that lay ahead:

Tues Oct. 10, 1899, Navy Yard, NY
    At 3:05 p.m. this vessel was placed in commission, and the ensign and pennant hoisted by Captain Frank Wildes, U.S. Navy, representing the commandant [of the New York Navy Yard], Rear Admiral John W. Philip. The crew was assembled, and Lt. I. V. Gillis read his orders and assumed command.

Following punishments assigned:

J. M. McAlevy (oiler), W. J. Powell (oiler), G. H. Reintarg (F1C). [All] drunk and unfit for duty on board ship. [Assigned] five-nights' confinement in double irons.[51]

Unlike his previous tour of the *Porter* with Lieutenant Fremont, Gillis was the only officer on board, and, of the twenty-six enlisted men in the crew, twenty were older than he. A variety of languages and accents was in evidence, as nearly half the crewmen were first-generation immigrants representing England (one), Ireland (five), Germany (two), Norway (one), Denmark (one), and Sweden (one). Gillis was the only person on board who had previously served on the *Porter* and was intimately familiar with its engineering and weapon-system idiosyncrasies.

It was fortunate that Gillis had a strong engineering bent because, during the year he commanded the *Porter*, he probably spent as much time belowdecks in the engineering spaces as he did topside. What seemed to be an endless number of minor repairs and system failures required constant attention. In fact, the *Porter*'s log resembles an engineering record more than a traditional deck log. For example, in the summer of 1900 the following entry, signed off by Gillis, reads in part as follows: "Steam on 'B' boiler. Overhauled and cleaned furnaces of 'A' and 'B' boilers. Renewed water in 'A' boiler. Renewed suction pipe from forward main feed pump heater bank and packed same. Re-babbited crank pin brasses of after blower engine. Filled tanks with fresh water."[52] When a nonengineering item did appear in the log, it often was in reference to some disciplinary matter. In July 1900, while moored in Newport, Rhode Island, the log makes note that a certain W. P. Bell "returned on board 4 hours overtime," and Gillis wasted little time meting out a severe punishment. He reduced the offender to fourth class.[53]

Interestingly, a month after Gillis took command of *Porter*, in late November, Admiral Dewey returned to Washington for a strategy meeting with Navy Secretary John D. Long about establishing a permanent U.S. naval base in the Philippines. Accompanying him was his old friend Rear Admiral James H. Gillis, whom Dewey was lobbying to be named the commandant of the new, temporary naval base at Cavite in the Philippines. Subsequently, James Gillis was not selected, as the Navy opted to give the command to a younger man.

Gillis' tour as commanding officer of the *Porter*, for the most part, was uneventful as he followed a routine operating schedule with the torpedo-boat flotilla. Over the next thirteen months the *Porter* alternated between Norfolk, Annapolis, and Newport while acting as a training ship. The torpedo boats generally headed south for the winter to Norfolk, Charleston, or Key West, where they conducted periodic maneuvers and trained naval militiamen. In early spring they would rendezvous at Annapolis and exercise in the Chesapeake Bay. The *Porter* did dock at one point in Annapolis, where Naval Academy midshipmen were introduced to the various weapon and engineering systems on board the ship. Some training was conducted for local naval militiamen. From Annapolis the ships typically would head to New York, where they would undergo repairs and upkeep at the Brooklyn Navy Yard.

The highlight of the year occurred in early summer when the boats returned to their home base at Torpedo Station, Newport, Rhode Island. In 1900 Newport was at the forefront of the Gilded Age, and many of the mansions for which the town would become famous already lined Bellevue Avenue. In fact, the officers and men of the flotilla were well known about Newport and often attracted much attention when they conducted high-speed runs in Narragansett Bay for the benefit of people like the Vanderbilts, the Whitneys, the Astons, and the Belmonts. These operations also had an official sanction, as Admiral Dewey was also in residence at Newport and was a popular figure at various supper parties and banquets hosted by Newport's elite.

Gillis and his fellow commanding officers also enjoyed participating in various festivities such as yacht racing and carnivals sponsored by the wealthy members of the "cottage colony." The torpedo station and the torpedo-boat captains also responded in kind by sponsoring "at home" dances for many of Newport's more influential citizens. One newspaper article described these events as "delightful entertainments" that had become a popular feature of the Newport social scene.[54] Sometimes the social whirl required the torpedo boats to ferry various government dignitaries or senior Navy officers about Narragansett Bay. On 5 September 1900 Gillis had the honor of welcoming Admiral Dewey and his wife on board the *Porter*. His assignment was to convey them from their cottage at Narragansett to Newport, where the following day the admiral was to preside over the Navy's newly created General Board.[55]

On the operational side, Gillis also performed duties as an instructor, both at the Naval War College and the torpedo station, on the subject of torpedo operations and tactics. His superior, Commander Newton E. Mason, who headed the torpedo station, rated him highly as an instructor, commenting in Gillis' report of fitness that Gillis delivered a "very fine performance."[56] Mason went on to become a rear admiral and subsequently headed the Navy's important Bureau of Ordnance.

One further event in the fall of 1900 occupied the torpedo-boat commanders. A major naval war game had been planned for the last week in September and would involve many units of the North Atlantic Squadron as well as the several Army forts that guarded the entrance to Narragansett Bay. The basic idea behind the war game was to test their readiness to defend Newport against a large hostile fleet attempting to force an entry at night into the bay, destroy the various defending units, and then support the landing of soldiers and marines ashore. Though never stated, the hostile force plainly represented the British Royal Navy. Interestingly, the U.S. Navy's only operational submarine, the *Holland*, would be part of the defending fleet. The entire torpedo-boat flotilla, comprised of six boats, was assigned to the hostile force.

The war game proved to be a bust for Gillis and the *Porter*, however. His assignment was to enter Narragansett Bay via the west passage while avoiding detection by the searchlights from Fort Greble on Dutch Island. In an audacious maneuver, he attempted to make a slow-speed approach well inside the main channel in the shallow waters on the island's western shore. However, the *Porter*, which drew only four feet of water, nevertheless ran aground on the mud flats and was detected. With no apparent damage to the ship, Gillis freed the *Porter* within several minutes but was declared "out-of-action" by the umpires and forced to return to the torpedo station.[57]

Somewhat abruptly, in late October 1900, less than eight weeks after the war game, the decision was made in Washington to again decommission the *Porter*. One month later, on 16 November, Gillis received new orders to a gunboat, the USS *Annapolis*, which was at Norfolk preparing for an extended deployment to the Far East. He was to be the ship's navigator. Commander Mason's final assessment of Gillis was again most complimentary, commenting in the young officer's report of fitness that his "duties [were] very well performed."[58]

CHAPTER 2

Sea Duty in the Pacific (I):
1900–1904

"*ANNIE*" IN THE PHILIPPINES: THE USS
ANNAPOLIS AND THE PHILIPPINE-AMERICAN
WAR, 1900–1902

Although commanding a ship is the ultimate goal of a naval officer, the challenge presented by the USS *Porter* was probably disappointing to Lieutenant Gillis. Throughout his command, the ship engaged in the rather monotonous series of assignments as a training vessel. Gillis reported on board the *Annapolis* on 20 November. By the end of December 1900, his ship proceeded to sail across the Atlantic into the Mediterranean and passed through the Suez Canal. The *Annapolis* arrived at Cavite in the Philippines on 24 April 1901.[1]

The *Annapolis,* or "*Annie,*" as she was affectionately known by the crew, had originally been scheduled for China duty.[2] Conditions in the Philippines, however, were more pressing. Key Filipino leaders had objected to the ceding of the islands to America for $20 million at the signing of the Treaty of Peace at Paris on 10 December 1898. On 15 September 1898 they had formed a new government and elected Emilio Aguinaldo president of the just-established Philippine Republic. The United States balked at this, deeming Filipinos to be unfit for self-rule and anarchy to be a sure result if an independent government were allowed to stand. This republic would not be satisfactory in light of the international power game that was now in full bloom in East and Southeast Asia. Accordingly, President McKinley issued his Benevolent Assimilation Proclamation refusing to recognize Aguinaldo's government.

USS *Annapolis* (PG 10)
(U.S. Naval Institute Photo Archive)

It was just a matter of time before hostilities erupted and, when American forces killed three Filipino soldiers in Manila on 4 February 1899, the Aguinaldo government declared war on the United States. By the time the *Annapolis* arrived in the Philippines in April 1901, the war had evolved into a bloody guerrilla campaign in the interior that promised to be enormously costly in terms of lives and dollars. The *Annapolis'* role in this was varied. The ship participated in patrols to interdict waterborne resupply efforts. It also ferried U.S. troops and provided valuable ship-based artillery support.[3]

Another activity included conducting hydrographic and land surveys of likely sites for a proposed permanent U.S. Navy base. Two primary locations under consideration were Subic Bay and Guimaras Island.[4] During the summer of 1901, just as he was receiving a promotion to full lieutenant, Gillis was ashore on Guimaras engaged in a survey when he was attacked by wasps and stung so badly that he nearly died. Fortunately he fully recovered.[5]

MAP 1

GILLIS' AREA OF INVOLVEMENT
DURING THE PHILIPPINE INSURRECTION OF 1902

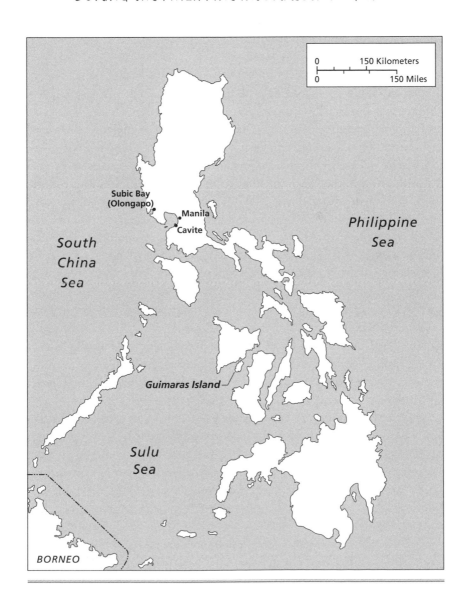

On 28 September a company of U.S. soldiers had been ambushed—as they say, "down for breakfast." Many were hacked to death by Filipino *bolomen* in the town of Balangiga. When news of the attack reached the United States the public set up a fierce clamor for retribution. Part of the demand for revenge was no doubt due to the nation's ugly mood in the wake of President McKinley's assassination only two weeks earlier. President Theodore Roosevelt ordered the pacification of Samar, and almost immediately every U.S. warship in the Philippines, including the *Annapolis*, was sent into the fray.[6]

With Gillis on board, *Annapolis* arrived in the vicinity of Balangiga for what would be a violent and vengeful campaign. General "Jake" Smith, the on-scene U.S. Army commander, ordered his force to turn the island of Samar, and particularly Balangiga, into a "howling wilderness" by killing anyone capable of bearing arms, including ten-year-old boys.[7] This latter activity undoubtedly introduced Lieutenant Gillis to the ugly feature of jungle guerrilla warfare, for the *Annapolis* did, in fact, provide ship-based artillery support for the Army ashore at various times, and the poorly equipped Filipino opposition forces took many casualties as a result. Over the next year the *Annapolis* continued to conduct patrols and survey work, ferry passengers and mail around the islands, and support U.S. Army combat operations.

By the spring of 1902 the fighting finally slowed when two important Filipino generals were captured. Although sporadic fighting would continue for more than another decade, Roosevelt was able to officially declare the war over on 4 July 1902.[8] The fourteen-year campaign (1899–1913) resulted in relatively high American casualties, with 4,324 U.S. soldiers and sailors killed in action as well as 2,818 wounded. The Filipinos lost more, and several Filipino generals were captured.[9]

With the cessation of fighting, the *Annapolis* once again returned to more mundane activities, such as performing more hydrographic surveys and basic shipboard maintenance. Attention also now could be given to catching up on naval policies and directives, which were always of second priority when in combat. One of these concerned the alarming and continuing shortage of engineering officers in the Navy that had begun to develop in the late 1890s.

When the USS *Annapolis* experienced a vacancy for chief engineer, the ship's commanding officer, Commander Karl Rohrer, probably under pressure to comply with a directive, reviewed the records of his officers.

He could not help but notice Gillis' mathematical competence and long, successful experience on the technically challenging torpedo boats. As a result, Gillis was designated the ship's engineering officer on 10 August 1902.[10] There can be little doubt that Gillis had the aptitude for such duty. As evidenced by his academic record, he possessed excellent mathematical abilities, understood complex machinery and systems, and could intellectually grasp as well as any junior officer the new career patterns then coming on line in the Navy. With his recent experience in USS *Porter*, he was familiar with the task.

President Roosevelt, when he was assistant secretary of the Navy, had urged that something be done quickly to attract more officers to the naval engineer ranks. He had listed a number of practical engineering training programs that needed to be implemented. One recommendation was that torpedo boats were excellent training platforms for new steam engineers and that they should be used for that purpose. He also argued strongly that Naval Academy graduates should no longer have a choice over line or engineering, but that they should instead be assigned in fair proportions so as to meet the increased demand.[11]

Perhaps the most important recommendation that the chief engineer of the Navy, George W. Melville, had forced through was that more junior line officers be detailed exclusively to engineering duties. Over time he had observed that such duty had been avoided by the line officer corps with few being detailed to the engine room. As a result, there was now an acute shortage of officer engineers and the responsibilities had "devolved upon warrant officers of limited education and doubtful fitness." Line officers having strong mathematical and technical competence found themselves being detailed to engineering duties. Since the Navy was becoming much more technical, he required that all future naval officers master the rudiments of steam engineering to enable both engineers and line officers to act as officer of deck, responsible for conning the ship, as well as engineering watch officers. Until then only the line officers could have that responsibility and shied away from engineering duty. The engineers, meanwhile, were considered second-class citizens in the Navy and advanced slowly up the ranks—unless they became line officers. Thus, at that time, the Navy dictated a change of policy that sought to eliminate a nearly fifty-year rivalry in the officer ranks.[12]

As the Melville policy finally reached the fleet in 1901, a temporary solution had been passed down to the fleet: to designate certain line officers for engineering duty. This was immediately met with stiff resistance within the Navy line ranks, and a severe rift soon developed within the naval officer corps, which finally broke out into open "rebellion" by 1902. Still, with the urgent need for better management of the new ships' engineering plants, the policy stood. Throughout this period Gillis must have spent much time studying for, and by August 1902 had subsequently passed, the requirements to become a qualified steam engineering officer. On 10 August 1902 the USS *Annapolis*' ship's log contained the following entry: "8AM—12 Sunday August 10, 1902 at Cavite, P. I. by order of the Commander in Chief Lieutenant I. V. Gillis assumed the duties of Senior Engineer Officer of the Annapolis, relieving Lieut. J. F. Luby."

It is not known how Gillis received what, in his mind, may have been a dubious assignment. It was, after all, a dirty, hot job and subject to severe criticism should a ship suffer a serious engineering casualty or failure. Because of this, an engineer was essentially on call twenty-four hours a day. He also had to oversee another unpleasant activity, that of recoaling the ship. This occurred when a ship arrived at a designated coaling station and inevitably meant fewer days of liberty (shore leave). Even when the coaling crew did get ashore in the Philippines, as was likely the case in other places, the coaling site for the *Annapolis* was a relatively unappealing port of call. Nevertheless, Gillis probably saw his sudden redesignation as a temporary challenge that would soon be over as he neared the end of his tour of duty on board the *Annapolis*. If indeed this was his view, he could not foresee a series of coincidental events that would soon alter his naval career and his life.

The *Annapolis* went into dry dock in Japan on 2 September 1902 and came out on 6 October. She remained at the Uraga shipyard for nearly another month as indigenous Japanese workmen continued to complete their work under the watchful eye of the senior engineer. Finally, on 1 November 1902, the *Annapolis* got under way for the return voyage to Cavite, arriving eight days later. Three weeks later Gillis received orders to detach and "report to the Senior Officer present at Amoy, China."[13]

That officer was Rear Admiral Robley "Fighting Bob" Evans, who had taken overall command of the U.S. Asiatic Fleet on 29 October 1902.[14] It may be recalled that Evans was a contemporary of James Henry Gillis and had been the commanding officer of the armored cruiser *New York*, on which I. V. Gillis had served his two-year midshipman cruise. Evans also had been ferried about on board the *Porter* during the

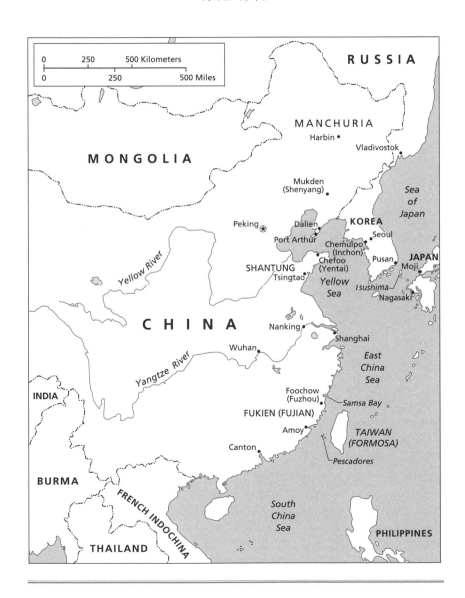

MAP 2

GILLIS' PROFESSIONAL AREA OF INTEREST, 1902–1948

0 250 500 Kilometers
0 250 500 Miles

RUSSIA

MONGOLIA

MANCHURIA

Harbin •

• Vladivostok

Mukden (Shenyang) •

Peking ⊛

Dalien •

KOREA

Port Arthur •

Seoul •

Chemulpo (Inchon) •

Chefoo (Yentai) •

Pusan •

JAPAN

Moji •

SHANTUNG

Tsingtao •

Yellow Sea

Tsushima

Nagasaki •

CHINA

Nanking •

Shanghai •

Wuhan •

East China Sea

Yellow River

Yangtze River

INDIA

Foochow (Fuzhou) •

Samsa Bay

FUKIEN (FUJIAN)

Amoy •

TAIWAN (FORMOSA)

Canton •

Pescadores

BURMA

FRENCH INDOCHINA

South China Sea

PHILIPPINES

THAILAND

Sea of Japan

Spanish-American War as he shuttled to battle-planning meetings from the battleship USS *Iowa*, which he then commanded.[15]

GILLIS AND HIS MONITOR IN CHINA: THE USS *KENTUCKY* AND THE USS *MONADNOCK*, 1902–1903

Upon arrival at Amoy in late November 1902, Gillis reported to Rear Admiral Evans, on board the battleship USS *Kentucky* (BB 6), for further reassignment instructions. He then was directed to report to the USS *Monadnock*, a 4,000-ton monitor sporting four 10-inch guns, which served as the U.S. Asiatic Fleet's station ship in Shanghai.[16] At the time it had just resumed duty to help protect the foreign settlement in that city.[17] This included American commercial and religious activities at Shanghai and upriver cities as well. Gillis was, again, to be the ship's senior engineering officer, a temporary assignment pending the arrival of a permanent chief engineer being ordered in from the United States by the Bureau of Navigation. Upon the arrival of the permanent engineer, Gillis was to detach from the *Monadnock* and report back on board the *Kentucky*. After two years of tedious duty in the Philippines on board the *Annapolis*, Gillis was surely eager to head north to China to report for his next assignment and the prospect of a change of scenery from the Philippines.

Gillis, in his brief stay on board the flagship, learned that the *Monadnock* had arrived at Amoy on 18 November to participate in a series of demanding fleet exercises that Evans had ordered.[18] Evans' staff probably let Gillis know that the *Monadnock* had certain problems that the admiral was anxious to correct. In fact, as soon as the *Monadnock* arrived, Evans had noted the poor condition of his two river station ships, the other being the USS *Monterey* (at Canton). He later wrote in his memoirs: "The two monitors had remained at anchor so long that the propriety of sending them to sea was doubtful, for they might meet some serious trouble because of the lack of experience of their engine room forces. The best way to determine this, and many other things as well, was to send them to sea and keep them there a reasonable time for practice."[19]

One of Evans' chief concerns after he took command of the Asiatic Fleet was its state of readiness to fight. Secret U.S. Navy battle plans for the Far East envisioned a general war among the powers with the United States, Japan, and Great Britain on one side, arrayed against Russia,

USS *Kentucky* (BB 6)
(U.S. Naval Institute Photo Archive)

France, and Germany on the other. Thus, Evans set about trying to whip his fleet into shape with a series of fleet evolutions, the first of which was to be conducted at Amoy. On Wednesday, 19 November, the Asiatic Fleet's flagship, the *Kentucky*, anchored at Amoy.[20] For the next two weeks, on a daily basis, ships conducted morning gunnery and maneuvering drills followed by afternoon physical-fitness training ashore. This included sporting activities in which units were divided into athletic teams that competed against each other in baseball, football, and track. Then, as a finale, Admiral Evans held a grand regatta during which sailing and oaring races were conducted. The crews for these races were manned by different classes of men: seamen, Marines, and engine room crews.[21] Gillis probably organized and led the *Monadnock* engineers' division in those races. It was all designed to build teamwork and raise morale—as well as fighting efficiency—among the crews of twenty-some old U.S. Navy ships. Upon conclusion of the training, Evans took the combined fleet south to Manila for more winter exercises.[22] The *Monadnock*, however,

A monitor of the same class as USS *Monadnock*

(U.S. Naval Institute Photo Archive)

was ordered to return to Shanghai and resume its station ship duties. It went without saying that everyone knew Evans was now determined to shake up and shape up his northern and southern ships.

Evans' poor assessment of the *Monadnock* and the *Monterey* was based on feedback from a warrant machinist on board the *Kentucky* who had visited the *Monadnock* shortly after its arrival. He had been sent to assess an engineering casualty the monitor had suffered on the short three-day transit to Amoy from Shanghai. Evans probably harbored private worries about the *Monadnock*'s three-stripe commanding officer, too. Commander Dennis H. Mahan, Naval Academy Class of 1896, had had a lackluster career, in part due to the long shadow cast by his famous elder brother, Admiral Alfred Thayer Mahan. A bitter man constantly in debt, Dennis Mahan had a reputation for alcohol abuse and even experimentation with opiates. Such information had a way of making the rounds among the officer corps, and there can be little doubt that Gillis knew the stories.

One of Evans' solutions to the *Monadnock*'s problems was to change the culture on board the ship. Accordingly, Evans, on 29 November, directed a wholesale swap of nearly one-third of the *Monadnock*'s crew with sailors from seven ships of the fleet. Informed of the fact that there were only two inexperienced enlisted warrant machinists on board, he quickly redirected Gillis to report to the *Monadnock* for temporary duty as the senior engineer. This occurred on 2 December 1902, only a few short hours after Gillis' arrival at Amoy.

Gillis boarded the ship at Amoy, and within days, with minimal time to acquaint himself with the ship's engineering plant, it got under way for Shanghai. There, it was to take up winter station until the following April, protecting American interests on the Yangtze River. Gillis was probably somewhat familiar with the *Monadnock* because it had served in the Philippines when he was there. Following a pleasant three-day transit, the ship arrived at Shanghai. During this time Gillis, besides familiarizing himself with the ship's engineering plant and his personnel, gained a keener appreciation for the ship's capabilities and shortcomings.

With Evans now the fleet commander, it went without saying that a high state of readiness was to be maintained and the ship had to be ready to sail at a moment's notice. There must have been a great deal of consternation and grumbling among the *Monadnock*'s crew, which had grown complacent while anchored comfortably for months at Shanghai. For most, there was no better "sea duty" than that of station ship, but now that they had come under Fighting Bob's scrutiny, things had undergone a drastic change. To the *Monadnock*'s engineering department, Gillis probably represented Evans' personal agent, sent to ensure that they were "squared away" and that all machinery would be maintained henceforth at a high state of readiness. An oft-quoted old Navy adage held that "a taut ship is a happy ship." The *Monadnock*'s crew may not have entirely agreed.

The function of the Shanghai station ship at its anchorage on 6 December 1902 was soon evident to Gillis, for it did not get under way again until June 1903.[23] Gillis passed his time overseeing routine maintenance and testing the ship's engineering plant. There was not even a need to coal the ship during that six-month period. The *Monadnock*'s log reflects that at daily quarters for muster there was a constant report of absentees and an endless series of courts-martial for unauthorized absence, drunkenness, alcoholism, and desertion. For Gillis this meant frequent assignment to special court-martial boards to determine guilt and punishment. That was an unpleasant duty, but not much different from that to which he had become accustomed on other ships.

However, there was time to go ashore and mix with and meet U.S. and foreign naval officers to glean information or absorb rumors making the rounds and then repeat them in wardroom gossip. The U.S. Asiatic Fleet's officer corps had immediately sensed a sea change in style and substance through the effort to conduct frequent drills and more underway "fleet work and maneuvers." Another sore point was Evans' Fleet General Order No. 4, which directed all officers to appear for each evening wardroom meal in full formal evening dress or mess jackets. This became a contentious issue, as some officers complained that "the commander-in-chief could not legally compel them to appear for their meals in any particular uniform."[24]

When the ship arrived in Shanghai on 6 December 1902, Evans had moved to "beef up" his meager presence by appointing the *Monadnock's* captain as operational commander over three other smaller U.S. vessels, the *Elcano, Villalobos*, and *Pompey*. Together, these four ships played a key role in supporting the new American Open Door Policy in the Yangtze River Valley along the central and northern China coasts, the genesis of what ultimately would become the "Yangtze Patrol."[25] Gillis, the only commissioned officer-engineer in the group, very likely found his engineering expertise to be in demand on board all four vessels.

Although the *Monadnock* was well suited for its river-gunboat-diplomacy role, it had a negative side: the 262-foot ship was slow and had a deep draft and little freeboard. Because of this, its main deck was usually awash even in a moderate sea, and it could only safely operate several hundred miles up the Yangtze. However, its four heavy 10-inch guns could, if required, deliver a devastating blow to any belligerents ashore, being capable of leveling several city blocks with one salvo. Equipped with this formidable firepower, minor operational missions in China were largely left to the purview of the Navy's Canton and Shanghai monitors, along with an assortment of small U.S. gunboats. The monitors' commanding officers often were the on-scene commanders involved in quelling disturbances that threatened U.S. interests upriver or at obscure ports. The *Monadnock*, while poorly suited for the open sea due to its main deck having little freeboard, was ideal for river and close-in coastal operations.[26]

Soon after his arrival in Shanghai, Gillis was also introduced to the political, military, and strategic realities that prevailed in a restless and volatile China. First, Gillis could not help but notice that despite the spectacular U.S. naval victory over the Spanish at Santiago and Manila and the continued buildup of American naval power, the U.S. Navy still lagged far behind the other major players in East Asia. For example, when the *Monadnock* arrived in Shanghai it likely received its usual anchorage assignment from the harbor authority, that of seventh position. This meant it had to anchor well down the Whangpoo River at an inconvenient distance from the center of activity at the Shanghai Bund. The anchor buoys were assigned in the following order of rank: England, France, Russia, Germany, Japan, Italy, and the United States.[27] Among the Asiatic Fleet's officer corps it was common knowledge that America's inferior position in East Asia was largely due to its reluctance to join in the "sphere of influence" chess game that threatened to divide China into a series of European colonies. As a result, the foreign navies tended to regard each other's activities with much more suspicion and wariness than they did the antiforeign sentiment rippling through the Chinese provinces. While it is not within the scope of this narrative to detail each foreign concession and outright territorial land grab, suffice it to say that by the time Gillis arrived on board the *Monadnock*, the various powers dominated entire provinces, including control over railways, mines, industries, and seaports.

Because the *Monadnock* did spend a great deal of time at anchor with only an occasional trip to Nanking, there was ample opportunity for Gillis to go ashore and experience China for the first time. What he found was a place simultaneously decadent yet vibrant with new ideas. Enlisted Navy men could indulge themselves in singsong bars while being exposed to the vices of wine and woman. Many succumbed to this lifestyle by reenlisting in exchange for a second or third tour in China. The sailor who did this was known by fleet sailors as having "gone Asiatic." On the other hand, Gillis witnessed the wave of new thought that pervaded Shanghai in the wake of the Boxer Rebellion. Many young Chinese intellectuals descended upon the city seeking more freedom from the hated Manchu regime. They found some protection in the proximity of the foreign settlement. Printing houses proliferated, and all forms of Western ideas and philosophies had begun to take root there. Eight years later the Shanghai ferment led to the Chinese Revolution of 1911.

America's role in all this drama was deepening. The aforementioned Open Door Policy had been enunciated by John Hay, the U.S. secretary of state, in 1899, just prior to the Boxer Rebellion. The Open Door Policy was intended to protect the integrity of China as well as support the continuance of a central government, asking the major powers to declare formally to uphold Chinese territorial, political, and administrative integrity. Additionally, they were asked to not interfere with the full use of the treaty ports that might lie within their respective spheres of influence. Though none of the nations complied formally as requested, Hay felt that enough of a consensus existed to announce in March 1900 that an agreement had been reached.[28] No one objected, and the Open Door became de facto international policy and would serve as America's foreign policy in China for the next thirty years. The potential it offered attracted two general groups of foreigners, each pursuing a different market: the commercial market and the "market of souls."[29]

By the time Gillis arrived on the *Monadnock*, the U.S. Navy had determined that devising a practical role for the U.S. Navy to enforce the Open Door Policy required a rethinking of its strategy in the East Asian theater. It was no secret that as of 1900 the region was not yet of major importance in overall U.S. strategy, and by 1902 not much had changed. Thus, the inability of the Navy to assume effectively its new enforcement role was not lost on U.S. Asiatic Fleet commanders and the Navy Department at home. Since the end of the Spanish-American War, U.S. naval strategy in the Pacific had been shaped by the dangerous territorial chess game being played out by the Western powers in China and had become a matter of serious concern.[30] By 1902 there arose three basic objectives. First, there was a need to create an effective Asiatic or Pacific Fleet as part of an evolving two-ocean strategy. Second, in order to support this fleet, it was paramount to establish a major naval base in the Philippines. Finally, and perhaps most delicate, it was essential to establish a second Asian naval base on the coast of China. The purpose of such a base was simple and twofold: to protect the Philippines by being able to counter any hostile move by the other naval forces in China, and to provide a rapid-reaction force, especially in support of the Open Door Policy.[31]

In the summer of 1902, the Navy's General Board made the China base a key element of its strategy as it related to coaling stations. The Navy had spelled out its preference for a chain of coaling stations that would extend from the U.S. eastern coast through the Caribbean and the Panama Canal to Hawaii, Guam, and the Philippines, and end in China. The coaling capacity would be 100,000 tons at the Hawaii station; 20,000 tons at Guam; 100,000 tons at Subic Bay in the Philippines; and 50,000 tons at a Chinese base. The Chinese site had yet to be determined, but the Navy's choices had narrowed to a port off the Yangtze River mouth and San Sha Bay (Samsa).[32] While much of this information was not generally known within the fleet, there was the usual wardroom gossip that made reference to studies and surveys that the Navy was conducting. As early as June 1900, just days before the Boxers attacked the legation compound in Peking, the *Army and Navy Journal* had warned that the United States should demand a Chinese port if the rebellion resulted in a grab for Chinese ports by the Western powers.[33]

American intentions were soon known, however, when several diplomatic overtures about a coaling base were made to Great Britain and to Japan. It seems that each had protected its interests in earlier agreements with the Chinese. Much territory, in fact, had been placed off-limits to foreign bases in an agreement Japan had concluded with China several years earlier. Japan reacted quickly with a resounding objection to the American request.[34] Soon thereafter the British also objected to the request. It also had obtained a promise from China, in 1846, to not allow a third power to have a leasehold on its claimed territories.

All of this was put on hold in the summer of 1903 when tensions with Russia flared. Russian encroachment on Port Arthur had become a sore point with U.S. diplomats in the north of China. During this time, several U.S. sailors had been imprisoned for fighting with their Russian counterparts while ashore on liberty. Eventually the sailors were freed, but the incident aroused great suspicion on the part of the U.S. consul, who thought the Russians were about to annex all of Manchuria despite assurances that they would withdraw their troops from the region by 8 October 1903. Things seemed to quiet down when the Russians made an initial effort to remove some of their force during the summer, but by October 1903 they had made no effort to complete the withdrawal as promised.[35]

Admiral Evans had previously ordered his fleet north to Chefoo (Yantai, on the northern Shantung Peninsula coast) for "exercises." He also alerted the five hundred Marines in detachments in the Philippines to be ready to move quickly to China.[36] In early June 1903, with Lieutenant Gillis on board, the *Monadnock* left its winter station to head north to Chefoo. Upon arrival, it joined three battleships, several cruisers, and a sister monitor.[37] They were now eyeball-to-eyeball with a similarly configured Russian fleet a hundred miles north across the Korea Bay (the northern Yellow Sea) at Port Arthur. The standoff continued, and the threat of war moved President Roosevelt to consider preparing the public for a possible war. Everyone was nervous. The sides seemed to shape up with Japan and Great Britain joining the United States and France and Germany joining Russia.

Admiral Evans, having returned with much of the northern squadron of the Asiatic Fleet from the Philippines, ordered a series of fleet gunnery exercises and drills.[38] The tension was broken in mid-July when Russia finally caved in and agreed to open ports in Manchuria for commercial purposes. Japan meanwhile had been negotiating separately with Russia and things remained unsettled until, in October, press reports began to circulate that war between those two nations would soon occur.[39]

The *Monadnock* remained at Chefoo for the summer.[40] On 20 July, the secretary of the Navy, William Henry Moody, in a letter that forwarded a letter from Admiral Evans, "warmly" commended Gillis for the *Monadnock*'s successful full-speed trial. In Admiral Evans' letter, he noted that he had ordered Gillis to assume charge of the "engineers' Department" due to the fact that *Monadnock*'s "motive power was in a very unsatisfactory condition and the excellent work accomplished is due, in the main, to him."[41] But at last, on 25 August, Gillis' relief finally arrived in the Far East, ending his temporary engineering duty on board the monitor. Gillis received orders to report back to the USS *Kentucky*, which lay at anchor in Chefoo harbor, where he would be reunited with Admiral Evans, whose staff was embarked.[42]

A TASTE OF THE FLAGSHIP AS WAR CLOUDS THICKEN: THE USS *KENTUCKY*, 1903–1904

It may be recalled that Evans had been the commanding officer of the armored cruiser *New York* when Gillis served on that ship. Evans had arrived in the Far East in April 1902 and subsequently assumed command of the northern squadron of the Asiatic Fleet. It was just following his promotion to fleet commander that Evans, a stern taskmaster, set about putting both the northern and southern squadrons into fighting trim. For Gillis, his assignment to the *Monadnock* was somewhat of a boost of confidence since Evans undoubtedly took a hand in the selection. But it also meant that Gillis had a great deal of pressure exerted on him to ensure that the *Monadnock*'s engineering force measured up. By the time he arrived on board the *Kentucky* on 26 August, Gillis likely still had a sympathetic ear in the person of Admiral Evans.[43]

This assignment on the Asiatic Fleet flagship afforded Gillis an even better place to observe the increasing war activities between Russia and Japan. By this time U.S. naval policy had evolved into four broad missions: (1) protecting American lives and property; (2) promoting American interests, both commercial and religious; (3) cultivating amicable relations with the central Chinese government and its provincial representations; and (4) gathering intelligence vis-à-vis the other foreign-power navies. There was an inclination to place the most emphasis on the fourth mission. The intelligence mission also appealed greatly to the newly emergent, technically oriented naval officer. As one expert put it, they "tended to view foreign relations and naval diplomacy quantitatively . . . counted ships and men, measured tonnages and weights of broadsides, and evolved mathematical ratios."

Admiral Evans paid much attention to the third mission—cultivating amicable relations—by initiating frequent contact with Chinese leaders, including a meeting with Dowager Empress Tz'u-hsi and Prince Ch'un in the spring of 1903, and establishing good relations with Chang Chih-tung, the Hunan and Hupeh viceroy protecting the upper Yangtze River Valley.[44] The thrust of Evans' reasoning—as well as the senior U.S. State Department officials in China, including the minister—was to generally side with the existing, and perhaps more predictable, Chinese Manchu government. On the other hand, as mentioned earlier, Gillis witnessed the wave of new thought that pervaded Shanghai in the wake of the Boxer Rebellion. Lieutenant Gillis, by that point, had seen China "up close and personal." And he received firsthand an education in the delicate strategic balancing regarding the chess game between the contending powers in East Asia.

On board the flagship, the USS *Kentucky*, Gillis was thankful to find himself no longer attached to the engineering department. Instead, he once again was involved in above-deck line duties. The *Kentucky*'s log shows him standing regular watches as officer of the deck under way and in port.[45] It was a very busy period for Gillis because Evans was frequently on the move, involving the flagship in various naval diplomatic missions and fleet readiness exercises.

Gillis also learned quickly that in his brief time on board the *Monadnock*, his initial mission of protecting U.S. interests against Chinese xenophobia on the Yangtze had changed and was now of secondary importance to that of keeping a watchful and suspicious eye on the activities of other big power navies. When he arrived on board the *Kentucky* in August, the top priority for Evans and his staff was to carefully monitor the rapidly deteriorating relations between Japan and Russia. That was the very reason that Evans had brought much of the U.S. Asiatic Fleet to Chefoo, which lay only a hundred miles across the Po Hai Strait from the Russian naval base of Port Arthur.[46] The Russian naval concentration there, as well as the recent movement of ground forces into Manchuria, had been a chief worry in Tokyo for quite some time. It also worried others, including the British, who gladly concluded a semisecret pact with the Japanese in 1902 that in essence stated that should either country become engaged in hostilities, the other would be obligated to remain neutral.[47]

Evans began to worry openly that a war might break out at any moment, and he decided to place the fleet close by the likely flashpoint of Port Arthur. Since May, he had been advising the secretary of the Navy that the situation was quite unstable. The following cipher message on 2 May offers an example of his state of mind: "The conditions of affairs in China, I regard as growing more and more serious. The extraordinary activity of the Russians in the accumulation of munitions at Port Arthur, their evident disinclination to evacuate Manchuria and the daily increasing uneasiness and antagonistic feeling among them . . . calls for deep and careful consideration of those in authority in regard to the protection of American interests in China."[48]

Once he placed the fleet at Chefoo, Evans probably played an important role in seeing that the Tokyo naval attaché, Lieutenant Commander Charles C. Marsh, gained permission to visit Port Arthur in the summer of 1903. Marsh, who happened to be Evans' son-in-law, probably met with the admiral on board the *Kentucky* sometime in July or August to brief him on his observations of conditions there. These included an estimate that there was an adequate coal supply in Port Arthur in the event of war, and a report that the Russians claimed to have enough forces there to withstand an assault of an army of 60,000 troops. Marsh probably also relayed to Evans that he believed there to be five battleships and three armored cruisers in the port, but, interestingly, there were no dry-dock facilities.

It was evident that the Russians suspected that American sympathies lay with Japan and were concerned enough about the assembled American fleet at Chefoo to send a high-ranking military observer there to report on U.S. Navy activities.[49] The Russian observer remained in

Chefoo for the summer, frequently seeking out American naval officers to engage in conversation.[50]

In late September the U.S. fleet was ordered back to Japan for much-needed repairs and coaling. Evans sent his cruiser division to Yokohama, while the *Kentucky* and three other ships headed for Nagasaki. En route they stopped at Tsingtao, China, where Evans and the various ships' officers and crews, including Gillis, were entertained lavishly at the German naval base there as well as by the large German expatriate population living in the surrounding city and suburbs. After nearly a week there, the ships sailed on to Nagasaki.[51]

At Nagasaki the four American warships underwent a brief upkeep and repair visit. It was evident to all that Japanese war preparations were at a fevered pace. Railroad lines were being laid to all wharves and docks so that men and supplies could be easily delivered to warships and transports. Evans noted that officers on several Russian warships in the harbor remained "curiously indifferent to what was going on under their very noses."[52]

Following the two-week stay, Evans took the squadron to Kobe, where his cruiser division at Yokohama was to join up for more drills before the ships headed on to Manila. At Kobe, however, he received the stunning orders from Washington to take the fleet to Honolulu. Evans was perplexed. A war was obviously imminent in China, but the orders had not indicated why he was now being sent to Hawaii. It was only some time later that he found out that President Roosevelt was about to acquire Panama and its Canal Zone. Several South American republics were rumored to be openly hostile to the American acquisition and were possibly preparing to fight.[53] In that event, the Asiatic Fleet would be needed in the South Pacific.[54] Evans immediately took his squadron on to Tokyo Bay to rendezvous with the cruiser division that was hurriedly finishing up repairs there. While in Tokyo, he was called upon by a Japanese cabinet minister, a close personal friend, who asked Evans to convey the following message to President Roosevelt: "Please say to the President that war between Japan and Russia is inevitable unless England and the United States interfere. We have done everything possible to prevent it and have failed."[55]

On 5 December 1903 the Asiatic Fleet sailed for Hawaii, arriving there on 18 December.[56] The *Kentucky*'s ship's log continued to reflect Gillis standing regular at-sea officer of the deck watches. It was a very rough passage, as the fleet had a following sea that constantly broke over the after section of the ships, preventing any crewman from safely going on deck. Evans commented that he had "rarely seen such a heavy sea."

Once the ships arrived at Honolulu, the situation in Panama seemed to settle down, and the fleet was not required to sail any farther east. The stay was most pleasant, in fact, and a grand party was sponsored by Evans several days after Christmas. The government pier where the battleships *Kentucky* and *Wisconsin* were moored was converted into a lavish outdoor garden ballroom. The two ships provided electric lighting by their generators, and tables with palms and flowers were set up. Evans again notes: "Two fine bands provided music, and officers and men, all in white uniforms, received and entertained our guests. Dancing was kept up until daylight brought an end to our frolic, which had been thoroughly enjoyed by all."[57]

A week later Evans was ordered to get under way and proceed back to Manila at best speed. Following brief stops at Wake Island and Guam, the Asiatic Fleet anchored off Cavite on 18 January 1904.[58] The admiral promptly paid a call on Governor William Howard Taft at Manila and received the latest update on the situation between Russia and Japan. President McKinley had asked Taft to head a commission in 1900 to oversee the transition of the Philippines from military to civilian governance, to prepare them for eventual independence, and appointed him the first governor. Part of that debriefing likely included reading the latest dispatches from Lieutenant Commander Marsh, the naval attaché in Tokyo, which warned that the situation had reached a "most critical" stage.[59] Evans also received orders to proceed immediately to investigate Subic Bay, north of Manila on the west coast of Luzon, for its suitability as a coaling station. On 20 January the *Kentucky* anchored in Subic Bay off the town of Olangapo.[60] On arrival, another cable from Marsh was waiting. It alerted the Navy Department that the Japanese navy had accumulated a large supply of high-quality smokeless Welsh coal, and the emperor had taken the extraordinary step to authorize war funds without bothering to obtain the approval of the Diet (the Japanese legislature). Marsh concluded that war was near at hand.[61]

Marsh's warning of impending hostilities was supported by other diplomatic and military reports reaching Washington. Most key American officials, as well as President Roosevelt, now saw that war was inevitable. Earlier, on 25 December, Commander Dennis H. Mahan, as senior officer present afloat (SOPA), Shanghai, ordered the USS *Vicksburg* to Chemulpo (Inchon, Korea) to protect American interests and transferred his Marines to that ship for the mission.[62] On 8 February 1904, the commanding officer of the *Vicksburg*, who at that point was SOPA, Chemulpo, received a letter from Rear Admiral S. Uriu, of the Imperial Japanese Navy, advising that he should notify any American merchant ships in port that he planned to attack any Russian ships there if they refused to leave port.[63] The news was received with excitement at the Office of Naval Intelligence (ONI). For some time, the ONI had viewed the anticipated contest of arms as an ideal opportunity to observe new weapons and tactics expected to be employed by each side. And the United States was not alone in this thinking. More than a dozen other nations were busily preparing to do the same.

During the *Kentucky*'s voyage back to the Philippines, the ONI set in motion a plan to place competent observers on board warships of both the Japanese and Russian fleets. An immediate action involved posting someone to Tokyo as assistant naval attaché who would be instantly available once permission was obtained from the Japanese.[64] It is unclear whether the ONI preselected the officer; however, it appears that in the interest of expediency the ONI deferred to Admiral Evans to select an officer from the Asiatic Fleet for reassignment to Tokyo. Whatever the process, the *Kentucky*'s log at Olangapo for 20 January 1904 reads in part as follows: "Lieutenant I. V. Gillis USN detached from this ship and ordered to take first mail steamer to Japan and report to naval attaché, Lt. Commander Marsh, USN for further instructions."[65]

When Gillis departed the USS *Kentucky* that morning, he had no way of knowing that with only a brief exception, his sea duty career was at an end. Instead, over the next sixteen years, his naval duties would find him ashore, heavily engaged in the contentious and strategic struggles as a player in the "Great Game," whose playing field had now shifted eastward from Central Asia. In the original Great Game, the only opponents were Russia and Great Britain. Now, in the Far East, many others had been added to the mix.[66]

CHAPTER 3

The Lure of Naval Intelligence: Ashore in Asia and Back to the Atlantic, 1904–1907

WAR AND INTELLIGENCE: ASSISTANT U.S. NAVAL ATTACHÉ IN TOKYO, JAPAN, 1904–1905

Evan's choice of Gillis for naval attaché was likely not a difficult decision. By then, the admiral was quite familiar with the young officer's competence and courage. He had demonstrated his technical proficiency by putting the *Monadnock*'s engineering system back in order and, on board the *Kentucky*, Evans had been able to observe Gillis' keen ship-handling abilities over the previous several months. Gillis' selection for attaché duty in Tokyo was probably predicated on several practical considerations. First, he was available on board the *Kentucky* as an officer "in excess." That is, all lieutenant billets were already filled by qualified individuals, so he was available for reassignment. Second, Gillis possessed ideal qualifications for what the Office of Naval Intelligence subsequently planned to do. The Navy believed that torpedo warfare was going to play a prominent role in any confrontation between the Russian and Japanese fleets. Also, Gillis possessed battleship experience and was well versed with tactics and gunnery associated with the "heavies." This, too, would be of key importance because Japan had seven battleships, and Russia had eight in the Northeast Asia region. Thus, from the Navy's point of view, Gillis possessed the perfect combination of courage and technical qualification to expertly record and report on any action to which he would be privy.

Gillis undoubtedly was excited about the prospect of covering a conflict that would command the attention of the highest officers of the U.S.

government and the Navy. Under normal peacetime conditions, however, he probably would not have been pleased with his assignment. Despite strong interest and backing by President Roosevelt, the ONI was still a nascent, unsophisticated organization, initially established by Secretary of the Navy General Order No. 292 on 23 March 1882 and formally, finally, and officially recognized by an act of Congress on 12 January 1899.[1] It operated on a meager budget and was forced to rely on the Bureau of Navigation to identify and order line officers to serve either at its bare-bones headquarters in Washington, D.C., or abroad as attachés.[2] The staff at the ONI's headquarters in Washington received, collected, studied, and published information from three principal sources: naval attachés, shipboard intelligence officers, and the media (i.e., newspapers and magazines).[3]

The prevailing Navy culture held that intelligence duty not only lacked prestige, but also that its product had only minimal value. As was the case with engineering duty, intelligence assignments (e.g., attaché posts) could seriously divert an officer of the line from the real business of operating and preparing a ship to fight at sea. Over the years Gillis had surely been exposed to secondhand wardroom gossip about attaché duty: the endless rounds of teas, dinners, and receptions; the ungentlemanly spylike activities connected with gathering information; and the ungenerous expense allowances. This is not to say that there were no officers who believed in intelligence or none that served ably in this period. In fact, there were a few who succeeded for a variety of reasons. Some were fluent in one or more foreign languages, which allowed them to move easily about in another country. Some grasped the strategic significance of understanding a potential enemy and its intentions. Others possessed a keen aptitude for analysis. Unfortunately for the ONI, there was little prospect for continuity. Also, attaché duty was comparatively rare among line officers because there were comparatively few duty stations. Inevitably these "few good men" had to return to sea duty or risk being failed for promotion. At the same time, the post of shipboard intelligence officer was merely a collateral duty assigned to an inexperienced junior officer.[4] As a result, this duty was performed for the most part without enthusiasm or interest and reported observations often lacked in useful detail. The real professional intelligence officers, of course, were the attachés. They observed their host nation's navy and tried to insert themselves into the elite social society of the diplomatic and naval communities. Also, as line officers, they were proficient observers, keenly interested in new naval weapons and technology. Their effectiveness during the Spanish-American War paid off with keen interest and support from people like Theodore Roosevelt.[5] By the time Gillis reported to Charles C. Marsh, all the world's eyes were firmly fixed on the war clouds, while the U.S. Navy anticipated useful reporting from their naval attachés.[6]

Gillis' understanding of the challenges that lay ahead for him was probably superficial at best. He was likely cheered by the hearty endorsement of Admiral Evans and had, without doubt, received a cursory briefing from the admiral's staff about the issues now propelling Russia and Japan toward all-out war. He may even have learned that efforts were under way to place him on board a Japanese warship to observe the anticipated naval action. Based on this knowledge, it can reasonably be argued that Gillis was excited about the prospect of going to Tokyo. He likely viewed it as temporary duty and assumed that he would be returned to sea duty upon the conclusion of the war. On the other hand, he probably gave only passing consideration to the fact that he knew little about the intrigue and secret struggles for strategic supremacy that the Russians called the "Tournament of Shadows." Even if he had considered this, he did not worry much about it. After all, he was being seconded to Lieutenant Commander Marsh, whom he knew would bear major responsibility for the many diplomatic functions that might be required. Marsh had been in Tokyo for nearly four years and also could quite expertly instruct Gillis on whatever arcane aspects there were about the business of intelligence.

For his part, any misgivings Admiral Evans may have had surely passed quickly when, only a week after Gillis reported to Marsh at the U.S. Legation, the war between Russia and Japan erupted. Lieutenant Commander Marsh, already sensing that hostilities were at hand, hurriedly assisted Gillis in getting "squared away." Other naval diplomatic calls and social activities would have to wait. Gillis busied himself in his first week calling upon the U.S. minister, Lloyd C. Griscom, and his two legation secretaries. The first thing Gillis noticed was their age. The minister was thirty-two and his first secretary, Francis M. Huntington-Wilson, was twenty-nine, the same age as Gillis. The second secretary, John Mackintosh Ferguson, was also young, being in his thirties. Gillis probably found some common ground to break the ice. Griscom hailed from a well-connected Philadelphia area family, Ferguson was from Pittsburgh, and Ransford Stevens Miller Jr., the legation's interpreter, was a New Yorker. Huntington-Wilson had been in Tokyo since May 1897. Miller was the legation's eldest staff member, in his forties. They were solidly Republican in their politics, which was comfortably compatible with Gillis' own political views.[7] Like Gillis, the staff also knew Admiral Evans well, since Marsh was his son-in-law and the admiral's wife and a second daughter had been living in Tokyo since Evans joined the Asiatic Fleet in 1902. Despite their youth, they were all enthusiastic and well situated in Tokyo. They also were well connected politically in the United States through family and by marriage. For example, Griscom's father, Clement, was a prominent Pennsylvania shipping magnate, at ease with John Hay, Henry Cabot Lodge, J. P. Morgan, and Mark Hanna.[8]

Eventually Marsh arranged for Gillis to make many rounds of official calls. After the legation staff, he introduced Gillis to whatever Japanese navy officials there were in Tokyo, and letters of introduction also were arranged with other key foreign naval attachés. This was important for, until 1914 and the onset of World War I, it was standard practice for attachés to trade information with their foreign counterparts. In this regard it was particularly important to be on good terms with the British naval attachés, who, because of the 1902 Anglo-Japanese Alliance, enjoyed special entree with the Imperial Japanese Navy. The senior British attaché was Captain Ernest Troubridge. Gillis could not help but be envious of the British influence on Japan's navy. Not only were many of Japan's warships designed and built by the British, but Captain Troubridge had accompanied the Japanese fleet in early February to Port Arthur (Lüshun), where he witnessed the opening naval salvos of the war.[9] Moreover, the British military even had a cadre of Japanese-speaking officers available as observers. Japanese approval for that training had been granted some months earlier, in September, and by February four language-proficient British officers were resident in Japan. Shortly after the war began, Britain ordered four more language officers to Tokyo.

In the larger political-military context, very simply, the emerging war had its origins ten years earlier, when Japan defeated China in 1894. As a consequence of the Treaty of Shimonoseki signed on 17 April 1895, China ceded Taiwan, the Pescadores, and the Liao-tung Peninsula in southern Manchuria to Japan. The latter contained the two strategic ports of Ta-lien (Dalian), a commercial center, and Port Arthur, an ice-free naval base guarding the entrance to the Po Hai Strait. China also was forced to recognize Korea's independence and open more treaty ports as well as grant Japan all the privileges that the Western powers enjoyed in China. Adding insult to injury, the Chinese were also assessed 200 million taels indemnity. Almost immediately, alarm bells went off in St. Petersburg over Japan's success, which now threatened to checkmate Russia's own ambitions in Manchuria. In short order the czar convinced Germany and France to "advise" Japan to give up its claim over the Liao-tung Peninsula—including the two ports. Japan bowed to the pressure in late April 1895, accepting a further 30 million taels indemnity. By 1903 Russia had continued its blatant activities in Manchuria, which included construction of a series of railways connecting the newly built Trans-Siberian Railway with Vladivostok, Port Arthur, Ta-lien, Mukden, and Harbin. Troops and supplies were flowing into the area, and the Russians were poised to reap the rewards of the rich industrial resources in Manchuria. As Japan watched, it felt betrayed, finally concluding that it could no longer tolerate the Russian encroachments. In later years, Japanese diplomats would often point out that the strategic area of Manchuria was viewed in the context of Japan's own version of an Asian Monroe Doctrine: they would not stand idly by and watch their strategic interests violated.[10]

On 6 February Gillis' indoctrination gave way to on-the-job training when Marsh cabled the Navy Department that Japanese troop transports had sailed for Korea. During the evening of 8 February 1904, a Japanese destroyer squadron carried out a surprise torpedo attack on the Russian fleet at Port Arthur. By midnight two Russian battleships and a cruiser had been heavily damaged and put out of action. The next day, another Japanese naval squadron fired on and crippled Russian warships at Chemulpo, Korea, as Japanese troops occupied Seoul. Meanwhile, Admiral Heihachiro Togo arrived with the bulk of the Japanese fleet at Port Arthur and commenced an unmerciful shelling of the harbor and surrounding facilities. It was not until the third day, 10 February, that Japan officially declared war on Russia.[11] Marsh and Gillis, without hesitation, set about organizing their activities to meet the immediate demand for information now streaming in from the Asiatic Fleet, the White House, and various key Navy commands in Washington, submitting reports on military events as they unfolded. Initially they learned little of immediate value but were able to pass along the official daily war reports by Griscom obtained from Japanese Imperial Military Headquarters. As the Japanese gradually loosened up on their censorship, local press items soon proved to be of some value in piecing together reported actions into useful news.

On a monthly basis they prepared a location report of all foreign naval vessels in the Asian theater. Biographies of key Japanese naval officers were also produced, including those of Admiral Togo and various staff and operational commanders.

In response to pressure from Roosevelt and the U.S. military, reacting quickly following the war announcement, John Hay, the U.S. secretary of state, directed Griscom to approach the Japanese government with a request to send U.S. attachés to the war zone as observers. Several weeks went by before the Japanese responded. They finally authorized military attachés to go to Korea with the Japanese army, but no naval attachés were permitted to embark on board Japanese warships.[12] This came as a sharp disappointment to Gillis, who had now been officially designated by the ONI to act as the forward naval observer attached to the Japanese fleet. He was one of three officers selected to try to get to the war zone, which was expected to be concentrated in China's Liao-tung Peninsula. This strategically important peninsula was connected by the Manchurian Railway linking Siberia via Harbin across inner Manchuria. Passenger and supply traffic from St. Petersburg to Vladivostok across the Trans-Siberian Railway had started in 1903, and Westerners simply referred to the strategic rail system as the Manchuria Railway.

The other two U.S. attachés selected to observe the war zone were Lieutenant Newton A. McCully and Lieutenant Lloyd H. Chandler. Each of the three officers was instructed to carry out his assignment from differing means of access. McCully was to go to St. Petersburg and attempt to gain Russian approval to go to Port Arthur. Chandler apparently was tasked with trying to cover the fight, possibly, from Korea. Gillis seemed to have the best assignment.[13] When Griscom protested the decision not to allow Gillis to go, the Japanese offered a slight compromise. They granted Gillis and Marsh access to the Imperial Military Headquarters, where they could receive periodic briefings by Japanese navy officials. This soon proved to be a disingenuous gesture, since Griscom frequently had to remind Hay that the information given to the attachés was "only bare official reports very carefully censored and interesting details . . . generally withheld."[14]

Thwarted in the effort to place an observer with the Japanese fleet, the two naval attachés began reading and clipping news articles, for nearly every key office in Washington, from the White House to the various U.S. Navy commands, clamored for news of the war. Even this, however, was of only slight value. In the early weeks of the war, correspondents from around the world poured into Tokyo thinking they would be able to quickly move on to the war front. Griscom was under similar pressure from the White House and the State Department to report on diplomatic matters. The Japanese, however, were of another mind. They implemented a news blackout and exercised strict censorship over any war-related articles. About the only thing the correspondents were allowed to do was sightsee about Tokyo and write articles favorable to Japan. Most, however, just "holed up" at the Imperial Hotel, where they would gather daily at the bar to drink and commiserate about the lack of Japanese cooperation. The American contingent was an illustrious and colorful group that included Jack London, representing the Hearst papers; James Dunn, the *New York Globe*; Frederick Palmer, *Collier's*; Willard Straight and Robert Collins, Reuters; Richard Harding Davis, *Harper's Weekly*; John Bass and Stanley Washburn, the *Chicago Herald*; Lionel James, the *Times* of London; and John Fox, *Scribner's Magazine*. Finally, in late March, they were granted permission to go to Korea. Once there, however, few reached the actual war front as the Japanese military authorities continually blocked them. Instead, like Gillis and Marsh, they were given official news releases that often were misleading and inaccurate.[15] When Jack London found himself arrested in Korea by the Japanese military for accusing a low-ranking Japanese soldier of stealing food from his house, Roosevelt made strong representation through Griscom to ask for London's release—which ultimately was accomplished.[16] By July many reporters had straggled back to Tokyo, fed up with Japanese obfuscation. It rankled both American correspondents and attachés alike, however, that British military personnel and newspapermen enjoyed near-complete access to the battle front.

Assistant U.S. naval attachés also assigned to cover the war elsewhere were faring no better. Lieutenant McCully, who the ONI had detailed to St. Petersburg, was upon arrival to obtain permission from the Russians to travel overland via the Trans-Siberian Railway, eventually connecting to Port Arthur. Once there, he was to seek approval from the naval authorities at the port to board a Russian warship as an observer. McCully encountered much hostility in St. Petersburg due to Russian suspicions that the United States was sympathetic to Japan. He eventually made it to Port Arthur, but the same resentment of Americans existed there, too, and he was never able to observe any of the subsequent naval actions at sea.[17] Other nations' reporters and attachés were treated similarly. The one exception was that of Britain. Captain Sir William Christopher Pakenham had been approved to accompany Admiral Togo on board the Japanese battleship *Asahi*, which served as the Imperial Japanese Navy's flagship. Pakenham left nothing to chance, however. He remained on board the *Asahi* for fourteen months, fearing that if he disembarked he would be left behind. As a result, he was able to gain the confidence of Togo and observe the two major naval fights of the war, the Battle of the Yellow Sea on 10 August 1904 and the Battle of Tsushima on 27 and 28 May 1905. Marsh and Gillis were unable to receive any meaningful information from the British, however. Pakenham was wary of Japanese censorship and did not wish to incur their distrust. Early on, he informed the British Admiralty that "you will have to understand the limitations that the wishes of my kind and generous host impose on the scope of my reports." As a result, the full report of his observations was not published until some months after the war ended in 1905.[18]

Despite the initial disappointment of not gaining approval to accompany the Japanese fleet as an observer, Gillis' first encounter with intelligence duty was on the whole quite rewarding. Not only was it a welcome change from the nearly ten years of sea duty, but he undoubtedly was exhilarated with being at the center of intelligence activities, documenting the most significant naval battles, in the Yellow Sea and at Tsushima, since the Machine Age began some fifty years earlier. Gillis and Marsh could not help but recognize the sudden emergence of Japan as a world naval power. Nor could the authorities in Washington, including the U.S. Navy and President Roosevelt, miss the significance of Japan's victories. The Imperial Japanese Navy had adopted and mastered the latest in naval technology. Moreover, it appeared that Japan's sailors were well skilled in all facets of war at sea. They were an offensive force to be reckoned with in the Pacific. A wary President Roosevelt wrote: "In a dozen years, English, Americans and Germans, who now dread one another as rivals in the trade of the Pacific, will have each to dread the Japanese more than they do any other nation. . . . If we show that we regard the Japanese as an inferior and alien race, and try to treat them as we have treated the Chinese, and if at the same time we fail to keep our navy at the highest point of efficiency and size then we shall invite disaster."[19]

Meanwhile, in Tokyo, Marsh helped Gillis find a rental residence that had office space and a personal safe. The U.S. Legation, located not far from the Japanese Foreign Office and the Shimbashi railway station, had no space for the attachés except for classified file storage. Marsh, in fact, operated from his home in the Tokyo suburbs, and so would Gillis. Already at this early date, the legation was aware of the Japanese Secret Service's efforts to gather information from the foreign legations. Griscom assumed that the mail was being tampered with and learned the Japanese had a collection of seals of most countries that allowed them to break into diplomatic pouches "without leaving a trace."[20] To circumvent the efforts of the Japanese Secret Service, Marsh had instructed Gillis on a new code that the Navy had specially issued for use in enciphering. Moreover, in 1901 the ONI had introduced an intelligence "kit" for all attachés. It included a pocket-sized Kodak camera (Marsh was a skilled photographer), a vest-pocket Navy code book, and an Underwood type-writer. The typewriter was new, but the volume of material being sent to the ONI from the field now demanded that reports be typewritten for clarity. This probably explains not only Gillis' lifelong proclivity to type all his correspondence but also his subsequently acquired ability to micro-analyze typewritten matter. Gillis learned that attachés were assigned a letter cue to distinguish their correspondence from others. This included X for London, Y for Paris, T for Rome, Z for Berlin, and W for Tokyo.[21] Marsh also familiarized Gillis with the informant system. Attachés frequently tapped American businessmen, reporters, or missionaries who were located near or traveled to various ports or naval facilities of interest. The selection of such individuals was done with care and usually accomplished by appealing to the patriotic feelings of the individual informant.[22]

Marsh opened other doors by obtaining a membership for Gillis in several of the key clubs in Tokyo where meals could be taken and contacts made and maintained with club members from Japan and other nations. The Tokyo Club was one such place. Huntington-Wilson, whom Gillis would later record as knowing "very well," frequented this club and often met Henry W. Denison (about whom more will be related later) there. The Maple Club was another such gathering spot. Clubs were also handy for holding luncheons or dinners for entertaining a variety of U.S. naval officers. Marsh was an excellent mentor for Gillis in this, Gillis' first exposure to the attaché and intelligence business. One could dwell at length on the multitude of information they collected and reports that they generated. Suffice it to say that they did a creditable job while under strict censorship, and what Gillis came away with was a much keener understanding of how the system worked and a multitude of acquaintances, several of whom would play an instrumental role in his career in the not-too-distant future. To help pay for travel, club membership, subscriptions, and "business" dinners, Marsh introduced Gillis to the legation's so-called Maintenance Fund. Both officers could draw upon this money while awaiting reimbursement from the Navy. Even with the help of this financial resource, they sometimes had to borrow money from each other to get through the month. For example, in 1904, among the memorabilia Gillis later sent to the New-York Historical Society, there was a 10,000 yen (about $500) IOU signed over to Marsh by Gillis.[23]

With the observer issue at a stalemate, Marsh set about introducing his new assistant to the world of naval diplomacy and intelligence. Aside from the social whirl in Tokyo, Marsh undoubtedly shared local travel with Gillis to observe Japanese naval activities. Most of the places they likely visited were in proximity to various shipyards and naval staging areas, such as Kyoto, Nagasaki, Sasebo, Yokohama, and Moji. Moji, located on the western entrance to the Island Sea, was where many Japanese naval ships staged from as they sortied to meet the Russian fleet at Tsushima in late May 1905. As a result, it was a sensitive area; Jack London had been arrested there by the Japanese and his camera confiscated. As information collection continued, Marsh organized a systematic reporting system. On a daily basis both he and Gillis forwarded official Japanese war releases and relevant newspaper items to Washington. These were usually first encrypted using a special naval code and then transmitted via cable. The pair also forwarded any other information using the same code on an as-occurring basis. A monthly report was also transmitted to Washington that listed the locations of all foreign warships in East Asian waters.[24]

In Washington, the ONI, hampered by the censorship, cobbled together reports from all its sources and produced a weekly war bulletin that went to the White House. The ONI also forwarded memoranda containing more analytic "meat" that were briefed at weekly cabinet meetings. The ONI created a large war map of sea areas in East Asia for Roosevelt, placing small national flags at the estimated positions of Japanese and Russian naval units. An example of the ONI intelligence passed to Roosevelt, undoubtedly drawn from data forwarded by Marsh and Gillis, reflected a keen awareness of Japanese military competency and zealotry. It essentially described the coordinated amphibious landing in Korea involving thousands of troops that was executed by the Japanese army and navy. Some of the information was obviously gleaned from accounts by Lionel James, who, as a British reporter, had more access than most. One part reads as follows: "It was deliberate but rapid as the situation required and entirely without noise, fuss, or confusion. Every man knew exactly what to do and where to go. The behavior of all the Japanese was excellent and they all seemed to be stirred by an all-powerful sense of loyalty to their nation."[25]

Under normal peacetime circumstances the attaché's job usually proceeded at a comfortable pace. There were no reporting deadlines to meet, and success or failure usually depended upon the inclination of the officer to take his responsibilities seriously. The typical task was to appraise the host country's warships and manpower, calculating tonnages and weight of broadsides, and estimating maximum speed and coaling ranges as well as the proficiency of its personnel. It was unexciting, dull work, and most viewed such duty as lacking in prestige and as a serious impediment to their career. But, in a wartime setting, over the next twelve months, Gillis would learn much from Marsh, who was a seasoned attaché, having been in Tokyo since November 1901. When Marsh was ordered to the attaché position in Tokyo, he also had responsibility for China. Prior to that, he had held a position at the ONI's headquarters, where he helped develop a new filing system for incoming intelligence reports. The system was useful in cataloging the vast amount of data that had accumulated at the ONI since 1882, when it was founded. It has already been noted that Marsh was Robley Evans' son-in-law, and in his memoir the admiral made mention of Marsh's professionalism: "During the time he had been on duty in the East this officer had shown astonishing aptitude for the work given him. His ability to deal with Asians, his . . . tact and courtesy in his intercourse with them, added to his professional qualification, which . . . had enabled him to collect a mass of information most useful to his government."[26]

The fact that Marsh was Admiral Evans' son-in-law opened many doors for him in Tokyo. For example, Evans was fast friends with Baron Kaneko, a Harvard Law School graduate, the main architect of the Meiji Constitution, and a member of the emperor's Privy Council. Kaneko left Japan in late February 1904 and, as a measure of his stature and fame, was sent on a public relations mission that subsequently evolved into the inclusion of Japan at the Portsmouth Peace Conference.[27] Evans also was friendly with the Japanese minister of marine, a Vice Admiral Baron Enomoto. These connections could well explain Marsh's ability to gain access to the Imperial Military Headquarters for Gillis. He also ensured that Gillis met nearly all the most prominent Japanese officers.[28]

As the war progressed following the initial naval battle, the Russian squadron, which suffered little damage, retired to Port Arthur protected by the base's shore batteries. The Japanese fleet, under the command of Admiral Heihachiro Togo, maintained a naval blockade in the area around the port while contenting itself with laying mines and firing an occasional naval barrage to drive Russian army forces back across the Yalu River. Other Japanese naval units protected their army's eastern and southern flanks by keeping watch over the Russian Vladivostok squadron. The Japanese strategy seemed plain to all—neutralize or defeat the Russian Pacific Fleet while the Imperial Japanese Army consolidated control over the Korean mainland, and then cross the Yalu and seize the Liao-tung Peninsula so as to isolate Port Arthur. The final land action was predicted to be a move north into Manchuria, where the rail links with the Trans-Siberian Railway could be severed. This would deny the Russians the capability to resupply its ground forces as well to support an eventual naval fight, the end game being to consolidate Japanese control over Korea, Manchuria, and the Liao-tung Peninsula, including the ports of Ta-lien and Port Arthur.

Meanwhile, Lieutenant Lloyd Chandler, commanding a torpedo-boat flotilla based at Cavite in the Philippines, was ordered to go north, probably with the U.S. Asiatic Fleet's cruiser division. Admiral Evans had received a report that the Russians "were forcibly detaining an American ship at Port Arthur." In late January Evans ordered Admiral Philip Cooper to take his cruisers to Shanghai and then proceed in the USS *New Orleans*, the flagship, to Port Arthur to retrieve the American vessel, as well as report back on conditions there. This latter task was probably going to be Chandler's responsibility. The *New Orleans* never went farther than Shanghai, however, as the forcible detention report proved to be false. The Navy Department intervened, and Cooper was ordered not to proceed north of Shanghai, at least in part because there was apprehension in Washington that the United States might be placed in an embarrassing situation should the *New Orleans* find itself in the midst of a naval confrontation between Russian and Japanese fleet units. By July Chandler reported that he had nothing to report, and he returned to Cavite.[29]

During all this, Marsh and Gillis labored on in Tokyo, submitting periodic reports on military events. Both continued to pressure Griscom and the Japanese to allow Gillis to embark on board Japanese fleet units as a naval observer, but to no avail. The correspondents also remained a disgruntled group, continuously complaining bitterly to Griscom about censorship. The U.S. minister would, in turn, pass along to John Hay the exasperation he felt in dealing with the attachés and the correspondents. Regarding the latter, he occasionally complained to Hay about their increasing uncooperativeness.[30] Nevertheless, Marsh and Gillis drew upon a variety of sources that sometimes yielded clues to tactics and weaponry and provided a fuller understanding of the tactical and strategic picture. The quest for better information on the war led Griscom to conduct a very active social calendar, frequently attending or hosting high-level diplomatic soirees. Both Marsh and Gillis were likely in attendance at some of these functions, where they would have exchanged war gossip with their foreign military and naval counterparts.

During this busy period Gillis also experienced a fortuitous, near-perfect harmony of effort between the Navy and State Departments. This was due in part to the congenial and collaborative atmosphere created by Griscom and his staff. Compatibility played a role as Gillis found himself at ease and accepted among the legation staff.[31] Gillis also learned early on to appreciate Marsh's close and friendly relationship with Japanese officials. From his tenure as naval attaché, Gillis also developed a grudging respect for the use of military force as an instrument to further Japanese ambitions in the Pacific and, as we shall see, later in Asia. His reports to the ONI would show Gillis to be fervent in warning of a coming conflict between Japan and the United States. His strategic thinking at this early period was undoubtedly influenced by what he observed and heard as an attaché. Whereas before the war the Russians were viewed as a principal concern for the U.S. Navy, now Japan was to be closely watched.

A key source tapped by Griscom and Huntington-Wilson was Henry W. Denison. He was a highly placed and influential American who had been a special adviser to the Japanese Foreign Office since 1875. By 1904 the Japanese entrusted Denison to draft all treaties, declarations, and vital diplomatic documents. Huntington-Wilson, who was on intimate terms with Denison, later recorded in his memoir that he thought Denison "wished to help Japan to become a sort of miniature Britain in the Far East, and believed it necessary, for this, to take measures of protection against the constant Russian threat." While Denison never betrayed any confidences, he did provide valuable insights into Japanese strategic thinking, which always were conveyed to the White House, the State Department, the Navy Department, and the ONI.[32] Griscom also enjoyed a special relationship with the writer Richard Harding Davis, with whom he was a close friend. In fact, they had been together in Central America in 1895, and their adventures were chronicled in Davis' book *Three Gringos in Venezuela and Central America*.[33] The Davises (Richard's wife, Cecil, accompanied him to Tokyo) were frequently included in the Griscoms' social circle.

A significant acquaintanceship made by Gillis was with the Reuters reporter Willard Straight. Again, it was through Wilson that this developed. Straight had gone to Korea just ahead of the first press contingent, eventually reaching the Yalu River with the Imperial Japanese Army. Increasingly frustrated with Japanese intelligence and red tape, he returned to Tokyo in July. A frequent guest at the Huntington-Wilsons', where he sang and played the guitar, he also knew the Far East quite intimately, having lived in Japan as a boy and later serving as private secretary to the famous Sir Robert Hart, inspector general of the Imperial Chinese Maritime Customs Service. He spoke Chinese well and possibly could converse in Japanese. Possessed of a charismatic quality that drew people naturally to him, he moved in the highest of social and business circles in the United States and counted among his close friends Edward Harriman, J. P. Morgan, Taft, and Roosevelt. Later, he benefited from his marriage to Dorothy Payne Whitney, the daughter of W. C. Whitney, the political leader, financier, and former secretary of the Navy. He was very much a progressive Republican who strongly promoted American business interests in China, and particularly in Manchuria.[34]

Several other journalists were also recruited to provide any sensitive information they might learn in their travels to the war zone. Griscom likely utilized both Richard Harding Davis and Willard Straight for such matters as details of battle damage to the Russian ship *Askold*, which had sought refuge in Shanghai in April 1904.[35]

During the first several months of the war, one of the best sources of information available to the attachés was Lionel James, the British correspondent representing both the *London Times* and the *New York Times*. James was the only reporter who actually witnessed naval activity at Port Arthur with the blessing of the Japanese government. Moreover, he was the first man to send wireless news reports while at sea. He accomplished this feat by boarding a steamer in Shanghai shortly after the war began. After a coincidental meeting with Dr. Lee De Forest, in London in December, James had been intrigued with the American inventor's idea that a radio transmitter at sea could instantly send reports to a station ashore, which, in turn, could be converted to newsprint within hours of receipt. After successfully rigging the steamer with an antenna and placing De Forest's equipment on board, James had sailed to Wei Hai Wei. There, he set up a relay station that could within minutes send cables to London. By late February he was at sea and operating just a few short miles from Port Arthur, and over the next several months he transfixed readers the world over with accounts of the sea war. Unfortunately, his reporting was so good that not only did the Russians try to label him a spy, but the Japanese as well thought it best to not give up too much tactical insight into the Port Arthur campaign. By July his operation had ended.[36]

Until mid-August the war's action was principally focused on the ground. By 1 May the Japanese army had succeeded in pushing the Russians back across the Yalu River, essentially placing Korea under Japan's control. By late May, after having crossed the Yalu, the Japanese forces gained another victory at Anshan that allowed them to occupy the commercial port of Ta-lien. Russia now had to consider seriously that Port Arthur might also be lost. After the initial naval battle at the outset of the war in early February, the Russian fleet had retired to Port Arthur, protected by the base's shore batteries. Admiral Togo continued to maintain a naval blockade in the Po Hai Strait, with his destroyers occasionally dashing in to fire a barrage. The noose around Port Arthur slowly tightened over the next three months as the Russians were defeated in a series of bloody skirmishes on the Liao-tung Peninsula. These actions resulted in the final encirclement of the port, preventing resupply and escape on the northern flank.

The Japanese pushed relentlessly forward, and on 15 June at Telissu they were able to completely sever Russian links from Manchuria to the southern Liao-tung Peninsula and Port Arthur, where the bulk of the Russian Pacific Fleet was now effectively sealed off by land as well as sea. The siege of that port began as Russian troops attempted to reopen links to the beleaguered navy and army forces dug in around the naval base. It was a bloody affair throughout the rest of 1904, with casualties climbing into the tens of thousands. In this moment of desperation, the Russians gambled on a naval confrontation in an attempt to cripple the Japanese fleet and end the blockade of Port Arthur.

The Russian fleet sallied forth from the port on 10 August with six battleships, four cruisers, and thirteen destroyers. Admiral Togo's opposing force consisted of four battleships, ten cruisers, eighteen destroyers, and thirty torpedo boats. The battle was a furious one, but within hours the Russian Yellow Sea squadron was resoundingly defeated. Fifteen damaged Russian ships were able to limp back to Port Arthur. These included five battleships, one cruiser, and nine destroyers. The rest were captured or scattered along the Chinese littoral, seeking refuge at various ports. The Japanese suffered damage to four battleships. The ultimate result was an overwhelming tactical and strategic victory for Japan. We now know what happened there, but, at the time it was happening, Marsh and Gillis remained relatively uninformed about the tactical aspect of this battle and could only report piecemeal on events as fragmentary accounts reached them.

By August Port Arthur was sealed for good and the port of Vladivostok was badly mauled. When news finally reached St. Petersburg, the Russians were stunned. Their dismay was further compounded as ground losses began to mount. By mid-October the Russians on the Manchurian front had lost a fifth of their 200,000-man ground force, while the Japanese had suffered 20,000 killed. Port Arthur was surrounded but hung on doggedly; word had come that a relief Russian naval expedition was on its way from the Baltic via the Indian Ocean and was expected to arrive in the early spring of 1905. That fleet, under the command of Admiral Zinovy Rozhestvensky, had been preparing itself for the voyage since early summer, but because of its magnitude the undertaking would take nearly eight months to complete. The fleet's arrival in 1905 came as no surprise to the waiting Japanese.

The Japanese were determined to conquer Port Arthur before the Russian relief fleet arrived, and on 2 January 1905 the city finally surrendered. Casualty figures vary depending on the source: the total of Russian soldiers killed numbered between 40,000 and 70,000, while the Japanese lost from 47,000 to 80,000. Many were killed in pushing the Russians back to Mukden (Manchuria), where the last land battle of the war took place in February.[37]

As the world watched the slow progress of the Russian relief fleet and learned of the surrender of Port Arthur and the Japanese army's victories in Manchuria, changes were occurring at the U.S. Legation in Tokyo. In January 1905 Marsh received orders to report as the executive officer of a cruiser, and Gillis relieved him as the naval attaché. It was a temporary assignment for Gillis, however, for Lieutenant Frank Marble had been ordered in February to proceed to Tokyo and relieve Gillis.[38] Upon being relieved by Marble on 31 March, Gillis was once again the assistant naval attaché, but by then he had received orders to report to the ONI's headquarters in Washington for temporary duty. In early April, however, the Russian Baltic Fleet was sighted near Singapore. One week later, on 14 April, the Russian fleet had anchored at Cam Ranh Bay in Vietnam. It was obvious that the long-anticipated naval showdown was near at hand. Because of this, Gillis would remain in Tokyo and assist Marble in reporting on what promised to be a singular event in naval history. There is little doubt that with a decisive naval fight looming, a final plea to the Japanese was made by Griscom to place Gillis on board a naval unit as an observer. Approval never came, however, and the naval attachés once again were forced to play a secondary role in recording the largest naval battle in history to date.

The Battle of Tsushima took place on two successive days in late May 1905. On paper, at least, it appeared that the Russians had the advantage with big ships. But the Japanese more than made up for that with the speed and maneuverability of their smaller, more-numerous units. At the end of the second day, 28 May, the once-proud Imperial Russian Navy no longer existed. Twenty-one of its ships had been sunk and thirteen disarmed and captured. More than 4,000 Russian sailors were dead and another 6,000 injured. The Japanese had lost but three torpedo boats and just over 100 dead and 500 wounded. The battle could not have been more lopsided.[39] Back in Tokyo, Gillis and Marble could only wait for press reports and official Japanese statements. Gillis' frustration over the previous sixteen months was summed up in a *New York Times* news item on 1 June 1905 with the headline "Togo Lost but Three Boats." The article stated in part:

> Secretary [of the Navy] Morton today conferred with the President regarding the sea battle. Naval officers are very anxious to get the details of the conflict. The relatively small loss by the Japanese is especially interesting to them. The questions naturally suggested to the technical mind are: Was it superior marksman-

ship and proficiency in the handling of guns, or was it a swarm of torpedo boats or submarine mines that did the effective work?

The Japanese have been so reticent regarding the movements of their armies and fleets that it is regarded as doubtful whether they will be disposed to furnish any information on these points.[40]

The war reduced the Russian navy to a second-rate power, a condition from which it needed fifty years to recover. Japan, meanwhile, now took its place as the second most powerful navy in the Far East, and its domination over Korea and Manchuria was generally recognized by the European powers and the United States.

Shortly after the Tsushima battle, Gillis detached from Tokyo and headed back to Washington, where he was to perform temporary duty with the ONI.[41] There were likely three impressions that Gillis took away from his experience in Tokyo. The first was a dislike for civilian bureaucracy. He probably felt betrayed by the State Department for its failure to gain permission for him to be a forward naval observer with the Japanese fleet and did not blame Griscom so much as he did the civilian bureaucracy. Second, his experience with the various national rivalries then prevalent in Asia had given him a deep-seated suspicion of other nations' motives and activities. Sobered by Japan's victory over Russia and the ascendency of its navy within the ranks of the world's imperial powers, he also developed a strong suspicion of Japanese intentions that would greatly influence both his naval and civilian careers for the rest of his life.

There was a third factor that would impact significantly on Gillis' career over the next decade. He became acquainted with two men who would come to play key roles in his career over the next decade. The first was Francis Huntington-Wilson, the legation's first secretary. Huntington-Wilson harbored strong alarm over Japan's rising power in the Pacific and its relative easy conquest of the Russian army and navy. He, like Griscom, would write later in his memoirs about the "arrogance and power" of the Japanese military after the battle.[42] Only four short years later, Huntington-Wilson would become the assistant secretary under Secretary of State Philander Knox within the Taft administration. He would be credited with being the architect of Taft's "Dollar Diplomacy," as well as the driving force behind a reorganization of the State Department.

The second person was the aforementioned Willard Straight, the Reuters reporter, a close personal friend of Griscom who spent much time in Tokyo, and who it is certain Gillis would have met. Straight had strong reservations about the Japanese presence in Manchuria and Korea and did not hide his suspicions about Japan's intentions in the region. He would, over the next four years, be the U.S. consul in Manchuria and the head of Far East Division at the State Department. Both he and Huntington-Wilson would have a lasting influence on Gillis.

At this point, with the Russo-Japanese War winding down and culminating in the peace conference arranged by President Roosevelt at the naval shipyard near Portsmouth, New Hampshire, Gillis could take great personal satisfaction from the contributions he undoubtedly made during his first tour of duty in naval intelligence.[43] The disappointment of being unable to report firsthand from the deck of a Japanese warship had passed. It had been tempered by the exhilaration that obtains from helping create a rich archive of data that once analyzed leads to a keener understanding of a potential rival.

BACK TO OLD VIRGINIA AND MORE SEA DUTY: THE ONI, THE RESERVE TORPEDO FLOTILLA, AND THE USS *ATLANTA*, 1905–1907

Upon his departure from the Far East in May 1905, Gillis proceeded to Norfolk, Virginia. From there he went to Washington, where he stopped from 8 May to 20 May for special duty at the Office of Naval Intelligence, probably to wrap up a compilation of lessons learned from the Russo-Japanese War.

Over the next few months, several important diplomatic events occurred that significantly altered the Asian landscape. William Braisted, professor of history at the University of Texas, characterized the resultant agreements and alliances as "tripartite policies of the Pacific."[44]

The first of these events was the secret agreement signed in July 1905 between Secretary of War William Howard Taft and Japanese prime minister Taro Katsura. In this document the United States essentially agreed to Japanese control over Korea in return for Japanese recognition of American interests in the Philippines. Following on the heels of this agreement was the famous Treaty of Portsmouth, in which President Roosevelt mediated a settlement of the war between Japan and Russia. Signed on 5 September 1905, the treaty contained language that essentially ratified the Taft-Katsura agreement. Russia and Japan also agreed to leave

Manchuria, returning it to Chinese sovereignty. Japan, however, was granted a leasehold of the Liao-tung Peninsula, which gave it control over the port and city of Ta-lien as well as the Russian rail system in southern Manchuria. Japan also gained the southern half of Sakhalin Island.[45] The Japanese public reacted negatively to the agreement, however. Many felt that the entire island of Sakhalin should have been ceded to Japan and that Russia should pay a significant indemnity. That resentment boiled over in 1906 when a series of events hastened the collapse of the Katsura cabinet. Much of the anger was also directed at the United States because of its role in orchestrating the Treaty of Portsmouth.[46] As these various diplomatic events unfolded, the ONI carried out an analysis and assessment of Japan's sudden emergence as a naval power. The ONI files were sifted, and Gillis undoubtedly participated in these activities.

In Norfolk, on 3 June 1905, Gillis took command of the Reserve Torpedo Flotilla, which was based there.[47] In September 1905 he was assigned additional duty as commanding officer of the USS *Atlanta*, formerly a "protected cruiser," one of four ships built in the 1880s with steel-protected vital areas, powered primarily by sail but with steam power in battle. These were the pioneers of the U.S. Navy's steel warships. At this point, however, the *Atlanta* was a barracks ship that housed the sailors of the Reserve Torpedo Flotilla in Norfolk.[48] At first glance the command of a barracks ship could be construed as a rather minor assignment, of not much significance. The *Atlanta* did not often go to sea and served as a place where Reserve Torpedo Flotilla sailors could live while their boats, with their cramped quarters, were in port. As such, the *Atlanta* operated with a reduced crew that was primarily responsible for order and discipline among the various crews housed on board the old cruiser. On the other hand, the assignment was undeniably a stepping-stone to higher rank and more important status. For example, there were six vessels in reserve in the Atlantic Fleet in January 1907. Among the commanding officers of those ships, two, Bradley Fiske and Alfred Reynolds, would eventually rise to the rank of rear admiral. Another, Washington Chambers, eventually founded U.S. Navy aviation and retired as a captain. Lieutenant Gillis, the youngest of these commanding officers, was again under the command of Admiral Evans, who now was commander in chief of the Atlantic Fleet.[49]

Little has been uncovered concerning Gillis' official activities during this tour of sea duty, but we do know that his time back in the United

USS *Atlanta* (protected cruiser)
(U.S. Naval Institute Photo Archive)

States allowed him to renew family ties. Harry and his wife, Emma, were only a short distance from Norfolk, in Richmond, Virginia, where Harry was a mechanical engineer. James Henry and his new wife, Ursa Canfield Gillis, visited fairly often with his children, coming north from his home in Melbourne, Florida. Brother Lyle was in Alexandria, Virginia, with his wife, Grace. Sister Carol had married David Murray, a patent attorney from Binghamton, New York, where he was also a U.S. commissioner. Murray practiced law in New York City.[50]

The Navy Department's Board of Inspection and Survey conducted an inspection of the Reserve Torpedo Flotilla from 29 January to 1 February 1907. Its report on that inspection resulted in a letter from the secretary of the Navy to Gillis that indicated the Navy Department was pleased to note the general satisfactory and efficient condition of the vessels of the Reserve Torpedo Flotilla and quoted the board's words regarding how the unit's work had been "done with a plant that has been, in a great measure, improvised by the force of the Reserve Torpedo Flotilla and speaks well for its intelligent organization and administration."[51]

The Office of Naval Intelligence sent Gillis' nomination for promotion to lieutenant commander to the secretary of the Navy on 12
April 1907 for the secretary's endorsement to the president of the Naval
Examining Board. The board's positive recommendation was approved
by President Roosevelt on 15 April.[52]

On 20 May 1907 Gillis attended the unveiling of a statue in Raleigh,
North Carolina, honoring Ensign Worth Bagley, a U.S. Navy hero of the
Spanish-American War.[53] It may be recalled that Bagley was killed in
action in Cuban waters on board the USS *Winslow*, a torpedo boat similar to the USS *Porter*, to which Gillis was assigned at the time. Bagley was
the only U.S. naval officer killed in that war.[54]

Meanwhile, many political and military events occurred that con-
verged and bore on the situation in China, to which Gillis would later
head. From the earlier work at the ONI in which Gillis had participated
emerged an initial assessment and "lessons learned study." Much of the
information ended up being published in an essay that appeared in the
U.S. Naval Institute Proceedings in March 1906 under the authorship of
Captain Seaton Schroeder, then the chief of the ONI. The essay, entitled
"Gleanings from the Sea of Japan," ranged across a series of naval systems
and tactics that were in evidence at Tsushima. The list included torpedo
warfare, wireless technology, guns and armor, big ships' advantages, and
speed. Schroeder also addressed the proficiency of the Japanese and their
fighting spirit. President Roosevelt concurred in the assessment, and he
concluded that the balance of power in Asia had suddenly been altered.[55]

This conclusion was reinforced in October 1906 when an ONI
study showed that the Japanese fleet in the western Pacific posed a serious threat to both the Philippines and Hawaii. For example, of the fifteen battleships in the U.S. Navy, only one was then in the Pacific. In the
event of a war, the U.S. fleet in the Pacific could not be reinforced rapidly enough from the Atlantic to counter a Japanese threat to the islands
of Hawaii or Guam. Also of concern was the eruption of anti-Japanese
immigration activities in California at this time.[56] All this produced war
jitters in the United States that were serious enough to prompt Roosevelt
to review plans for war with Japan in June 1907. Among the fallout from
this review was the decision to send the U.S. Atlantic Fleet to the Pacific
as a bold show of force.[57]

Captain Schroeder left the ONI in the spring of 1906, having been
promoted to rear admiral. His replacement was fifty-seven-year-old

Captain Raymond Perry Rodgers, a well-respected line officer and an experienced former naval attaché who had done much in the late 1880s to demonstrate, as second in command there, the value of the ONI.[58] He also had been acquainted with James Henry Gillis, having graduated from Annapolis in 1868 and subsequently serving extensively at sea. In his earlier tour at the ONI, Rodgers distinguished himself as an innovator and keen student of new intelligence methods. For example, he introduced cryptography and traveled about Europe observing and collecting intelligence. He had likely had contact with Irvin Gillis at Santiago, Cuba, where, as the executive officer of the USS *Iowa,* he was well aware of Gillis' heroism in the Spanish torpedo-recovery incident.[59] Gillis also must have impressed Rodgers with his understanding of the Asian naval situation and his performance of duty in that theater. In addition, Rodgers would have had occasion to speak with Lieutenant Commander Marsh, who arrived in Washington in the fall of 1906 for duty as a member of the Board of Inspection and Survey. By the winter of 1906 Rodgers had concluded that conditions in Asia had been changed so greatly that previously aborted plans to place an attaché in China required review.[60]

In January 1907 the Army and the Navy agreed to conduct joint studies for a possible war with Japan, and Congress approved funding for two U.S. "dreadnought" battleships. It is likely that at least in part due to the ONI's observation the previous fall that fourteen of the fifteen U.S. battleships were in the Atlantic and that Pearl Harbor and the Philippines were vulnerable, the Navy established the Pacific Fleet in February. This "new" fleet was actually a realignment of naval forces in the Pacific that included a squadron of armored cruisers and heavy cruisers that patrolled the U.S. West Coast and another that performed police duties in China and the Philippines. A third squadron remained in the Atlantic area of operations. The fleet's biggest concern remained the lack of a suitable base in the western Pacific.[61]

In the same month, President Roosevelt signed an immigration bill that denied entry into the United States to Japanese laborers who had no passports.[62] The U.S. naval attaché in Berlin reported in March that he was convinced that war between the United States and Japan was inevitable. He also reported that the British and German admiralties were convinced that Japan would win such a conflict. A rumor circulated by the Italians had Japan building eight battleships, but later in the summer

Commander John A. Dougherty, the U.S. naval attaché in Tokyo at that time, said that no such battleships were being built.[63]

Riots against Japanese residents occurred in San Francisco in May 1907 and, as a result, vigorous protests were published in Japanese newspapers. In June President Roosevelt sent the Atlantic Fleet to the Pacific, giving rise to the concept of the "Great White Fleet"—so named because of the white-painted hulls of the U.S. warships. Also in June, France and Japan reached an agreement in which they recognized each other's spheres of interest in China. More disturbing was the agreement reached between Russia and Japan that included a rapprochement concerning Manchuria, defining their respective spheres of influence. With this in mind, Admiral George Dewey, then head of the General Board, asked the War College to study what effect the current situation might have on a possible war between the United States and Japan.[64] In July Commander Dougherty forwarded an alarming statement by Admiral Sakamoto of the Japanese Hydrographic Office that stressed the principal U.S. Navy weakness: "Where will the U.S. have a base for such a fleet?"[65]

Meanwhile, back in Washington, Captain Rodgers learned that all of the focus at the ONI's Tokyo office from 1903 through 1905 had been concentrated on the Russo-Japanese conflict. Marsh reminded Rodgers that the last time any detailed intelligence gathering had been conducted in China was in the fall of 1902, when he accompanied Admiral Evans up the Yangtze River.[66] In late 1906 Rodgers had begun to lay the groundwork for what he envisioned would be the mission of a Peking attaché. By January 1907 Rodgers made the decision to press his superior, Admiral George Converse, chief of the Bureau of Navigation, to consider improving intelligence collection in Asia by creating a separate billet for an attaché in Peking. In making his case, Rodgers emphasized that he believed new sources of information needed to be developed in China, recognizing that an autonomous attaché would be able to collect and report information relative to relations between China and Japan. He further argued that an independent attaché in China might well fulfill the duty for which secret agents had been contemplated and, if deemed necessary, later establish a system of agents in the principal centers of interest. One source of concern to the U.S. Navy was the reports in late 1905 of a potential naval relationship between the Chinese and Japanese. A news item suggested that Japanese naval advisers would soon be detailed to China to assist in rebuilding its Beiyang (North Sea) squadron, which had essentially been destroyed in the 1884 War. More rumors circulated that many Chinese, impressed by the recent Japanese victory over Russia, "saw Japanese naval assistance to China as an opportunity to get out from under the yoke of European commercialism."[67] As a result, Rodgers advised Converse of the need to better understand the Chinese navy and its capabilities.

Rodgers not only was familiar with Gillis' father but also the son's exceptional professional abilities and technical acumen. Furthermore, Gillis' five years of duty in Asia certainly qualified him as someone who could be reasonably expected to comprehend and report on the ever-changing conditions and delicate strategic relationships then extant in China. Rodgers initially may have considered appointing Marsh as the China attaché, as had been planned prior to the war, but the veteran Tokyo attaché had now become too senior and had to consider his own career as a line officer. Most likely, Marsh urged Rodgers to consider Gillis, who had acquitted himself well as Marsh's assistant in Tokyo. By a curious coincidence of timing, an article appeared in a London-based journal, the *English Illustrated Magazine*, in February 1907. It was written by William B. Northrop and entitled "Capturing a Plunging Torpedo." The short story, replete with dramatic drawings, extolled the daring actions of I. V. Gillis in the Spanish-American War, leaving the impression that future histories of naval actions would no doubt come to recognize Gillis as in the forefront of American heroes.

As a consequence of all of this, the Navy began preparing to send Lieutenant Gillis to Peking. In April 1907 Commander Dougherty had relieved Commander Marble as the Tokyo naval attaché and was also designated as naval attaché in China. According to a rather secretive June letter of explanation from Captain Rodgers to Commander Dougherty, "It has been the intention to send a Naval Attaché to China for some time; a memo to do so was sent last January." Up until receipt of that letter, Dougherty had no knowledge of Rodger's plan to eliminate his China responsibilities. But in June Rodgers advised the Tokyo attaché that official approval of a separate attaché billet for Peking had finally been approved and Gillis had received orders to fill the position. He further advised that Gillis would be directed to stop in Japan en route to China. Rodgers seemed uncertain of the security of the mail system and informed Dougherty that Gillis would "explain orally many things which can be better described in conversation than by letter." Rodgers also explained his reasons for not informing Dougherty earlier, noting that Gillis should arrive in Yokohama, Japan, at the end of August.[68]

Even after Gillis' appointment, Rodgers continued to expand on what the China attaché's mission would be. In addition to establishing a network of agents, he thought it wise to obtain permission from key foreign diplomatic missions in China to permit the U.S. attaché to visit their naval facilities in their respective spheres of influence. It was contemplated that this would include French naval bases, the German naval enclave at Tsingtao, and the Russian naval forces at Vladivostok and along the Amur and Ussuri Rivers on the Manchurian border. The Royal Navy and its facilities in China also were to be observed. Interestingly, the U.S. naval attaché in Tokyo would retain responsibility for Japanese naval activities at Ta-lien and Port Arthur—then and still very much part of China.

On 14 May the secretary of the Navy sent a letter to the secretary of state, Elihu Root, formally requesting that Lieutenant Gillis become naval attaché in Peking. Secretary Root responded directly to Gillis on 23 May, designating him as "Naval Attaché to the Legation of the United States in Peking vice Commander John A. Dougherty, U.S.N."[69] On 31 May Captain Rodgers informed Gillis that he was working on Gillis' orders.[70]

CHAPTER 4

⌒

China Naval Attaché and Rocks and Shoals: 1907–1908

ONI AND U.S. NAVAL ATTACHÉ TO PEKING (I): 1907–1908

Gillis detached from his afloat assignments on 6 June 1907 and was ordered to the Office of Naval Intelligence (ONI) of the Navy Bureau of Navigation for additional duty.[1] Capt. Raymond Rodgers, chief intelligence officer and head of ONI, soon thereafter sent a memo to the Bureau of Navigation nominating Gillis for orders to Brooklyn, New York, Newport, Rhode Island, and South Bethlehem, Pennsylvania, on "special temporary duty," because to be the naval attaché in China, he should "acquaint himself with recent developments in the manufacture of torpedoes, steel forgings, armor, etc."[2] Upon his return to Washington, Gillis was directed to proceed to the U.S. Naval Powder Factory at Indian Head, Maryland, and the Naval Gun Factory at the Washington Navy Yard—for which it was noted no written orders were necessary. Also, on 3 June, Rodgers sent a letter to the president of the Fore River Shipbuilding Company at Quincy, Massachusetts, and to the general manager of W. & A. Fletcher Company at North River Iron Works in Hoboken, New Jersey, requesting that they permit Gillis to visit to "observe the developments of the marine turbine."[3] These were the beginnings of a long association between Gillis and U.S. Navy–related industries in conjunction with his activities in China, and those visits must have been a fascinating opening to a new world for him.

Official orders were issued on 25 June telling Gillis to detach from his duties at the Bureau of Navigation on 15 July and proceed to San

Francisco by 25 July to board the Pacific Mail steamship *Siberia*. He was to stop in Japan en route to consult with the naval attaché in Tokyo, Commander Dougherty, and to "receive from him such archives and other public property as pertain to the Office of the Naval Attaché Peking." He was ordered then to report to the U.S. minister at Peking for duty, relieving Commander Dougherty of his China responsibilities. His orders unequivocally directed him that "during your service as Naval Attaché you will regard our Minister at Peking as your superior officer and will at all times comply with such instruction as he may give you."[4] Gillis departed Washington on 18 July.

Gillis was promoted to lieutenant commander on 1 July 1907, and Rodgers apparently felt it necessary on that date to inform the Department of State of that fact in order that it might convey this to the Chinese government, which may have been concerned about Gillis' relatively junior rank of lieutenant.[5]

On 25 July 1907 Lieutenant Commander Gillis boarded the SS *Siberia* in San Francisco. It sailed that afternoon. The next day a small item appeared in the *New York Times*, headlined "Distinguished Men Sail," that indicated a number of prominent passengers were on board, including the secretaries of commerce and labor; an Ohio congressman, Nicholas Longworth; the congressman's wife, Alice Roosevelt Longworth, President Roosevelt's daughter; and Governor George R. Carter of the Territory of Hawaii. It also recorded that prominent naval officers were also on board, including "Lieut. Commander Gillis."[6]

Upon Gillis' arrival in Japan, he conferred with Commander Dougherty on the work Dougherty had been doing regarding China and received archives that included a chart of China telegraph lines, a *1908 Naval Pocket Book*, and two files of reports on China. According to Dougherty, Gillis declined to take the offered charts of China because he had already been furnished a set by the Navy Department.[7] Curiously, Gillis remained in Japan for a month, reporting to the secretary of the Navy and the ONI on 21 September that he had visited Tokyo, Karuizawa, Kobe, Kyoto, Moji, and Nagasaki. He did not explain why he had embarked on such a grand tour of Japan before proceeding to China.[8]

It would take nearly two months before Gillis received Rodgers' instructions regarding his new post. In the interim, he had determined not to go to Peking directly but rather to establish his office and residence initially in Shanghai, where the main naval activity in China was obviously centered. Apparently he made an error of judgment by not making a personal appearance in Peking to meet the U.S. minister, William Woodville Rockhill, before the latter left on a lengthy leave of absence in the United States in October.[9] Gillis stated in a letter the following spring to Rodgers that he had decided to make Shanghai a base for a while because, as the "metropolis of the East, it is visited by many people from the other ports." In the first several weeks at Shanghai, Gillis was fortunate to quickly become acquainted with the American consul general, Charles Denby Jr.[10] Denby's father had been the U.S. minister to China from 1885 to 1898, but there had been bad blood between him and Rockhill during that period.[11] While there did not seem to be the degree of enmity between the younger Denby and Rockhill, he did not share the minister's somewhat sanguine attitude toward Japanese activities in Manchuria. Very likely Gillis' own wariness of Japanese intentions was wholly compatible with Denby's viewpoint, and the two shared a common suspicion of the Japanese.

The relationship with Denby paid immediate dividends for Gillis. He was able to gain an invitation to attend Secretary of War William Howard Taft's reception and speech on 9 October sponsored by the U.S. Chamber of Commerce in Shanghai, where Denby received special thanks from Taft for his service as consul general.[12] Gillis was the only U.S. Navy officer in attendance who appeared in uniform. There is little doubt that Taft noticed him and that they had occasion to chat about his new assignment. For Gillis, his attendance was essential, as it immediately enabled him to make the acquaintance of nearly every wealthy and influential American and Chinese business leader at Shanghai. Also present were H. E. Morse, an official with the Imperial Chinese Maritime Customs Service, and Admiral Sa Chen-ping, the British-trained chief of the Imperial Chinese Navy, who also made his headquarters at Shanghai.

Taft's speech was well received by the nearly three hundred persons in attendance. Taft made several key points. First, he assured the Chinese that the interest of America in China was that of a good neighbor. Japanese influence would be held in check by the U.S. Navy's continued presence in the western Pacific. Second, Taft, with great vigor, declared that the United States would actively interfere if it became necessary to defend its Open Door Policy in China. He emphasized that this policy would obtain "in all parts of the empire." Journalist Thomas Millard commented that the speech was welcomed by "Americans and others who are becoming uneasy about the status of Manchuria and the trend of some foreign policies." Millard reported that in nearly every aspect the Taft speech was worthwhile, concluding: "It was his belief that it would aid in maintaining the integrity of China, and contribute to the advancement of America's interests in the Far East."[13]

Following the speech, Gillis, who was still living in a hotel, set about finding suitable quarters, eventually taking up Denby's offer to occupy a small apartment with an office at the consul general's residence. He then undertook to develop his contacts by joining various clubs in China. For example, he joined a social club, the Shanghai Club, a golf club, and a dance club.[14] He made it a primary objective to keep on friendly terms with the head of the Chinese navy, Admiral Sa Chen-ping, and over the next several months hosted dinners for Sa while attempting to learn what he could about the state of China's navy. Gillis discovered early on that the British-trained Sa was not readily forthcoming with information, primarily because he had been much disappointed with the U.S. Navy Department's earlier refusal of a Chinese request to train Chinese midshipmen at Annapolis and to allow them on U.S. warships. Nevertheless, despite this obstacle, Gillis' persistence over time did seem to pay off, and eventually he established a good relationship with Sa.

Sa was an interesting figure. He had first entered the Imperial Chinese Navy in 1873 as a fifteen-year-old midshipman at the Foochow Naval Academy, where he achieved high academic honors. Upon graduation in 1877, he was chosen to attend the Royal Navy Academy at Greenwich, England, where he studied navigation, natural science, and English. He missed action at the Battle of the Yalu in 1894 because he was serving as head of the Navigation Department at Tientsin Naval Academy. In 1897 he became the commanding officer of a new Chinese cruiser, the *Hai Chi*. He later became a good friend of Admiral Evans, who described Sa in his memoirs: "During our stay in Chefoo [summer 1902] I came to know Captain Sa of the Chinese Navy very well, and found him an officer of great tact and ability. He is now in command of the Chinese Navy. The cruiser he commanded, the *Hai Chi*, was the cleanest thing in the shape of a warship that I ever saw. From keel to truck she was in the pink of condition. Her decks were as white as snow, her guns in perfect order and her crew in neat uniforms and excellent discipline."[15]

It also is interesting to note that at this time Gillis was not comfortable with the Chinese language and in fact probably had no facility in it at all. He mentioned to Rodgers in his letter of 8 January 1908 that "on the question of an interpreter I am going slowly, although I am handicapped now by not having one." He went on to indicate that he preferred a person who was not only a proficient interpreter but could also assist him on collecting information.

Meanwhile, the Japanese in Washington may have questioned the need for a U.S. naval attaché in China. Japan had had a naval attaché in China for some time, and the arrival of Gillis immediately raised alarm bells. It had only been three years since the issue of a Chinese naval base for the U.S. Navy had surfaced, and the Japanese could have been suspicious that Gillis was up to something during the sensitive time of the Japanese immigration problems in California. The Japanese had been most careful to control the movements of Marsh and Gillis in their own country during the war, and now here was an officer, one who they knew pretty well, suddenly in China. To them it did not bode well.[16] They in fact already were having great trouble with Willard Straight, the colorful "China Hand," in Manchuria.

In any event, Lieutenant Commander Gillis, after his trip from Japan, reported officially for duty as the U.S. naval attaché in Peking on 16 September 1907.[17] Upon his arrival in China, Gillis had commenced receiving a $150 monthly "maintenance" allowance for the purpose of covering extraordinary expenses for his duties, including official entertainment. This allowance was in addition to his "actual and necessary" expenses for travel, stationery, postage, telegram, and wages for clerical help. His office expenses were fixed at $25 per month.[18] For official travel, he was to submit a quarterly statement of his disbursements. In addition, the Navy Department arranged, without giving a reason, for its agents at Seligman Brothers in London to transfer 400 pounds sterling to Gillis.[19] On 9 July, before Gillis departed Washington, the ONI had forwarded him the following items and requested that he sign for them:

- Confidential Instructions regarding Naval Intelligence Duty, Register No. 57.

- *Coaling, Docking and Repairing Facilities of the Ports of the World,* 4th edition, 1900.

- Supplement to the 4th edition, *Coaling, Docking and Repairing Facilities of the Ports of the World,* 1905.

- *Naval Reconnaissance, Instructions for the Reconnaissance of Bays, Harbors and Adjacent Country.* By Major Dion Williams, U.S. Marine Corps.

- One set of metric conversion tables, nos. I and II.

- 12 quarterly returns of Confidential Publications.[20]

Authority also was granted for Gillis to purchase a "No. 4" Underwood typewriter for $62.50, to be paid from the maintenance funds he was already authorized, and a telescopic camera with a small supply of photographic material, its cost not to exceed $80.[21]

Finally, on 18 November 1907, Rodgers, possibly prodded by Secretary of the Navy Victor Metcalf, expanded on Gillis' assignment. In a short letter he advised Gillis that in addition to recruiting reliable agents in China, he also should undertake to produce a detached study of the Imperial Chinese Navy. Rodgers directed him to write a report on his evaluation of the Chinese navy and its salient characteristics "in the near future" and submit it by the first of March. The report was to include Gillis' sentiments and to discuss the value and efficiency of the Chinese navy's material, personnel, organization, readiness for war, the "general idea of the tactics it favored" and in force, the range at which battle was preferred to be engaged and pressed, the role intended for its different classes of vessels from battleships to submarines, and the value of its torpedoes.[22]

By 9 December Gillis had submitted an intelligence report to the ONI, not in response to the 18 November tasking—for he had not yet received that letter—but in which he discussed a strong desire on the part of the "metropolitan [Chinese] officials" to reorganize their navy and put it on a "proper basis." The navy was to have been removed from under the Board of War, and General Yuan Shih-k'ai recommended that Rear Admiral Sa Chen-ping be placed in charge. Gillis speculated that "because he is a Fukien man" (and presumably not among the Peking elite) Admiral Sa would probably become the second, not the first, in charge. Gillis went on to report that it was extremely difficult to obtain exact information on shipbuilding programs. Rumors were plentiful, however, and frequently mentioned were four battleships with cruisers, gunboats, and torpedo craft. The Chinese navy was proposing to establish suitable naval schools and colleges, this in the context of "several Chinese boys" who were then studying English in the United States "with a view to attending our Naval

Academy later on." In contrast with the U.S. Navy's earlier hesitance to train Chinese midshipmen at Annapolis or allow them on U.S. warships, Gillis noted that during the previous month eight Chinese midshipmen were received on board British men-of-war, and three young officers had trained on board a Japanese mercantile training ship. Funding for the navy's reorganization, totaling about $7.5 million, was to come from the Imperial House, each of the provinces under Nan-yang and Peking's jurisdiction, and, perhaps, a further $7.5 million from a foreign loan— although this was not a popular option at the time. Gillis concluded, noting that "under the present form of government there can be no definite [naval] policy."[23]

In early January 1908 Gillis responded to Captain Rodgers that he had received his "confidential instruction" tasking a survey of the Chinese navy. He reported that he had not yet "gone into details or pushed matters very strongly" and proceeded to explain why. Observing that he was the first resident naval attaché of any Western power in China, he cautioned that the Chinese were "at the present time more than usually suspicious of foreign intentions toward China." This, he said, "has made it seem very wise to go very, very slowly asking for information or permission to visit forts, arsenals, etc." as "a little patience may bring about the desired result without trouble or annoyance." This must not have provided much encouragement to Captain Rodgers that Gillis would accomplish his task on time.

Gillis, in the same letter, reported that he was making arrangements with the manager of a U.S. firm doing a large, native retail business throughout China to keep him informed of "military and other doings of interest through its Chinese staff in the interior." At the same time he noted that his best source of information on naval technical matters was Sa and that he was doing his best to keep on friendly terms with the admiral. He reported, as mentioned earlier, that a sore point with the Chinese was the U.S. refusal to admit Chinese midshipmen to the Naval Academy, while Chinese trainees had been welcomed by the British, French, and Japanese navies, a fact that might incline the Chinese not to buy new warships from the United States.

Also reported in this letter was the fact that the Chinese had no national navy. The two principal navies were the Pei-yang and the Nan-yang (north and south oceans), each under its own viceroy but recently placed under Admiral Sa as one command. There also was a flotilla under the viceroy of Wu-ch'ang (central China) and another under the two viceroys at Canton (south China). Gillis concluded with a long plea to Rodgers for understanding that the situation in China did not lend itself to readily obtaining the tasked information, which he characterized as "of doubtful value at the present time owing to the marked probability of an entire reorganization in the near future, a high price to pay for a loss of relations with the Chinese." He closed with the reassurance that he would carry out Rodgers' wishes, no matter what the latter directed him to do, "without undue annoyance to the Chinese authorities." Gillis was unquestionably correct in his assessment of the Chinese navy but, unfortunately, it did not satisfy Secretary of the Navy Metcalf.[24]

Gillis received another letter from Captain Rodgers, in January, that raised an issue concerning Gillis' accreditation to "the possessions of other powers," including Great Britain, Germany, and Russia, characterized as an extension of his duties as naval attaché. Rodgers said that he assumed Gillis had received copies of letters that went from the embassies in St. Petersburg and Berlin conveying to the State Department replies from the respective governments to the request that Gillis should be allowed to visit their possessions. The matter resulted from an apparently innocent and undefined visit Gillis made to the State Department on the eve of his departure for China. He replied that he had paid a courtesy call on Francis Huntington-Wilson, his friend from his days assigned to the U.S. Embassy in Tokyo, to discuss his impending assignment. Huntington-Wilson now held an influential post in State as the third assistant secretary, and his opinions carried much weight.

Part of the discussion between Huntington-Wilson and Gillis apparently centered on whether the Navy Department had authorized Gillis to visit the possessions of the other Western powers in China. Gillis volunteered to Huntington-Wilson that he understood that this was to be one of his tasks but did not know whether the question had been put to the State Department by the Navy. According to Gillis, Huntington-Wilson promised to "make a note of it," and Gillis explained to Captain Rodgers that he did not request Huntington-Wilson to take any action in this matter.[25] The State Department subsequently sent letters to the British, the Germans, and the Russians, informing them that Gillis' duties extended to their possessions in the Far East. It is not readily apparent in the correspondence just why Rodgers expressed concern over this except that the Germans, on the grounds of an international law technicality, stated that a visit by Gillis to the German territory of Tsingtao (Shantung Peninsula) "does not seem soon practicable."[26] Rodgers had said that the State Department had sent a letter to Gillis, which the attaché denied ever having received. Gillis responded to Rodgers on 16 January 1908 that he regretted "very much the turn that the question has taken."

Gillis then changed the subject and asked Rodgers if the ONI could send him and other naval attachés a "small confidential bulletin" that would keep them informed of the "general points of interest in our own Navy." He also asked if Rodgers had obtained any information on the guns that were being made in the United States for Japan, explaining that the information had been requested by one of his contacts and providing it would help him, as a reciprocal gesture, to receive more intelligence from his contact.[27]

On 20 January Gillis wrote Rodgers, calling his attention to the "desirability of indicating in some way the value to be placed on information submitted to the Office of Naval Intelligence." He suggested that the value depended on the source: personal observation of the attaché or from somebody else. He attached a table that presented a proposed "Scheme of Valuation [to attaché reports]," enabling the ONI to "judge the weight to be attached to them and their usefulness." The scale went from 0 for "Rumor" to 10 for "Personal Observation."[28] No response to Gillis' suggestion was found, but similar ratings are applied to modern intelligence reports from the field. Perhaps his was the first.

Rodgers responded to Gillis' 16 January letter on 12 February and enclosed copies of all the correspondence to and from the U.S. embassies in St. Petersburg, Berlin, and Russia and the U.S. State Department about the extension of Gillis' duties. Rodgers said that he had already sent Gillis copies of the correspondence with Great Britain on 30 January. He did not say if permission had or had not been granted. Rodgers also discussed the matter of keeping naval attachés informed about developments in the U.S. Navy, pointing out that Gillis already was in receipt of many items, such as hearings by the various Navy bureaus plus other important documents as they appeared. He declined, however, to prepare a confidential bulletin. He explained that this had been tried a few years before but was considered to be a lot of trouble and was abandoned. Rodgers said, "With these service papers and documents that are sent you, I think that you can keep fairly well posted." He also explained that he fully appreciated and understood what Gillis had said about his duties being new and the need to proceed slowly.

Rodgers also suggested that the matter of sending Chinese midshipmen to the Naval Academy be taken up by China's Foreign Office and that the Chinese minister in Washington "endeavor to have an act of Congress passed." In this letter he also raised the subject of Gillis' tasked report on the Chinese navy, noting that the words "near future" might better have been omitted in the directive. Nevertheless, he told Gillis that the "entire situation in China should be gone over by you and reported." Citing pending naval-related activities in Congress, he told Gillis that such a report would be of use and added, "I beg you not lose sight of the fact that it is not well to postpone reports too long." Rodgers closed by noting that the U.S. minister to China, Rockhill, who was at that moment in the United States, was sailing back to China on 2 March and that he would endeavor to see the minister before his departure to converse with him concerning Gillis' work.[29] It appears that at that point Gillis' career as an attaché was beginning to sail into some rough waters.

It is pure speculation to believe that during Gillis' earlier visit to the State Department, he and Huntington-Wilson discussed the various people at the U.S. Legation in Peking. Heading the list, of course, would be the minister, William Woodville Rockhill. Rockhill had been appointed minister to China by President Roosevelt in December 1904. Rockhill had arrived in Peking in June 1905, days after the Japanese defeat of the Russian fleet at Tsushima. Huntington-Wilson could have cautioned Gillis that the congenial atmosphere they had experienced in Tokyo in 1904–1905 with Minister Griscom would not be repeated under Rockhill. It was well known that Rockhill was subject to somewhat strange behavior, which junior staff members referred to as "mental gout." He was also antisocial with strong misanthropic tendencies. Dr. Paul A. Varg points out that Rockhill's motto was "love things, don't love people—things will give you pleasure." A description of Rockhill written by a member of his staff in August 1905 perhaps sums it up best: "Mr. Rockhill is a tremendously hard worker and has no pleasure outside of his work. He has no amusement whatsoever, which is bad for any man. He is a difficult man to solve and difficult to get on with unless you are careful, and I never feel that if I stand well with him for the present it means much for the future. That is, he takes a violent fancy to a person and as quickly changes around to a dislike which he doesn't attempt to conceal. I have already seen several instances of this."[30]

Of course, there was another side to Rockhill that had appealed to Roosevelt in naming him minister to China. It lay in the recent past and in Rockhill's love of adventure, which obviously resonated with Roosevelt. Rockhill began his adult life first as a cadet and then as an officer for nearly four years with the French Foreign Legion in Algeria. Coming into an inheritance, he then pursued his next love as a scholar, mastering the Sanskrit, Chinese, and Tibetan languages and then undertaking the full-time study of Tibet. Over a four-year period beginning in 1884, Rockhill served as second secretary of the U.S. legations in Peking and Seoul. After resigning from the Foreign Service under a bit of a cloud, in 1889 and again in 1891, he took advantage of the sudden opportunity to explore Mongolia and Tibet on foot. His breathtaking account of his adventures were published to the world in a series of articles in *Century* magazine and in a book entitled *Diary of a Journey through Mongolia and Tibet in 1891 and 1892* (Washington, D.C.: W. P. Roberts for the Smithsonian Institution, 1894). Now established as a noted scholar-explorer, he quickly gained the admiration and friendship of an assortment of influential people, including Roosevelt, Henry Adams, John Hay, and Alfred Mahan. In 1893 Rockhill was asked to rejoin the Department of State, and by 1896 he had been appointed assistant secretary. In 1899 Hay was named secretary of state, and Rockhill distinguished himself as the chief author of Hay's China Open Door Policy, subsequently promulgated as notes over Hay's signature. A year later, in the aftermath of the Boxer Rebellion, he was detailed to China as a special commissioner. There, he successfully negotiated a protocol with the Chinese. Another aspect of Roosevelt's attraction to Rockhill was the scholar-diplomat's relationship with the Dalai Lama. From 1905 to 1908 Rockhill corresponded with the holy man, perhaps the first Westerner ever to do so, and the ever-curious Roosevelt was kept informed of the correspondence.[31]

Another important U.S. official at Peking was Edward T. Williams. He had been in China for twenty years, first as a missionary. In 1896 he undertook a series of positions as an interpreter-translator with the Chinese government and then a similar position with the U.S. Consulate in Shanghai until 1901, when he became the U.S. Legation's Chinese secretary at Peking. As Rockhill's right-hand man, he had earned the minister's confidence primarily due to his excellent Chinese-language capability and his friendships with various Manchu officials.[32]

A third significant figure at the legation was the U.S. military attaché, Captain Henry Leonard, USMC. Leonard likely enjoyed the respect of Rockhill at least in part because of his heroism during the Boxer Rebellion. As a member of the international relief column, Leonard had lost an arm while scaling a wall during a battle. Despite the handicap, he remained on active duty until 1911 as the U.S. military attaché. Over a period of years, Leonard had been compiling information on the Chinese military organization that was periodically provided to the State Department through the U.S. minister.[33]

Finally, Willard Straight's name probably came up in the course of the meeting between Gillis and Huntington-Wilson. Straight had returned to China in June 1906, having been appointed consul general at Mukden in Manchuria. As such, he promoted the Open Door Policy and American interests in Manchuria while monitoring Japan's consolidation of its position there.

TROUBLES, TRAVELS, AND TRANSFER: 1908

When Gillis returned to his office in Shanghai in April 1908 from Peking, where he had gone to discuss his planned future official travels, he was not happy when he opened his mail from Washington. This time it was about his quarterly account for his "Allowance for Maintenance" that ended 31 December 1907. The secretary of the Navy had disallowed his claims for hiring a carriage and office rental pending further explanation; denied reimbursement for the expenditure of $120 for dinners pending receipt of further information; and rejected his explanation as to why he had hired a launch for $13.10 to visit the flagship instead of using a Navy launch from the flagship.[34]

Gillis told Rodgers in an eight-page letter dated 30 April 1908 that he learned of the disapproval "with much annoyance and disgust." He said that much as he would be willing, he was not in a position to pay these expenses himself, but that he felt an obligation, since he had been placed in a position of trust, to personally explain his claims.

Referring to his lack of progress on his tasked report on the Chinese navy, he said that he was annoyed at the secretary's "commercial, corner grocery way of looking at the situation, in other words considering reports from an attaché as so much copy for a newspaper to be paid for at so much a column or thousand words." Gillis went on to explain briefly the situation as he then saw it in China, noting that the Chinese navy was in a state of transition and that little could be said about the vessels or their organization while tactics, target practice, and maneuvers were all in either an embryonic state or did not exist at all. He lamented the great difficulty in traveling in China with its primitive facilities and with determining just what he should see when he got to a destination, while also explaining that knowledgeable contacts of "appropriate character in China" were few and far between. He told Rodgers that all of his requests for information and travel had to be submitted by the American minister to the Chinese government and in practically every case "a way is found to kill it (presumably by the Chinese)." Gillis said that he had even asked Minister Rockhill about suggesting a Chinese official to whom he could go directly, but that he had neither received a reply yet nor was Minister Rockhill "in sympathy with the military or naval side of the situation." He expressed his regret at his current situation and noted that he was "losing the valuable experience that [he] would gain professionally by being with the fleet at a time when such great strides are being made in naval progress, but also what little reputation [he] had for a conscientious performance of duty." He reported that he had remained in Shanghai in part to consult with Admiral Sa and in part because it was the "metropolis of the East," but that he was returning to Peking in a few days. Upon returning to Peking, Gillis said that he planned to visit various forts and arsenals as soon as he got permission from the Chinese. He had asked Minister Rockhill to obtain those permissions while he was away from Peking but was not optimistic that much effort would be made to get them.

There was perhaps more going on here than was readily apparent. Rockhill, while in Washington, likely had had contact with Secretary of the Navy Metcalf, pointing out that he had never met Gillis and that he doubted the value of having a naval attaché specifically assigned to China. While there is no record of any conversations or correspondence between Rockhill and the Navy secretary on this matter, Gillis did explain to Rodgers that a serious problem existed. He then announced that in the fall and early winter he planned to visit the French possessions in the south and to go to Singapore.

Gillis also went into great detail in justifying his denied expenses, explaining that such expenses had been allowed in Tokyo without question in the past and that he was disconcerted that instead of cautioning him not to make such expenditures in the future, he was being denied reimbursement for expenses already made. Gillis cited all this by way of explaining to Rodgers why he had not made much progress on his assigned tasks and that another person might be better qualified to do his job. He, therefore, announced that he was sending to Rodgers a letter to forward to the Navy secretary requesting that he be provided a relief and that he be assigned to some other duty. If Rodgers still wanted him to continue on to the best of his ability, Gillis assured him that he, of course, would and Rodgers could destroy Gillis' letter to the secretary. Finally, Gillis mentioned the pending U.S. Great White Fleet visit to Amoy, China, and his own planned trip to Korea or Ta-lien to meet with Commander Dougherty at Dougherty's request because their letters had been opened and Dougherty wanted to discuss a sensitive matter.[35] Gillis then wrote a detailed letter to the Navy secretary on 2 May 1908 requesting that most of the disallowed items be reimbursed.[36]

When Rockhill returned to China in April, Gillis found that his attempt to visit various Chinese shipyards and arsenals had been blocked by the U.S. minister and his staff. Gillis advised Rodgers that he had finally met with Rockhill in early April and found that he was still not in sympathy with either the military or the naval side of the situation. Gillis indicated that Rockhill had asked that the attaché write him a memorandum stating what places he wished to visit. Subsequently, according to Gillis, both Rockhill and the legation's first secretary were apathetic about the request and in fact did nothing about it. In conversations with Captain Leonard, Gillis discovered that Rockhill regarded his attachés as spies and was apparently of the opinion that all attachés were spies. Gillis wrote to Rodgers that he believed that no aid could be expected from the minister at Peking as far as naval or military questions were concerned, and "this was plainly recognized by Mr. Taft, who, in discussing this question with General Edwards, an aide with Taft on board USS *Rainbow* in Vladivistok when Straight visited them in 1907, intimated that he suspected that the difficulty in getting information was due to Mr. W's [Edward T. Williams, the legation's Chinese secretary] apathy."[37]

On 17 June 1908 the secretary of the Navy announced in a formal letter that the Navy Department had decided to discontinue maintaining a naval attaché at the legation in Peking for service in China alone. The letter also stated that the State Department would, as a consequence, detach Lieutenant Commander Gillis from his duty as naval attaché in Peking and revert to the former arrangement, whereby the naval attaché in Japan would be assigned additional duty in China but continue to reside in Japan.[38] Gillis was informed that day by the Navy Department that he was detached and was to report, by cable, to the commander of the Third Squadron, U.S. Pacific Fleet, Rear Admiral G. B. Harber, for duty. He was directed to deliver all archives from his Peking office and his secret codes to the commander of the Third Squadron and report to the department when he had done so.[39] Captain Rodgers, in a formal letter dated 18 June, directed Gillis to "furnish the Naval Attaché in Tokyo with a copy of any reports and memoranda of conditions in China that might be of value to him and for his guidance."[40] Gillis filed his last report on China in August 1908.

But this part of the Gillis saga is not complete without further explanation. In another, informal letter to Gillis dated 18 June, Captain Rodgers explained to Gillis that Secretary Metcalf had told him that the question of Gillis' accounts did not enter into his decision to recall Gillis from China. Rodgers said that he had suggested that any decision on discontinuing the position be made in the autumn to give Gillis time to "accomplish important results," but that the secretary had determined that the matter had to be decided without delay. Rodgers pointed out that the matter of the accounts had been brought to the secretary's attention and had made a "disagreeable impression," which Rodgers regretted very much, as it prevented the realization of his hope that Gillis would provide valuable and consequential results from his mission in China. He, in closing, offered Gillis "best wishes for a pleasant cruise, believe me."[41]

Gillis was probably very busy wrapping up matters in Peking and did not until August get around to responding in more detail to the news that his China post had been disestablished.[42] After Gillis had reported to his next duty station, the USS *Rainbow* in Shanghai, he wrote a letter to Rodgers, now an admiral, on 21 August 1908. In his final report as a naval attaché, he summarized in five single-spaced, typewritten, legal-sized pages his activities that past spring and early summer in China. The first item was his meeting with Commander Dougherty. Gillis had planned to meet Dougherty either in Moji, Japan, or Pusan, Korea, and then return to Peking, but Dougherty asked Gillis to meet him instead in Kobe, Japan. Gillis said that the trip was useless as far as he was concerned. Gillis had then planned to go to Vladivostok in far eastern Russia

MAP 3

GILLIS' TRAVELS IN MANCHURIA
WITH WILLARD STRAIGHT, SPRING 1908

RUSSIA

Blagoveshchensk

Khabarovsk

Amur River

Sungari River

Gillis and Straight
traveled to and from
Khabarovsk along this
segment.

Tsitsihar

M A N C H U R I A

Harbin

Ningan

Vladivostok

Ch'angchun

Chilin

Hunchun

Gillis and Straight
traveled from and
back to Mukden along
this segment.

Mukden
(Shenyang)

K O R E A

Sea of
Japan

| 0 | 50 | 100 Kilometers |
| 0 | 50 | 100 Miles |

and take a short trip to Khabarovsk on the northeastern Chinese-Russian border. But when he arrived in Mukden, Manchuria, he was offered the opportunity to accompany his friend Willard Straight, the consul general, on a more extensive trip. According to Gillis, this gave him a chance to obtain information on relations between China and Japan as well as relations between those countries and Russia. He again apologized to Rodgers for not obtaining more about the Chinese navy as tasked, but said that he felt he was on the verge of getting information "of an important character" just when he was advised that his post would be abolished.[43]

Gillis' trip with Willard Straight deserves elaboration at this point. Starting on 7 May, it lasted some sixty-seven days and covered more than 2,500 miles. Much of it was done by train or boat. According to Herbert Croly, Straight's biographer, the consul general had been planning for some time "to explore Manchuria and to investigate its agricultural and commercial possibilities." At the end of April, Secretary of State Root had finally approved the plan. The approval, however, had likely more to do with getting Straight away from Mukden, where only a few weeks earlier he had been involved in an embarrassing situation with the Japanese consul. News of the so-called Mukden Incident traveled quickly back to Washington, where the Japanese ambassador, Kogoro Takahira, went to Secretary Root to demand an explanation. Unfortunately for Straight, the incident coincided with the U.S. diplomatic problems with Japan over Japanese immigration in California.

Both Straight and Gillis had wanted to explore this region of China, particularly to observe Russian and Japanese activities there. During one part of the journey, they happened upon some old ruins near an ancient capital in Kirin (Jilin) Province. According to Croly, "these ruins were spacious and spectacular enough to suggest to Gillis, Willard's companion, that they might have before them the remains of Kubla Khan's palace, located by Coleridge at Shangtu." Croly goes on to quote an article that subsequently appeared in the *Journal of the Northern Chinese Branch of the Royal Banti Society*:

> It is interesting in connection with these rhythmic fancies that in 1908 two American travelers, Mr. Willard Straight and Commander Gillis, described ruins in the neighborhood of the old Manchurian capital of Tungking in Kirin Province, which they found to correspond to the "image" of Coleridge's poem.

A lazy river flowed through matchless scenes and disappeared; there were wells in which ice could be seen although it was July; the foundations of a summer house on an islet that at one time cast its shadow over the water, were reached by a ruined bridge; there was a waterfall, and rustics told a legend of a hapless maiden princess, buried beneath. There was also in the neighborhood a legend concerning a venerable tortoise which lived under the water surrounding the islet. In fact the coincidences of the features of the poet's city with the site of this ancient Manchurian capital were so striking as to have partly convinced the travelers that Coleridge had produced a description of a place he had erroneously assigned to Shangtu.

The two also traveled by horseback from Hunchun to Ningan. This was the busiest part of the journey, covering nearly two hundred miles. Straight had arranged with Manchurian officials to have a military escort accompany them during this stretch.[44] The two travelers must have had a good time.

There is every likelihood that the twenty-eight-year-old Straight welcomed Gillis as a traveling partner. Their paths had crossed in Tokyo and, during the Russia-Japanese War, Gillis was probably attracted to the charismatic Straight both for the latter's knowledge of Japan's activities in Manchuria and his repeated assertions that continued activity by Japan in the region threatened to undermine the Open Door Policy's principals. These activities, after all, matched one of Gillis' primary intelligence collection priorities as outlined by Rodgers. As to Gillis' way of thinking, it did not hurt that a suspicious attitude regarding the Japanese was more in line with similar thinking within the Navy. It also was helpful that Straight, like all consular officers in China, was directly responsible to the State Department, and only indirectly to the Peking legation, and thus was able to send his dispatches to Secretary of State Root without going through Minister Rockhill.[45]

Gillis likely told Straight in confidence about Rockhill's lack of interest in and support for Gillis' attaché mission. For his part Straight probably introduced his ideas for American business investments in Manchuria. Straight had a close relationship with E. H. Harriman, the wealthy and influential American industrialist. Harriman had agreed to provide a loan of $20 million to establish a bank that could help fund new Chinese investments in railroads, mines, and agriculture in Manchuria. All that remained for Straight to do was to obtain a memorandum of agreement with Hsu Shih-Chang, the viceroy of the so-called Three Eastern Provinces (Feng-tien, Kirin, and Heilun-chiang). Hsu's aide was Tang Shao-Yi, who had studied at Columbia University and was also a friend of Straight. Tang wanted to see Japanese influence in Manchuria countered by American business investment.[46]

The two men also probably talked politics. It was well known that William Howard Taft was a candidate for president, for Roosevelt had declared that he would only serve one term, and would have the best chance for nomination at the Republican convention, which would be held while Gillis and Straight were touring Manchuria. Gillis' past associations with Taft could not match Straight's, however. Straight definitely held the ear of Taft and, in fact, had met with the latter in November 1907. Taft's itinerary after leaving Shanghai in October had taken him to Vladivostok, where he had planned to take the Trans-Siberian Railway en route home. Straight had joined him there and had ridden with Taft as far as Harbin. According to Croly, Straight had an outline for his plan for American investment in China.[47] Straight seemed encouraged by the secretary of war, who was receptive to his ideas. Now, during their long journey together, Straight shared his views and ideas with Gillis and probably lent a sympathetic ear of understanding to the naval officer's difficulties with Rockhill. In the end, the trip for Gillis was a fortuitous one that would pay dividends several years down the road. A bright future, however, was not apparent to either man once they reached Tsitsihar in July. Telegrams awaited both, telling them that their jobs as consul general and naval attaché had been terminated. Straight was to return to Washington for consultations, and Gillis was to be returned to sea duty. The Peking naval attaché's duties would once again be run from the Tokyo office.[48]

Returning to other matters in Gillis' August letter to Admiral Rodgers, Gillis complained that Rockhill would not support Gillis' efforts in view of his opinion (noted earlier) that military attaches were all spies, "forgetting apparently that his function to a certain extent is of the same nature." Within the past year, Gillis noted, a lot of official Chinese telegrams had been leaked and several officials had been beheaded and others sent to confinement, with the result that officials were courting death if they were even seen to be talking with a foreigner. He countered Marsh's earlier observation that discussions with the Chinese were not difficult, noting that he had made it soon after the Western suppression of the Boxer Rebellion and the Chinese at that time were "only too willing to avoid . . . further trouble." By 1908 the Chinese had been impressed with Japanese successes that were, according to Gillis, "to a great measure due to keeping military and naval matters secret."

Gillis went on to mention French vessels on station in China and that if he were to get any information from them he would have to visit them himself in China's southern waters. Of interest, he commented that "the French papers seem to think that Japanese encroachments on China will eventually end in a partition and they want their share." Gillis also reported that he had made contact with a Chinese cook in the Russian navy who provided a lot of corroborated information and whom Gillis had intended to send to Vladivostok, apparently in an attempt to get a closer picture of Russian intentions. Gillis said that he had also wanted to visit Vladivostok to see firsthand what was going on in the northern Korean border area along the Amur River and with the increased presence of Chinese troops in Manchuria.

Gillis reported to Admiral Rodgers that in the previous few weeks there had been many incidents causing friction between the Chinese and the Japanese, giving rise to apprehension as to possible "untoward results." He said the U.S. Legation paid little heed to these indicators, but several factors were at issue: (1) the Fakumen Railway, (2) the Chientao dispute; (3) the *Tatsu Maru* case; (4) a Japanese smuggling case in Fukien; (5) riots in Hankow; (6) a Japanese break-in at a Chinese house in Peking; and (7) the establishment of post and telegraph offices outside the Japanese "railway zone." Gillis does not elaborate on all of these incidents, but noted that in Chientao, an area disputed between China and Korea, he had seen an increase in Chinese troops and barracks and had learned of plans for new, permanent buildings there. With the Chinese sending in more police to the district and the Japanese more gendarmes, Gillis noted that it would take but a "rash or foolish act on the part of some subordinate to explode the mine," whereupon the Japanese would use that as an excuse to rush in troops under the guise of maintaining order, and "that will be the last China will ever see of this piece of her soil." He cautioned that such a Japanese incursion would not be the same as sending U.S. troops to Cuba in 1898, for in China there would be no rioting, as there had been in Cuba, as the Chinese had the local situation well in hand. Gillis suggested that presence of the U.S. fleet would probably influence China, presumably to resist further Japanese incursions.

The next subject addressed by Gillis was the Russian presence in the region. He explained how he had deduced Russian troop numbers totaling 250,000 to 300,000 in the area from various contacts, beef contracts, and the size and quantity of barracks. He estimated that the number of Russian troops "out here" was doubling and noted that he had observed firsthand that following their poor performance in the last war they were being intensely trained in aiming, skirmish tactics, and mapmaking. The Russians were thoroughly colonizing the district along the Amur and Ussuri Rivers and were pushing the Amur Railway, which was to be built well to the north of the river with six or seven branch lines and a light railway. Military post roads were under construction from Khabarovsk to Nikkolak Ussurisk and along the Amur toward Khabarovsk. Gillis reported that the Japanese also were "all up through this region." He noted in the closing paragraphs of the letter that even with money issues and the empress dowager's death as yet another factor, the ONI should "not depend upon what the newspapers say. There is no doubt now that something will be done to reorganize the sea forces but when and how is hard to say." He suggested that the U.S. Navy read the State Department files for their valuable reporting on railroads, the military situation, and other matters.

In the last paragraph of his final intelligence report, Gillis commented on the visit by the U.S. Great White Fleet, noting that nobody seemed to know what was intended by it. He accused the legation of being "apathetic if not antagonistic" and claimed that the Chinese had no one to go to about the visit, suggesting that the United States should have someone on the scene at Amoy when the fleet units arrived.[49] Gillis' assessment of Rockhill's position was correct. According to biographer Kenneth Wimmel, "the Chinese government's enthusiastic acceptance of the idea was precisely the reason Rockhill questioned its wisdom. He feared that a highly publicized visit by a fleet of American battleships would send the wrong signal to the Chinese, leading them to believe that the United States would strongly defend the Open Door in China, even with force if necessary."[50]

Gillis closed the letter with regret that "such a thing as money" would interfere with what promised to be a successful mission and for all the annoyance the matter had caused Admiral Rodgers. He proposed establishing a correspondence school for Navy officers at the Naval War College "so we all could keep in touch with modern conditions." This probably refers to the fact that naval officers at foreign stations might become increasingly out of touch, and a correspondence course could help them stay abreast of changing conditions, technology, and doctrine. In fact, such a school and courses were developed later. He closed by expressing his appreciation to Rodgers and said that he hoped to have the "pleasure and honor of serving under you in your new grade."[51]

CHAPTER 5

Sea Duty in the Pacific (II), Then Dollar Diplomacy in China: 1908–1914

COMMAND IN CHINA; HAWAII AND MORE WAR CLOUDS; THEN BACK AS A "GREASER": THE USS *RAINBOW*, USS *OHIO*, AND USS *MICHIGAN*, 1908–1910

Upon leaving China in August 1908, Gillis returned to sea duty and once again excelled—the beginning of his redemption. He had a brief tour in USS *Rainbow* before he was detailed to the battleship USS *Ohio* (BB 12) as navigator for its return trip to the United States to become part of President Roosevelt's Great White Fleet. In the fall of 1909 he reported on board a new battleship, USS *Michigan* (BB 27), as its chief engineer, a tour that would last until 1910.

Gillis traveled from Peking in August 1908 only as far as Shanghai. It turned out that the USS *Rainbow*, the flagship of the U.S. Pacific Fleet's Third Squadron, was at that port and in need of a new commanding officer. When Gillis checked on board the *Rainbow* on 21 August, he likely was much relieved at being back in an environment he understood well.[1] The *Rainbow*, originally a merchant ship and later to become a submarine tender (AS 7), was both the station ship at Manila and the flagship of the Philippine Squadron. This unit, made up of torpedo boats and assorted gunboats, was assigned to the Fifth Division, Third Squadron, Pacific Fleet.[2] He was detailed by Rear Admiral Giles B. Harber, the commander of the Third Squadron, to become the flagship's commanding officer. Harber had been present at Santiago when Gillis performed his torpedo-boat heroics in June 1898. At that time Harber was the executive officer of the USS *Texas*, which eventually saw much action when the Spanish admiral Cervera attempted his escape. Harber could be expected to provide a sympathetic ear upon being told by Gillis about the latter's unfortunate and brief tour as the Peking naval attaché, for the admiral was no stranger to the naval intelligence game, having been one of the original founders of the ONI in 1882 and a former naval attaché himself, to St. Petersburg. He was a contemporary of James Henry Gillis, commencing his career as a line officer in 1869 following his graduation from the Naval Academy.

It may not have been a coincidence that on 2 September, less than two weeks after Gillis took command, the *Rainbow* arrived in northern China. The next day, Rear Admiral Harber and members of his staff were in Peking to confer with Minister Rockhill, probably about the upcoming visit of the Great White Fleet to China.[3] Gillis had explained to Harber that no one in the Peking legation seemed to know much about the planned visit, and they were generally unenthusiastic about it.[4] The main

USS *Rainbow* (AS 7)
(U.S. Naval Institute Photo Archive)

drawback was that Rockhill believed that a fleet visit would be evidence to the Chinese government that the United States intended to support China against Japanese encroachment in Manchuria. Gillis was, uncharacteristically, in apparent agreement with Rockhill on this assessment. The main sticking point was that President Roosevelt, after Secretary of State Root had accepted the Chinese invitation without consulting the Department of the Navy, had agreed to a visit to China by the fleet. Chinese internal politics and security also factored into the discussions that ensued between State and the Navy.[5] Meanwhile, the *Rainbow* got under way on 7 September and headed back to its home port at Cavite, in the Philippines.

It was finally determined in October that upon the conclusion of the Great White Fleet's visit to Japan scheduled for late October, the Second Squadron, consisting of eight battleships under the command of Rear Admiral William H. Emory, would visit Amoy. The ships arrived there on 30 October and remained in port for a week without incident as the Chinese, somewhat reluctantly and without Rockhill's support, put on an elaborate show that cost an estimated $1 million. The Second Squadron then rejoined the rest of the fleet in the Philippines for training and exercises in the warmer waters of the South China Sea.[6]

Gillis remained busy in Cavite as the gunboats of the Pacific Fleet's Third Squadron engaged in extended target and tactics practice. Happily for Gillis, the *Rainbow* distinguished itself, exceeding all previous high scores in night firing by some 300 percent and leading the entire squadron in overall scoring. Admiral Harber extended hearty congratulations to Gillis and his ordnance officer for the "remarkable efficiency attained."[7] The new secretary of the Navy, George von Lengerke Meyer, commended Gillis for his "intelligent direction of the gunnery training of the personnel which has produced the gratifying results indicated by the score made by the vessel under your command."[8] Again, on 14 April 1909, Secretary Meyer commended Gillis for the ship's "excellent condition . . . while under your command," noting that the report of the results of an inspection by Rear Admiral Harber in November 1908 found the *Rainbow* to be a "smart ship" and that her "engineering department was very efficient" and her "landing force was excellent."[9]

During this period Gillis must have been surprised when he received a letter dated 4 October 1908 from the chief of the Bureau of Navigation confirming that two letters had been filed in his official record. The letters had been submitted by Gillis in 1905 and 1906. The first concerned Gillis' "detailed suggestions" on coal economy and additional ship engineering efficiencies, which were subsequently adopted, while the other letter addressed a proposed system of maintenance of stores on board ship, also "since adopted."[10] The wheels of bureaucracy must have turned particularly slowly for those two letters.

His tour of duty in the *Rainbow*, however successful, was not a long one. In a short ceremony on 26 November 1908, Gillis was relieved of command of the *Rainbow* and reported to the battleship USS *Ohio* (BB 12), commanded by Captain T. B. Howard, as part of the ship's regular complement of officers, in time for its return back to the United States via the Suez Canal to join the Great White Fleet's around-the-world cruise.

Gillis did not yet realize it, but when word came on 4 November that William Howard Taft, the former secretary of war, had won the election for president, his naval career would forever be changed. This was because his election ushered in the era of Dollar Diplomacy, as it was labeled by opponents. Two men whom Gillis knew well became key

USS *Ohio* (BB 12)
(U.S. Naval Institute Photo Archive)

players in developing and then implementing Taft's new foreign policy. These were Willard Straight and Francis Huntington-Wilson. By the late spring of 1909, Straight, a protégé of Theodore Roosevelt, had become the chief of the Far Eastern Division at the State Department, but soon Taft's new secretary of state, Philander Knox, named Huntington-Wilson as his assistant secretary.[11] Coincidentally, Rockhill had been reassigned to St. Petersburg as the new U.S. minister to Russia, relieving John Riddle.

On 14 and 15 November 1908 both the emperor Kuang-hsu and Dowager Empress Tz'u-hsi died mysteriously. Temporary rule now rested with the emperor's brother, Prince Ch'un. Within a year Ch'un, now the prince regent, in an attempt to unify control over the decentralized armed forces, appointed his brother Tsai Hsun and Admiral Sa Chen-ping to supervise the reorganization of the Chinese army and navy, respectively. There ensued a series of trips abroad for Gillis to study naval and military organizations and facilities.

Upon assuming office, Taft had named Meyer as his new Navy secretary. Meyer, a friend of Straight's, probably had visited China in the fall of 1906. After graduating from Harvard in 1879, Meyer had been a businessman until the early 1890s, when he entered politics as a member of the Massachusetts House of Representatives, in which he served from 1892 to 1897. In 1900 McKinley appointed him minister to Italy, a post he filled until 1905, when Roosevelt, a longtime friend, sent him to St. Petersburg as minister to Russia. In 1907 Roosevelt recalled Meyer and made him postmaster general in his cabinet.[12] Of further interest, in 1905, when Straight passed through St. Petersburg after covering the Russo-Japanese War, he was discovered to have contacted typhoid fever. Meyer and his family nursed him back to health, and they became fast friends.[13]

There were several other significant changes that followed Taft's inauguration in early 1909. For the ambassador post in Peking, the president appointed William J. Calhoun, a wealthy Chicago corporate lawyer who was much more in tune than his predecessor with the Dollar Diplomacy being espoused by the Taft administration. Just prior to the official announcement of his appointment, Calhoun offered the following observation: "If I go to China at this time it will be with an open mind. I have no leanings, preferences, or prejudices. I have not studied what is called the Eastern question. All I know about it is obtained from casual reading in the newspapers."[14] Calhoun did not arrive in Peking until 16 April 1910.[15]

By the early summer of 1909, Straight had left the State Department, taking a position in Peking as the representative of an American financial consortium, the American Group, made up of J. P. Morgan & Company, Kuhn, Loeb & Company, and the National City Bank of New York. Taft and Knox were eager to expand American influence and power in China through investment in various projects, particularly railroad construction. Straight was replaced at State by Ransford Miller, the former chief interpreter in Tokyo when Gillis had been the assistant naval attaché there during the Russia-Japanese War.[16]

The business consortium in Peking, with Straight as its point man, seemed the ideal instrument to achieve Taft's Dollar Diplomacy goals. There were problems, however, for a syndicate of British, French, and German financial houses was set to sign an agreement with the Chinese to provide loans for the building of the railroad to Canton. When Knox protested to the Chinese to allow the American consortium to join the Europeans, a series of negotiations ensued in which Straight was heavily involved. Finally, in May 1910, an agreement was reached, and the American Group was permitted to share in the Hukuang Railway loan, which amounted to about $10 million.[17]

In matters at this point that would directly affect Gillis, the U.S. State Department was engaged in activity that drew the U.S. Navy and the Bethlehem Steel Company into an informal alliance to sell warships to the Chinese navy. This began to take shape in early 1909 when Rockhill advised that a reorganization of the Chinese navy had been announced, and Tsai Hsun, brother of the prince regent, and Admiral Sa Chen-ping were to head a commission to visit naval facilities in Europe and the United States.[18] The Chinese naval entourage arrived in Europe in November 1909 and was promptly treated to a steady round of lavish parties by British shipbuilders and government officials. Admiral Sa was even knighted by King Edward VII during this visit.[19] American shipbuilders, apparently aware of all this, pressured the State Department and the U.S. minister in China, Calhoun, to urge the Chinese to send the pair to visit the United States.[20]

Meanwhile, on 17 May 1909 Gillis was reassigned from the USS *Ohio* to the fitting-out crew for "inspection of machinery" of the new battleship USS *Michigan*, then under construction at the New York Shipbuilding Corporation in Camden, New Jersey.[21] A milestone naval event had occurred earlier that had a major impact on Roosevelt and the

U.S. Navy. That was the launching in 1906 of the HMS *Dreadnought*, a 1,800-ton British battleship built at Portsmouth, England. It represented a significant leap forward in armored-warship design. Her "all-big-gun" battery consisted of ten 12-inch guns, and its steam turbine power plant could drive the large ship at twenty-one knots. The ONI and the rest of the world observed this development with great interest, and it moved the U.S. Navy's General Board to fund an "American Dreadnought." Subsequently, in 1910 and 1911 three U.S. dreadnought battleships were commissioned: the *Michigan*, *Nevada*, and *Oklahoma*. Gillis continued his duties on board the *Michigan*, which conducted an extensive shakedown cruise following its commissioning on 4 January 1910. After further shakedown cruises in the spring, the new battleship steamed in Caribbean waters and along the Atlantic coast for the next few months. This was followed by a training cruise to Western Europe during November–December.[22]

USS *Michigan* (BB 27)
(U.S. Naval Institute Photo Archive)

On 20 March the *Washington Post* announced that Prince Tsai T'ao, the brother of the Chinese regent and Tsai Hsun, would visit the United States in April to "study the American military system."[23] During his visit he was feted by various Americans, including President Taft, and visited a number of places and key persons across the United States.[24] A few months after Tsai T'ao's visit, on 2 August Minister Calhoun reported that Prince Tsai Hsun and Admiral Sa would visit the United States "as imperial naval commissioners . . . to study naval affairs."[25] On 6 September 1910 the *Washington Post* published the planned itinerary for Tsai Hsun and Admiral Sa Chen-ping's travels in the United States. They arrived on 16 September to carry out a series of visits over three weeks, sponsored by the U.S. Navy. Tsai and Sa were lavishly greeted, first in San Francisco and later in Washington. Tsai was received by President Taft in the White House, where the president hosted a state dinner. Thirty people attended the dinner, including Knox, Meyer, Captain Templin M. Potts, the new chief of the ONI, and Gillis. Also present from the State Department was Edward T. Williams.[26] Huntington-Wilson, however, did not attend due to illness. Following the White House dinner, the trip continued with sightseeing treks to Annapolis, West Point, and New York City and visits to naval facilities and dockyards. Finally the entire entourage headed back across country via train on 4 October.[27]

Nearly two weeks later it was reported that upon the party's arrival at San Francisco, Bethlehem Steel's president, Charles Schwab, and Tsai Hsun were meeting to "close a deal for the building of a fleet of war needs for China." While there was no announcement of a deal, a brief item appeared in the *New York Times* on 26 September that Schwab had paid $25,000 in entertaining and transportation costs for the Chinese imperial naval commission while it was in San Francisco and the subsequent private train rides across the United States. Gillis, perhaps as the former U.S. naval attaché to China, managed to be present during all of these activities.[28]

Tsai had, indeed, signed a contract with Bethlehem Steel totaling 25 million taels ($15 million) of Chinese expenditures. Bethlehem would receive 2 million taels to improve existing gun and arsenal facilities and construct new ones; 2 million taels more to improve or construct new port facilities and dockyards; and the remainder for construction of unspecified new vessels and guns. Bethlehem also agreed to obtain training for Chinese officers and midshipmen on board U.S. Navy vessels and admission to U.S. naval schools and academies.[29]

After the Chinese visitors arrived in Oakland, just half an hour before boarding the liner *Chiyo* for home, Prince Tsai was attacked by a Chinese-American member of an anti-Manchu organization who was wanted by the U.S. Secret Service. Gillis was an eyewitness to the assault. An 7 October 1910 *Washington Post* article about the incident (entitled "Tries to Kill Tsai") offered that the prince's plans to build a modern navy had met with much opposition in China. The *Post* pointed out that "a large element of the people were actively adverse to the policy of a greater navy, contending that it was foolish for China to have any money at all, because the powers of the world, jealous of control of China, wanted her security."

Whatever the criticism at home, Prince Tsai, upon his return to China, soon announced that the Manchu government had opened negotiations for a foreign loan of 25 million taels to be used for the development of the Navy. An additional announcement reported that Tsai was to become the head of a newly constituted Navy Department and that his plans to reorganize and modernize the Imperial Chinese Navy had been approved.[30] These reports and others prompted Bethlehem Steel to request the services of Gillis to assist the company in further negotiations in Peking. The Navy was quick to respond and, on 18 October 1910, granted Gillis a leave of absence to perform extra duty in Peking with the Chinese imperial naval commission of Tsai and Sa.[31]

At this point it is interesting to note that in all three of his immediately preceding ship tours of duty, Gillis received "very good" to "excellent" grades in his reports of fitness from his superior officers. The USS *Michigan* turned out to be the final tour of sea duty in Gillis' naval career. Captain N. R. Usher, the *Michigan*'s commanding officer, assigned Gillis grades of "excellent" in all categories. In his remarks on the report of fitness dated 30 September 1910, just before Gillis' departure, Usher wrote that in "engineering, navigating and command of men, Mr. Gillis is one of the most talented and accomplished officers in our Navy." He also noted that Gillis had some knowledge of Japanese, Chinese, and Russian as well as the French and Spanish languages.[32]

Soon after his selection as a naval aide to the Chinese imperial naval commission, Gillis received a commemorative medal, awarded by the emperor of Japan in 1905. The State Department, up to that point, had taken the position that the U.S. Constitution forbade acceptance of foreign gifts or awards. It appears that, at least in Gillis' case, an exception had been granted.[33]

"ADDITIONAL NAVAL ATTACHÉ," BETHLEHEM STEEL, AND PEKING: BACK TO CHINA FOR SPECIAL DUTY, 1910–1914

In early December 1910 Gillis was in Washington again and likely attended a set of meetings at the State Department in which Secretary Knox conferred with a special envoy from China, Liang Tun-yen, who had been sent by Prince Ch'un to discuss potential naval contracts.[34] During these meetings Gillis was called away to attend the funeral of his father, who had died suddenly on 6 December 1910 in Florida and who, on 9 December, was interred at Arlington National Cemetery outside Washington. The funeral enabled Gillis to be reunited with his family, and there was an impressive number of naval and civilian figures in attendance. The U.S. Marine Band provided the music, which featured "Nearer My God to Thee" as the cortege entered Covenant Presbyterian Church.[35] With his father laid to rest, Gillis returned to the negotiations. Gillis did not remain long in Washington, however. He and Lieutenant Commander Frank Upham, the assistant naval attaché to Tokyo and Peking, were dispatched to Peking to help promote, in-country, the sale of ships and munitions to the Chinese.[36] Upham, in fact, was an ordnance specialist who was expected to advise the Chinese on naval guns and weapon systems.[37] According to the *Washington Post* on 13 January 1911, a contract between the Chinese and Bethlehem was signed.[38]

The talks, however, dragged on into April 1911 as the two sides attempted to gain some common understanding. One of the matters under discussion was the nature of the naval assistance that the United States was prepared to offer. Secretary Meyer had, in fact, earlier approved the release of classified naval specifications to the Chinese, and the U.S. aid was later expanded to include guns, training, and naval advisers. Other issues arose primarily due to the fact that the Chinese negotiators in Washington had to communicate with officials in Peking to report on the talks and obtain necessary guidance. These issues compounded a gloomy report from Lieutenant Commander Upham, the assistant naval attaché, who volunteered the observation that China's naval plans would surely come to naught.[39]

Meanwhile, Admiral Sa's plans to reorganize the Chinese naval ministry were approved on 9 February 1911, and Chinese government action on his request for the purchase of three cruisers, two training ships, two torpedo boats, and one large, unspecified oceangoing war vessel was still pending.[40] Also at this time, Secretary Meyer was having second thoughts about the legality of Bethlehem Steel's request for Gillis' services. After an exchange with the Navy's judge advocate general and the U.S. attorney general, it was subsequently ruled that officers detailed to work with American shipbuilding companies had to be on active duty and in no way in the pay of those companies.[41] On 15 April 1911 Gillis was immediately ordered back to active duty with the title of "additional naval attaché" to the legation at Peking. He was instructed that he "was not to perform any of the duties of Naval Attaché and to confine his activities to his 'special mission.'" Nominally, under the ONI chain of command, Lieutenant Commander James H. Sears would have been his official superior officer, but Gillis would appear to have retained a wide latitude of action.[42]

Throughout the spring and summer of 1911, Gillis, Archibald Johnston, Bethlehem Steel's vice president, and Charles Schwab, the company's president, negotiated relentlessly with the Manchu government. The Manchus, of course, were distracted by another pressing matter: a potential revolution. In the south of China, anti-Manchu forces were active with work that would bring down the imperial government in less than a year. Gillis and his Bethlehem counterparts apparently dismissed the seriousness of the revolution and likely believed that in the end the Manchu military would prevail. But the tumultuous political events in China threatened to short-circuit the naval negotiations.[43]

Across the Sea of Japan there were events occurring in Japan that indirectly could have affected the negotiations since a weakened China was aware that Japan was looking for opportunities to assert increasing control over China. Another war scare involving Japan and the United States had flared up in December 1910 when more anti-Japanese animosities erupted in California.[44] A Japanese official responded in an article that stated in part: "Japan must ask herself what object an element of United States citizens have in view when they advocate the expenditure of enormous sums on furnishing the Pacific with a big fleet; of creating a powerful army on the Pacific slope; of building a huge coal depot and naval station in Hawaii; and of forts in the Philippines, Hawaii, and Panama."[45] The already chilly relationship with Tokyo grew colder still in early 1911 when the U.S. Secret Service reported that Japan had undertaken secret negotiations with the Mexican government to acquire a naval base in Mexico. This prompted the ONI to send several officers under cover to reconnoiter Veracruz, Tampico, and the Gulf of Mexico.[46] The situation also motivated U.S. naval war planners to go into high gear as the ONI and the War College collaborated in developing War Plan Orange, aimed directly at Japan. The drafters of U.S. war plans gave color code names to the various countries addressed in the regional strategies; Japan was assigned "Orange." War Plan Orange was the U.S. Pacific strategy from this time until World War II. The plan evolved over the decades, but the name was retained until 1940. Its main premise was that "despite historically friendly relations, a war would erupt someday between the United States and Japan, a war in which neither could rely on help of [its] allies." Japan's quest for "national greatness by attempting to dominate the land, people, and resources of the Far East" would inevitably clash with America's self-appointed role as guardian of Western influence in the Orient.[47]

The Japanese, not unaware of American concern, countered in March 1911 that Japan had no desire to acquire a base in Mexico, at the time rumored to be at Magdalena Key. This notification brought little comfort to those hawks in Congress who refused to acknowledge the conciliatory Japanese posture. The rumblings in Washington continued, and the naval war planners moved ahead with War Plan Orange. Tokyo's concern was again heightened when, late in 1911, the channel at Pearl Harbor was finished and the first large American warship, the USS *California*, safely navigated its way to the new naval base there. The United States became even more concerned as rumors continued to swirl that a combine of Japanese businessman were in the process of buying the Baja Peninsula from Mexico.[48] Eventually the furor died down, but War Plan Orange, still on the books, was to come in handy in December 1941.

In April Liang Tun-yen, the special Chinese envoy, again met in Washington with Secretary of State Knox to commit $15 million to the purchase of warships and to request the services of U.S. Navy officers in a model Chinese naval squadron.[49] In June the *Washington Post* reported that the Chinese cruiser *Hai Chi* was to visit New York. Normally the visit would have been a significant one, but other events were soon to overtake the dying Manchu government. On 10 October 1911 the revolution in China erupted. In less than three days the large cities of Hanyang, Han-K'ou, and Wu-ch'ang were in the hands of revolutionaries.[50] Meanwhile, the Ch'ing (Manchu) government sent an army south to join the battle. Admiral Sa's naval force had been sent up the Yangtze River by

Peking to shell revolutionary units ashore at Wu-han. Sa's force did not prevail, and his flagship was compelled to haul down the Imperial Dragon Flag and run up a white one of surrender. The admiral escaped downriver to Shanghai, where he took refuge at the British consulate.[51] Despite all this, on 21 October a contract was signed by Tsai Hsun and Schwab, in the amount of 21 million taels ($13 million), for Bethlehem Steel to build warships for the Manchu government.[52]

One month after the contract was signed, the Imperial Chinese Navy mutinied. Rebel forces ashore continued to press their advantage, and by December General Yuan Shih-k'ai, a wily Han Chinese who, well familiar with the intrigues of the Chinese Imperial Court, had been fighting the rebels, decided to join them in a secret agreement. Dr. Sun Yat-sen became the first provisional president of the new republic on 1 January 1912 at Nanking. Yuan Shih-k'ai established his headquarters in Peking, refusing to move to Nanking, and in short order was handed the presidency by Sun, who stepped down peacefully. On 12 February Emperor Hsuan-t'ung (P'u-yi, the "Last Emperor") abdicated.[53] As these events unfolded, and it became readily apparent that the Manchu government no longer held power in China, Gillis and his Bethlehem Steel colleagues were forced to rethink their next course of action. Gillis advised Calhoun that he believed that the new government would honor the contract and still do business in the traditional way, in which personal relationships and gifts would be determining factors.[54]

By 1912 there were other matters for Gillis to ponder. Captain Potts left the directorship of the ONI and was replaced by Captain Thomas Slidell Rodgers. Thomas Rodgers, who was the younger brother of Raymond Perry Rodgers, was not at all like his elder sibling.[55] His leadership style was quite different, he was not especially suited for the intelligence business, and his support for the unusual task that had been assigned to Gillis in Peking might have been in jeopardy. This development, coupled with the election of Woodrow Wilson in the fall of 1912, threatened to undo the Bethlehem contract. Rodgers likely did not fully understand what Gillis was doing in China and thus was potentially unsupportive, while Wilson was not a supporter of the concept of selling military material to China. Wilson appointed well-known pacifist William Jennings Bryan as secretary of state, and together they pledged to abrogate the practices of Dollar Diplomacy as advocated by the Taft administration. Wilson's choice for secretary of the Navy, Josephus Daniels, did not help matters, either. He was at least indifferent toward close relationships with big business, which was standard practice under Taft, and at Wilson's direction he essentially terminated those relationships.[56]

The first test of the new administration came in early 1913 when the California legislature again opened old wounds with Japan. On 15 April it passed the Alien Land Law, which classified aliens as ineligible for citizenship or to own land. These restrictions applied to Japanese, Chinese, and Korean immigrants currently living in the state. Huge anti-American demonstrations immediately broke out in Tokyo. What followed was a crisis of significant proportions as the U.S. Navy again commenced preparations for war.[57] Gillis was directed on 2 May 1913 to proceed to Shanghai to establish an "information bureau" to furnish intelligence on Japanese intentions and the movements of their naval forces.

Soon thereafter, Gillis passed on the rumor that the Japanese fleet had put to sea, "ostensibly for target practice, destination unknown." Assistant Secretary of the Navy Franklin Delano Roosevelt, sitting in for Secretary Daniels, was immediately faced with pressure from the uniformed Navy leadership to begin moving ships and equipment into position in the Pacific to confront the Japanese threat. Franklin Delano Roosevelt's distant cousin, Theodore, had once been faced with a situation like this and had been given permission to reposition ships. However, FDR was forbidden by Wilson to direct the repositioning of ships. Nevertheless, he seemed to skirt around the order by approving the deployment of four submarines from Newport to Norfolk, pending a further move to the Pacific. Daniels returned to Washington four days later. Senior Navy and Army officers, including Admiral Bradley Fiske and General Leonard Wood, believed that war was a probability, and they chafed to begin massing military reinforcements, both within and outside the Pacific.[58] Wilson and Daniels held out in their policy of nonprovocation, and by the end of May the crisis seemed to have passed, an indicator that their restraint may have avoided a major war in the Pacific. That did not mollify much of the service leadership; their resentment smoldered, creating a division between the activist military "hawks" and their "dove" counterparts.[59]

Gillis had remained at his post in Shanghai watching and reporting on Japanese activities, but by early June 1913 he was urging the reopening of talks between the Chinese and Bethlehem Steel.[60] Bethlehem's Archibald Johnston quickly left the United States en route to China via Russia and the Trans-Siberian Railway, and forthwith requested that Secretary of the

Navy Daniels approve the reassignment of Gillis to Peking to assist in reopening the Bethlehem talks with Chinese naval authorities. Daniels approved, and about two weeks later Roosevelt telegraphed authorization to Gillis to go to Peking to work with Johnston, providing that it was at no expense to the Navy and that he could be spared from his intelligence duties at Shanghai. Gillis, for his part, had provided additional ammunition to the talks with his warning that Germany now posed a threat to American shipbuilders' interests in China. It was this rumor that led Johnston, then in the United States, to ask Daniels to permit Gillis to meet him in Peking. By the time Johnston arrived in China in August 1913, FDR had directed Gillis to return to the Chinese capital to meet Johnston, providing the trip involved no added Navy expense and Gillis could be spared from his Shanghai duties, in preparation for further discussions on the Bethlehem contract.[61] According to Gillis' reports of fitness for his time in Shanghai, he performed his duties "to the entire satisfaction of the [Navy] Department."[62] His reports of fitness, beginning with the one for 15 December 1913, also noted for the first time that he had studied the Chinese language and had a "slight knowledge of Japanese."[63]

At this point both Johnston and Gillis became ensnared in Chinese political-military maneuvering that presaged the general movement of China into warlordism. For many decades, the Chinese navy had been led by officers who largely came from Fukien Province on China's east coast. By 1913 nearly every senior officer in the Chinese navy, as well as those few who were ship commanders, were Fukienese. As such, they maintained a tight hold over all naval matters, and where profit might be made they acted to ensure that their interests would be served first. What many of the Fukienese hoped to see was the creation of a modern naval center in Fukien, where well-connected naval families could retain their resources and from which they could centralize operations to ensure that they might survive the turmoil that was enveloping the nation in the wake of the collapse of the Manchu empire. It became clear to Gillis and Johnston that if the Bethlehem contract were to ever come to fruition, building a naval base in Fukien would be a necessary first step before ship purchases could occur. Gillis was probably aware of the hesitation of the U.S. Navy to establish a base at Samsa in Fukien Province but saw this as an opportunity for it to gain an advantage.

From August until 7 November, when the new U.S. minister to China, Paul S. Reinsch, arrived, Gillis and Johnston worked hard to save the

Bethlehem agreement. Once Reinsch was in Peking, Gillis and Johnston began to educate the new legation minister on the background and content of the Bethlehem contract. Unsure of the new Wilson administration, they worked hard to enlist Reinsch's support, but he was quite cold to the idea that China needed modern battleships. Instead, he offered the observation that China would be better served with a fleet of police boats to combat piracy. Nevertheless, Gillis and Johnston had met with numerous Peking-based naval authorities and by late October had developed two proposals. Plan one was for $20.7 million that essentially would create a naval base and shipyard in Fukien that would be capable of building merchant ships and small cruisers. Plan two, the more expensive at $46 million, called for a more sophisticated manufacturing capability that would include battleships, armor, and guns. When Johnston forwarded his proposals to Schwab, the Bethlehem Steel president objected. He wanted to stick to the original 1911 contract agreement, which emphasized battleship construction in the United States. Schwab did not want to become entangled in the more-risky naval-base building. Johnston was caught in a dilemma, as he had already given the proposals to the Chinese. In a quick flurry of telegrams with Schwab, he succeeded in assuring his superior that the Chinese would buy battleships and that an excellent profit would be gained in the sale of big guns for shore batteries to protect the proposed naval base.[64]

It was at this time that an enduring player in Peking appeared on the scene. John Van Antwerp MacMurray, a "Diplomat and Photographer," according to his biographer, Lois MacMurray Starkey, landed in Yokohama, Japan, in November 1913 en route to his post at the legation in China. His first recorded meeting with Gillis was while "bowling at the Club" on 5 December 1913. On 16 December 1913 MacMurray, Gillis, and Johnston dined together, again "at the Club," presumably to discuss the progress of the Bethlehem Steel contract negotiations. Thereafter the diaries contain references to numerous meetings between the two men, such as having "tiffin" (lunch) and dinner with Gillis and other members and guests of the legation staff, including Minister Reinsch, up through 1918.[65] The two also collaborated in later years, as will be seen further along in this narrative.

In pursuing the base-building concept, according to William Braisted, Johnston and Gillis had virtually ignored the sphere of influence Japan had claimed in Fukien at least since 1898. The Japanese government began inquiring about Bethlehem's plans in the spring of 1914 soon after the appearance of newspaper reports that the company had contracted to build a naval base in the province. Both Reinsch and Secretary of State Bryan denied that a naval base contract had been signed. Bryan was probably ignorant of Bethlehem's involvement in China, but Reinsch obviously allowed his passion for China and his suspicion of Japan to influence his representation of the steel company's interests. The minister reported that Johnston and Gillis had only incidentally touched on coastal defenses during conversations with the Chinese that were primarily concerned with ship construction, and he suggested in his memoirs that the contract of 1911 provided only for the construction of merchant ships, convertible to cruisers, with which China proposed to establish a trans-Pacific steamship service. He was annoyed when Bryan telegraphed that the construction of a naval base in Fukien was highly objectionable to Japan and therefore would be unwise. Actually, the State Department did not definitively establish that Bethlehem Steel had not contracted to build a naval base in Fukien until 1921. That Japan was not satisfied with U.S. assurances was demonstrated when it presented its notorious Twenty-One Demands to China in January 1915.[66]

Braisted also observed that Johnston determined that it would be better to conduct his business with the Chinese without more changes if the Bethlehem contract were to survive. Reinsch and the legation staff eventually did support Bethlehem and Johnston in another way. They made strong representation to the State Department that the contract be honored, and they urged Gillis and Johnston to act in secrecy to prevent the British and the Royal Navy from gaining the upper hand. In fact, both Gillis and Johnston became convinced that their chief rival for naval business with China was the British. Shortly after he returned in May to the United States, Gillis wrote Johnston that the British intended to "exert themselves more than ever to do us in the eye if they can." Johnston reiterated the same sentiment to Charles Schwab at the same time and offered the opinion that more-aggressive tactics must be used by both businessmen and diplomats regarding improving China's navy.[67]

In the midst of all this, Gillis must have traveled from Peking to Washington, for the report of the Naval Examining Board and his reports of fitness reflect a period of temporary duty there. This was undoubtedly so that among other things, he could appear before the board on 4 May

1914 and take the necessary examinations to be considered for promotion.[68] On 7 May 1914 Assistant Secretary of the Navy Franklin Delano Roosevelt approved the promotion of Gillis to the rank of commander.[69] It seems, however, that by this time Gillis had made up his mind to leave the Navy and return to Peking as a civilian representative for U.S. shipbuilders and manufacturers.[70] It was not an idle decision by any means. But now, at age thirty-nine, he was probably more driven to secure his finances and prepare for the rest of his life as a civilian.

CHAPTER 6

⌐

Career Decision:
Gillis Retires and Returns to China,
1914–1917

RETIREMENT AND MORE DOLLAR DIPLOMACY: 1914–1915

Despite his long absences, Gillis had always kept in close touch with his family and was much devoted to them. He was regarded as the family hero, always dashing about the world engaged in some adventure. While Gillis was in Washington in spring of 1914, he took the opportunity to visit with his siblings. Brother Harry lived in Chevy Chase, Maryland, with his wife, Emma, and their newborn son, Hanford. Harry was a prominent engineer, a member of the exclusive Chevy Chase Country Club, and an active member of the Navy League. He undoubtedly maintained excellent connections in Washington and was able to update Irvin on current naval affairs. Lyle, who became a patent attorney, also lived in Washington. He and his wife, Grace, had two children: James Henry, age thirteen, and Josephine, who was seven.

Most likely Gillis also traveled to Binghamton, New York, to see and console his sister, Carol. She had been widowed in June 1913 when her husband, David Murray, a very successful lawyer, died suddenly of a heart attack. The Murrays had six children: Agnes, twenty-nine; Marjorie, twenty-three; William, twenty-one; David Jr., eighteen; Marion, sixteen; and Helen, fourteen. During the course of his reunion with his family, Gillis probably also learned that his first cousin Ansel W. Gillis had recently arrived in Korea with his wife and baby daughter, Elizabeth. Ansel was a Methodist missionary who would soon become friends with a young Syngman Rhee, the future president of South Korea.

Gillis' decision to seek an early retirement from the Navy and pursue a business career selling naval armaments to the Chinese was made despite the fact that he had invested all of his prime years in the pursuit of a naval career that remained exceptionally bright, placing him in a strong position to make captain within a few years. A successful captaincy would likely have resulted in his being selected for rear admiral sometime in the early 1920s. On the other hand, though he had once professed to then-Captain Rodgers that he was not much interested in money, the promise of handsome commissions on contracts concluded with China probably swayed him. By the time he was eligible to retire on 1 July 1914, with twenty years commissioned service, he had apparently worked out arrangements with a number of U.S. shipbuilders, including Bethlehem Steel and the Electric Boat Company, to represent their interests in Peking. He would receive retainers from individual companies that totaled as much as $6,000 per year per company (in dollars for that period), as well as commissions ranging from 0.5 to 1.0 percent on any contracts won.[1] This could be quite lucrative if one calculates that the two projected Bethlehem contracts offered to the Chinese in the fall of 1913 ranged between $20.7 million and $46 million. Gillis started to earn between $103,000 and $460,000 annually in today's dollars. Obviously he could live quite comfortably in China if he could summon that kind of income.

Gillis probably was under no illusions, however. Returning to Peking in late summer 1914, he found the business environment very uncertain, and his communications with Johnston pointed to heavy British involvement in Chinese naval affairs. In fact, just before he left the United States, Gillis had read a brief article in the U.S. Naval Institute's *Proceedings* that indicated that six billets had been approved by the Chinese for British naval officers to assist the Chinese navy.[2] The U.S. State Department was alerted by both Gillis and Johnston, prompting Secretary of State William Jennings Bryan to fire off a telegram to the U.S. minister, Paul S. Reinsch, stating that "British advisorship is regarded here as absolutely incompatible with the function of the officers to be engaged under agreement with American government."[3] All this became moot in August 1914, however, when World War I (the Great War) erupted in Europe. The British, as well as the other European powers, suddenly became quite disinterested in Chinese arms deals. For Gillis, this at first seemed to offer an opportunity to Bethlehem Steel, which no longer had to compete with the British or other European powers for China's naval business.[4] Two other forces were coming into play, however, that would work against Gillis' plans.

The first concerned the state of the newly founded Chinese Republic. Yuan Shih-k'ai, who maintained the loyalty of the best troops in China (the Pei-yang Army), had, as previously noted, secretly negotiated with the revolution's leaders and, while supposedly loyal to the Ch'ing government, helped engineer a settlement in February 1912 and was inaugurated on 10 March 1912 as provisional president of the Chinese Republic. He ostensibly was to run the new government from Nanking, which had been secured by the revolutionaries, but remained in Peking, where his source of strength, the army, was located. Thereafter, over the next four years, Yuan proceeded, through bribery and assassination, as well as sheer military force, to try and eradicate the revolutionary movement in China in order to establish himself as a successor to the Imperial Manchu Dynasty. Backed by the only effective military force in China, he moved quickly to undo parliamentary democracy while simultaneously negotiating huge loans amounting to more than $1.5 billion with various foreign powers, often under the most onerous of terms. He was also not enamored with the idea of creating an effective Chinese naval force, especially one located in Fukien. This, however, was nearly the only thing about which he agreed with the Japanese. For the most part, he harbored deep suspicions of Japanese aims in China, particularly in Manchuria, which was on the northern flank of his Peking region.

For their part, the Japanese had made steady inroads into Manchuria and Korea so that by 1914 both regions were under their total domination. Japan had also had a hand in the denouement of the Manchu Dynasty. Japan early on offered Chinese revolutionaries a safe haven in Japan, where they could study and indulge themselves with the benefits of the Japanese education system, military system, and unique brand of constitutionalism. Japan was eager to act as teacher, providing that the Chinese students did not present a conflict of national interest. Sun Yat-sen, of course, was perhaps the most prominent of these Chinese political students. He had escaped execution in 1895 by taking refuge in Japan and would operate out of that country off and on for a number of years. Another future Chinese leader who took advantage of the opportunity to study in Japan was Chiang Kai-shek, who attended the Imperial Japanese Army Academy from about 1907 to 1911.[5]

The eruption of World War I offered Japan an opportunity to make further significant encroachments in China and the Western Pacific. There was a minor hitch, however, when the United States declared its neutrality and the Panama Canal opened, presenting significant competition to Japan in the Far East. But the U.S. position was one of weakness. With the declaration of war in Europe, the United States decided that despite the new base at Hawaii and the availability of the canal, it would be wise to station most major combatants in the Atlantic. Spearheading that strategy was Assistant Secretary of the Navy Franklin Delano Roosevelt. The composition of the Asiatic Fleet, now called the Pacific Fleet, remained largely as it had been since 1910—aging cruisers and an assortment of gunboats.[6]

With its rear somewhat secure now that the U.S. Navy's attentions were focused elsewhere, and only four days after it declared war on Germany on 23 August 1914, Japan took advantage of its overwhelming naval superiority by blockading the lightly defended German naval base at Tsingtao. Troop landings on the Shantung coast in the vicinity of Tsingtao commenced on 2 September. By late October Japan had assembled an overwhelming force of nearly 50,000 soldiers. On 7 November, seven days after the bombardment of the rearguard defenders commenced, the Germans surrendered. Earlier in October another Japanese naval force had captured the German-held Caroline Islands, the Marianas, and the Marshall Islands.[7]

By the autumn of 1914 changes were taking place among the military contingent at the U.S. Legation in Peking. Captain Thomas Holcomb, USMC, who would become the commandant of the Marine Corps in 1936, was still there but had orders to depart in October.[8] Captain Pam Bigler, USMC, who had been the attaché in Peking since 1910, was reassigned in 1914, and Captain James Reeves, USA, had completed five years as U.S. military attaché in 1912 and moved on to the U.S. Army's 3rd Calvary, stationed on the Mexican border.[9] At the same time, the commencement of the Great War shook the Office of Naval Intelligence from its slumber. Among the many changes that took place was the decision to reestablish a full-time naval attaché in Peking. Fearing Japan and its designs for China in late summer, Lieutenant Commander Charles T. Hutchins Jr. was selected for that assignment. Hutchins was the son of Rear Admiral Charles T. Hutchins Sr., who was a contemporary of Gillis' father, James Henry. Young Charlie had graduated from the Naval Academy in 1901 and had followed the usual line officer career path with much sea duty, primarily in European waters.[10]

Accompanying Hutchins to Peking was his young, attractive, and vivacious wife, Eileen. She was the daughter of the Speaker of the Canadian House of Commons and had married Hutchins in 1910. She was no stranger to international lifestyles and had met her future husband in Melbourne, Australia, when the battleship USS *Louisiana* paid a port visit there as part of a goodwill mission. Eileen had been accompanying her older sister, Margaret, an accomplished international stage actress who happened to be starring in the play *The Thief* in Melbourne.[11]

The Hutchinses arrived in Peking in late August 1914, almost exactly the same time as Gillis returned there. This is pure speculation, but it would not be surprising that at some future point research would show that Gillis and the Hutchinses traveled together to China. It would have presented an excellent opportunity for Gillis to brief the new attaché on what to expect and who to trust. There is no doubt that Gillis and Hutchins did subsequently develop close working and personal relationships that extended nearly nine years. Hutchins became U.S. naval attaché in September 1914 and remained in that position until March 1917, when he received orders to assume command of the destroyer USS *Taylor* (DD 84) prior to the U.S. declaration of war against Germany.[12] The following month, Gillis returned to active duty and relieved Hutchins as U.S. naval attaché. Interestingly, Hutchins returned to China to once again take over as naval attaché when Gillis relinquished the position in late 1919.[13] Hutchins remained in that billet until relieved by Captain Arthur St. Clair Smith in October 1922.

Returning to events in Peking in 1914, Gillis either renewed his friendship with Thomas Sze or met the latter for the first time. Sze, who was from an affluent Chinese family and was sent to the United States to study, had graduated from Cornell University's engineering school in 1905.[14] While there he learned freehand drawing from Willard Straight and became a great admirer of the young American. At this time Sze encouraged Straight to apply for a position with the Imperial Chinese Maritime Customs Service. That launched Straight on his adventurous career in the Far East. Straight may have introduced Gillis to Sze some years earlier.[15]

Whatever the circumstances of how Gillis and Sze first met, Thomas Sze, writing sometime after 1949, seems to hint at having known Gillis prior to 1920. Sze, in fact, provides one of the best intimate looks at Gillis:

> In the year 1920 I joined the International Lodge, Peking, a Massachusetts Constitution Masonic Lodge, and inside that ancient and accepted lodge I met many friends of all nationalities. Among them was my good friend, Captain [*sic*] Gillis, who came to China some years before. He had served as naval attaché of the American Legation and had taken a great deal of interest in things Chinese. He studied the Chinese language both verbal and written and had a good many Chinese friends of culture and spent a considerable amount of time in studying the Chinese people, their history, culture and customs. He bought a house in his Chinese wife's name and prepared to remain in this ancient capital of China for the rest of his days. He was a very well educated and cultured person from New England and took great pains in cultivating friendship among all classes of people in Peking both foreigners and Chinese. He was popular and well liked, spent a considerable amount of time at the Peking Club and at the local hotels in social activities. Like most of the foreigners, he had acquired the cultivated taste of Chinese food and was an epicure in choice Chinese dishes. I often met him in purely Chinese gatherings and at dinners with Chinese families. The legation took advantage of his knowledge of things Chinese and his amiable qualities and he was often in demand when distinguished American visitors came to see Peking.[16]

In late 1914 Sze was preparing to go to the United States as a member of a high-powered Chinese commercial commission whose purpose was to stimulate trade between the United States and China. Probably through Sze's connections with Willard Straight, and perhaps Gillis, one of the commission's stops in early 1915 included a luncheon in New York that was attended by Straight and Charles Schwab of Bethlehem Steel. The main emphasis of the event, which was attended by twelve hundred businessmen, was that China needed banks and ships. Schwab, in fact, laid great stress on the necessity of China's need to create its own merchant marine fleet.

When it came his turn to address the gathering, Sze reminded them of the great untapped potential of China's vast consumer base:

> You would be surprised to see today, if you would come into a Chinese home of the middle classes, a house built with wood from Oregon, window glass imported from Belgium, brass window frames from Germany, and matches from Japan. The Chinaman buys everything. He imports millions in value each year he cannot get along without, such as cotton piece goods, yarn, flour, soap, and everything.
>
> Just imagine if the people of China should begin to wear foreign caps, and one-quarter of the 400,000,000 should buy a cap apiece, what a market would be created. Similarly, with other kinds of goods.[17]

Despite Sze's encouraging remarks, British obstruction and inadequate backing from the United States continued to pose challenges for Gillis and Johnston. In view of all this, the Americans tried in 1914 to protect Bethlehem Steel's concessions from British intruders. China canceled its contract for British assistance in return for indemnification, but Minister Reinsch could obtain no more than a verbal promise from Premier Hsiung Hsi-ling regarding Chinese arrangements previously concluded with the U.S. Legation. The U.S. government finally adopted the view in December 1914 that the Bethlehem concession should be regarded as in abeyance. The State and Navy Departments also agreed that European officers in China's employ should be denied access to U.S. naval secrets. This, however, would appear to have been nearly impossible to enforce.[18]

Commander I. V. Gillis (Ret.), ca. 1920s

(Naval History and Heritage Command, Washington, D.C.)

Another player appeared in the late summer of 1914 when Gillis probably met Guion Moore Gest, who indirectly assisted Gillis and the companies he represented. In his memoir, Minister Reinsch recalls that Gest had spent some time in Peking at that time touring with his family. Gest, who was identified by Reinsch as a New York contractor and whom the *Princeton University Library Chronicle* of spring 1954 describes as "a Quaker in religion and an engineer by profession," had conceived of an idea to build a system of tramways in Peking.[19] However, when Gest made his initial inquiries, he found that the French had apparently already concluded an agreement with China to both build a port works on the Yangtze River as well as a tramway system for the Chinese capital. Digging a little deeper, Gest discovered that the French loan was basically a political payoff but was being advertised as an "industrial loan." Gest immediately initiated efforts to secure a loan contract from the Bank of China, which he succeeded in doing before he left the country. He also had made up his mind to pursue his venture with American financial interests once he returned to the United States.[20]

Upon his arrival in the United States, Gest learned from his contacts with financiers that while they remained enthusiastic about such projects in China, they believed that the Wilson administration no longer supported such Dollar Diplomacy activities. They advised Gest that in order for any such project to succeed, he must be able to demonstrate U.S. government approval. Accordingly, Gest went to Washington and sought out officials at the State Department. Refusing to accept a negative response, he subsequently succeeded in obtaining a letter signed by Secretary of State Bryan stating that "this government will, in accordance with its usual policy, give all proper diplomatic support to any legitimate enterprise of that character." According to Reinsch, the letter received wide attention and led U.S. businessmen to understand that the administration had apparently had "a change of heart." Unfortunately, Gest's success was soon overtaken by the events in Sarajevo that set off World War I. Most U.S. businessmen and entrepreneurs turned their attention to that conflict and the possibilities it offered for lucrative contracts.[21] This included Gest, who, among other activities, subsequently gained a valuable contract to modernize the Presidio at San Francisco. Gillis' and Gest's stars crossed significantly a few years later when, together, they left an enormous legacy, the Gest Oriental Library. (That story will be related briefly in chapter 8.)

Gillis' return to Peking as a representative of various U.S. shipping companies bent on doing business in China likely did not go unnoticed by the Japanese. By now his activities on behalf of Bethlehem Steel, particularly its rumored $30 million loan to China for the construction of naval facilities in Fukien, had alarmed them. In January 1915 they received another jolt when news leaked out that Gillis was attempting to coordinate the sale of submarines to the Chinese on behalf of the Electric Boat Company. Apparently Gillis had briefed the Chinese on Germany's successful employment of submarine warfare against surface ships in the early months of World War I, and Electric Boat had agreed to train the Chinese in submarine operations at its works in Groton, Connecticut. Gillis' sales pitch prompted Peking to query Washington in January 1915 as to the feasibility of permitting Chinese midshipmen to come to America to study the operation and manufacture of submarines. In the late summer of 1915, Vice Admiral Wei Han and about thirty young Chinese were installed by the company in a New London, Connecticut, boardinghouse under the supervision of a former American naval lieutenant. The president of Electric Boat, George C. Davison, wired Gillis that Wei Han had "delighted company officials by announcing that China needed a fleet of two hundred submarines." Secretary of the Navy Josephus Daniels allowed that the Chinese might be employed on submarines then being built for the United States by Electric Boat providing they pledged to refrain from giving confidential information "to other foreigners." And, since the Bethlehem Steel Company's shipyards worked with Electric Boat in submarine construction, Charles Schwab obtained a promise from the National City Bank of New York to finance the purchase by China of a dozen submarines. The bank agreed to accept $6 million in unsecured Chinese government bonds at 75 to 80 percent of face value. Davison wired Gillis of the details on 1 November 1915. But the dream of a Chinese flotilla of American-built submarines collapsed after the National City Bank lost confidence in the regime of Yuan Shih-k'ai.[22]

JAPAN'S TWENTY-ONE DEMANDS, A CHINA BASE FOR THE NAVIES, AND NEW INTELLIGENCE COLLECTION DUTIES: 1915–1917

Whether the timing was coincidental to or deliberately because of the U.S. Navy's approaches to the Chinese, Japan, on the evening of 18 January

1915, secretly presented its infamous Twenty-One Demands to Yuan Shih-k'ai. The demands, which were divided into five groups and backed by threats of war, were essentially in the form of grievances that demanded immediate Chinese agreement to remedial measures. The main thrust of the demands were for the Chinese government to end its practice of leasing out any harbor, bay, or coastal island to foreign powers; recognize Japan's predominant position in Manchuria, Mongolia, and Shantung; and accept Japanese "advisers" to assist with developing and enforcing Chinese government policies. Among other things, the fifth group of demands also required the Chinese government to engage Japanese as military advisers and required that Japan be consulted first whenever foreign capital was to be needed in the construction of railways, mines, and harbor works (including dockyards) in Fukien Province.[23]

The U.S. government was not pleased. Three of the four points in the demands against which the United States took specific exception bore on the proposed American assistance to the Chinese navy: those relating to Fukien, foreign advisers, and arms purchases. The biographers of Takaaki Kato, the Japanese foreign minister, contend that this Fukien article was framed to halt imperialist penetration by either American capital or by the U.S. Navy. In the articles relating to arms and advisers, Japan proposed that China undertake to award a certain percentage of foreign adviserships to Japanese to build an arsenal as a joint Sino-Japanese enterprise and to purchase a fixed amount of arms in Japan.

Once the demands became known, Minister Reinsch objected most strenuously, particularly to those of Group V. The Japanese backed off slightly by informing U.S. diplomats that they were offered only as "requests." Edward T. Williams, then the chief of the Far East Division at the U.S. State Department, quickly sensed that the arms and arsenal proposals might affect Bethlehem Steel and that China's acceptance of Japanese military advisers would "make impossible for the U.S. to lend the naval officers as promised." It was obvious to the Americans, however, that the Group V demands were aimed squarely at ending U.S. naval assistance to the Chinese and particularly the potential for a U.S. naval foothold in Fukien Province.[24]

Subsequently, Secretary Bryan and Williams convinced President Wilson that the Group V demands must be challenged, and a lengthy note was passed to Japan on 13 March 1915 posing American objections, particularly to Group V. In his famous note Bryan specifically objected to the Fukien article and the other objectionable points as prejudicial to U.S. treaty rights, the Open Door, and China's independence. But Kato responded from Tokyo that Japan had made its proposal regarding Fukien to China because it was disturbed by published reports of Bethlehem Steel's plan to improve Samsa Bay, where the U.S. Navy had unsuccessfully sought a base since 1900.[25]

Although Japan opposed the movement of American capital into Fukien on the ground that even the most innocent business undertaking tended to assume a political coloration in China, Bryan concluded that Tokyo could be satisfied with a simple guarantee that the United States would acquire no naval base in the province. With President Wilson's approval, but without consulting China, the secretary proposed to Tokyo that Japan and China, with the concurrence of the United States, enter an accord that would address the construction of a harbor or naval base in Fukien. But to Bryan's formula, which would have left space in Fukien for Bethlehem Steel, Foreign Minister Kato added the significant proviso that China itself should desist from building a naval base in the province with foreign capital. This amended article was presented to the Peking government by Eki Hioki, the Japanese minister, with a warning that Asians should unite to oppose the increase in U.S. naval power that would follow the opening of the Panama Canal. According to the Japanese version, the Chinese negotiators were speechless when Hioki asked how China would protect itself should "the squadron of a certain power [the United States]" occupy Samsa Bay.[26]

When Bryan learned how Kato had amended his Fukien proposal, he again unsuccessfully urged the Japanese government to permit foreign loans for naval and harbor improvements in Fukien so long as these advances to China involved no mortgage on the properties concerned. It was a delicate time as Bryan and the Japanese ambassador to the United States, Viscount Chinda, maneuvered over the wording and intent of the demands. On 7 May the Japanese delivered a final ultimatum to the Chinese government. Within a few days, Bryan advised both governments that the United States would not recognize any agreement that "infringed on American treaty rights, the Open Door, or the independence of China."

The next day, however, China reluctantly agreed to the Japanese demands—which did have some significant revisions due to both British and U.S. pressure. For example, China was not required to accept governing "policy" advisers from Japan. The Group V demands were not included in the initial set that China agreed to. However, the Chinese, in an exchange of notes with Japan, subsequently promised to place in abeyance its plans to build a base in Fukien.[27] This accord effectively ruled out the plans for a naval base at Samsa Bay that Johnston and Gillis had pressed on the Chinese in 1913 and 1914. Because Japan consented to postpone negotiations regarding arms and advisers, the Sino-Japanese accords arising from the Twenty-One Demands of 1915 left intact the Bethlehem Steel Company's contract of 1911. The accords also left the door open for U.S. firms to tempt China with other naval schemes. One last attempt was made by the Chinese navy in September 1915 to get Yuan Shih-k'ai to reconsider plans to build a base south of Shanghai. This time Yuan sought the council of the British, whose representative condemned it as too expensive and technically beyond China's capability.

During this particularly sensitive period, Gillis continued to add fuel to the fire on behalf of his other U.S. company. Despite early reluctance by the U.S. Navy Department to consider the Chinese request to send personnel to study submarines, the Electric Boat Company was currently building submarines for the Royal Navy and perhaps intended to use them as models for the Chinese to use. The activities of Electric Boat and the Chinese understandably attracted the Navy Department's attention. Josephus Daniels had hosted Wei Han and some of his officers on board the Atlantic Fleet flagship, the *Wyoming*, in Boston in late summer 1915 and praised the qualities of submarines. Subsequently, he approved the assignment of the Chinese on board U.S. submarines then being constructed by Electric Boat.

Gillis immediately set about laying the groundwork to gain the approval of Yuan Shih-k'ai for the venture. Again, bad timing led to the collapse of the negotiations. Yuan still was in the midst of reestablishing the Chinese monarchy, intending to name himself emperor. The purchase of submarines was far down on his list of priorities. Then, in June 1916, as opposition to his imperial scheming was growing, Yuan died unexpectedly, throwing China into chaos as it collapsed into the warlord era. Part of Gillis' strategy had rested on a successful effort by Yuan to restart the monarchy. It was believed by Gillis that if Yuan Shih-k'ai succeeded in being named emperor, the submarine deal would be quickly approved. In fact, in the early spring of 1916 Wei Han had returned to China and immediately passed on to government authorities an Electric Boat Company offer to provide up to six submarines in exchange for

Chinese funds. Electric Boat, however, preferred that China agree to pay a quarter of the contract value in cash. The deal collapsed ninety days later because of Yuan Shih-k'ai's death. Official notification of China's rejection of the offer would not reach Gillis, however, until January 1917. As the Electric Boat effort collapsed, the Bethlehem Steel agreement also finally ground to a halt.[28] As China sank into confusion after the death of Yuan Shih-k'ai, its arms purchases were redirected toward the needs of its land-based warlords.[29] Although Minister Reinsch obtained confirmation from Premier Tuan Ch'i-jui that China would purchase ships from Bethlehem Steel at the earliest suitable moment, the Americans and their Chinese friends were more immediately concerned with preventing the Chinese navy from falling under Japanese domination.

In 1915 the ONI had reentered the picture for Gillis. Morale had dropped precipitously under the brief directorship of Captain Thomas Slidell Rodgers, but in January 1914 one of the Navy's best and brightest strategists, Captain James H. Oliver, assumed command of the organization. As a young officer, Oliver had been considered an activist who, in 1904, had confided to William Sims, then the naval aide to Theodore Roosevelt, that he believed "that the tender juniors will eventually succeed in lighting a warm little fire under the tough seniors." Oliver's strong suits included a keen knowledge of naval matters and three tours of duty (between 1904 and 1914) at the Naval War College, where he helped conceptualize a national maritime strategy that encompassed war planning and foreign policy analyses.[30] Within weeks after he became the ONI's director, Oliver began building his staff by adding four officers who were close to him as well as war-planning experts. Together, they instituted a rapid reform of the ONI that focused on four areas: general administration of the intelligence organization, collection of information, collation (analysis), and dissemination. By October 1915, with World War I in full swing in Europe, the ONI formed two services in the area of intelligence collection. The War Information Service was primarily concerned with homeland information collection activities. A counterpart service called the Naval Information Service (NIS) was also formed that concentrated on overseas information collection. Initially six posts were established—in England, Germany, Japan, China, Argentina, and Chile. It was envisioned that the collection of information would be done by attachés, retired officers living abroad, resident businesspeople overseas, journalists and their organizations, foreign nautical intelligence agencies, and other friendly overseas Americans, such as missionaries and teachers.[31]

Gillis received a confidential letter dated 15 November 1915 from Captain Oliver referring to the "strained relations with a certain power [obviously referring to Japan]" that required the appointment of a "Chief Intelligence Officer" in China. Oliver emphasized the urgency of the assignment, stating to Gillis that "if you are willing to undertake this work and to cooperate in so important a part of our National Defense, for which you are exceptionally fitted, it is desirable that you commence at once." The position was being offered to Gillis with the knowledge and consent of Eugene G. Grace, the new president of Bethlehem Steel, providing the company with a convenient opportunity to sever its agreement with Gillis. The terms of reimbursement for Gillis' new job were not disclosed, but it was believed that he would access pay equal to his active-duty commander's salary. Oliver admonished Gillis "to keep the whole matter as quiet as possible until such a time as it may be necessary to place things on a more formal basis." The letter went on to advise Gillis that should he accept the position, he was to work closely with the naval attaché at Peking, Lieutenant Commander Hutchins, who would "afford you all facilities and aid in his power." Despite the still-pending Electric Boat deal, Gillis readily accepted the post and commenced organizing his new office.[32]

On 15 November 1915 the director of naval intelligence (DNI) sent a letter to Hutchins that forwarded a set of orders, oddly, for him to pass to Lieutenant Commander Frederick Joseph Horne, the U.S. naval attaché in Tokyo. The orders directed Hutchins to ask Gillis—who, of course, was retired at the time—to be present at a meeting in Peking when Horne arrived there. Horne was to read to the other two the information he possessed about the plans for the Naval Information Service and the instructions for a "Special Intelligence Service (SIS)." Horne was also directed not to furnish Gillis anything in writing, or to retain anything in writing, about these plans in Tokyo.

Hutchins also was to inform Gillis and Horne that the meeting between the three men was to "study and discuss all matters in connection with the General Plan for the NIS and SIS and to agree on such preliminary arrangements and details as are now possible and advisable." No one, outside of the three principals, was to be informed of the conference's purpose or proceedings, and they were to postpone informing the ambassador "until relations become strained or at the discretion of the Naval Attaché in Peking." To others the visit was to be described as merely an "inspection."[33] In a separate letter on the subject to Lieutenant Commander Horne, the DNI told him to inform his ambassador, who would inform the Japanese government that he (Horne) was proceeding to Peking to inspect the naval attaché's office there.[34] A separate set of orders to Horne was transmitted by Secretary of the Navy Daniels on 17 November, directing him, among other things, to take a temporary leave of absence but to ensure that the leave "will in no way prejudice your return to Japan and the resumption of your present duties and status."[35] It was a strange business, indeed.

Apparently in implementing whatever had been decided at the unusual meeting of Gillis, Hutchins, and Horne in Peking the previous November, in February 1916 the DNI sent Hutchins a copy of "Instructions Concerning Special Intelligence Service, which copy is blinded and accompanied by key [?]." Hutchins also was instructed to "burn with this letter" his original copy, which was in plain language.[36]

After this point in time there is a paucity of information about Gillis' professional and personal lives. For example, the only records uncovered concerning Gillis' activities as chief intelligence officer in China are found during the period from 1917 to 1919, when he was again on active duty as naval attaché in Peking. Otherwise, no records of his reports and network building or to whom he was reporting have been found. It is likely that since there was no Central Intelligence Agency or Defense Intelligence Agency in those days, he still reported to the DNI. There is no evidence found in the ONI records, however, for this period confirming that was the case.

Documents revealing details about Gillis' personal life in 1916 are similarly lacking. Any records that Gillis might have retained, revealing such facts as when he was married or by whom he was paid in 1916, are presumed to have disappeared from Gillis' home in Peking while he was imprisoned by the Japanese during World War II. It is noted in the final chapter of this biography that Gillis, following his release at the end of the war, told Dr. Nancy Lee Swann at Princeton University's Gest Oriental Library that the Japanese appeared to have taken almost everything from his home. A number of Gillis' living family members were interviewed for this biography, and they told the authors that they, too, had no documents relating to Gillis' personal or professional life during this time.

CHAPTER 7

~

World War I and Recall to Active Duty:

Naval Attaché in Peking,

1917–1919

RECALL TO ACTIVE DUTY: A NETWORK OF SPIES, 1917–1918

The American entry into World War I on 6 April 1917 resulted, not surprisingly, in increased responsibilities for Gillis. At that time Hutchins received orders to Mare Island, California, where he subsequently took command of a newly commissioned destroyer, the *Taylor*, as Gillis accepted recall to active duty, becoming once again the U.S. naval attaché in Peking for the duration of the war. World War I proved to be a busy time for Gillis, who continued to build his network of informants but now also had to keep the ONI informed of conditions in China, paying particular attention to Japanese activities. Over the next three years, he would provide a steady flow of reports that ranged across a variety of subjects. These included Japanese activities in Manchuria, Shantung, and Siberia. He also reported on political conditions in China, collecting and translating articles from the Chinese newspapers and magazines, while his informants provided excellent information on mining, railroads, and shipyards. All this was done in the context of the maneuvering between the great powers in Asia as a result of the Great War.

On the larger world stage, a major (and in light of later events, particularly ironic) upshot of the Japanese wartime naval relationship with Great Britain was a similar, if much smaller, relationship with the United States. In effect the Imperial Japanese Navy now extended further, if roundabout, aid to the Royal Navy by making it possible for the U.S. Navy to assist the British directly. The Royal Navy's most pressing lack at his point was escort ships. British officials importuned their American counterparts to help make good that shortage. Doing so meant shifting U.S. naval forces to the Atlantic from the Pacific, producing for the Americans a shortfall of their own in the latter theater. To fill the gap in 1917 they, like the British in 1914, approached their new Pacific "ally," Japan.

This was because U.S. intervention in the European war required a complete rethinking of American naval strategy and construction policies, which, before 1917, had assumed an allied defeat followed by an attack by German and Japanese forces against the United States. Shortly after the U.S. entry into the war, a British mission headed by Arthur Balfour sought to alter the American naval construction program, which consisted of a massive buildup of capital warships, in part to remain capable of fighting combined German-Japanese forces. In April and May 1917 Balfour entered into secret discussions with the United States and proposed that the Americans construct, instead, large numbers of desperately needed escort ships in return for a promise of British help in case of a Japanese-American conflict. The two parties ultimately demurred at this late stage of the war. Nonetheless, that these negotiations occurred demonstrates the depth of Anglo-U.S. antipathy and mistrust toward Japan in 1917.[1]

American leaders viewed their relations with Japan through a prism of concern about China and racial bigotry. James Reed described some of the sources of anti-Japanese feeling in the United States before World War I: "Pacific Coast politicians; labor union leaders; Hearst Chain journalists (whose idea of news embraced lovely white maidens found dead in the flea-bag hotels of debauched Japanese); and, perhaps not least of all, the Navy officer corps, whose War Plan Orange was really a war plan yellow." That sentiment joined with a determination to adhere to the Open Door Policy concerning China to turn American opinion against Japan. U.S. leaders viewed Japan as seeking unfair territorial and political advantage in China, a state known to most Americans mainly through the eyes of the many missionaries serving there.

Nevertheless, the U.S. entry into World War I dictated a renewed attempt to resolve the impasse in American-Japanese relations. Like Great Britain at the beginning of the war, the United States now found itself dependent on Japanese goodwill and assistance in the Pacific. A Japanese mission to Washington led by Viscount Ishii Kikujiro concluded an agreement in November 1917 that permitted U.S. warships to redeploy to the Atlantic and support the British fleet. Under that agreement, Japanese warships patrolled the waters of the Hawaiian Islands for the remainder of the conflict. The cruiser *Tokiwa* commenced its patrol there in August 1918 and protected commerce in Hawaiian waters until it returned to Japan in February 1919.[2]

In related activity during the Great War, British leaders, who also depended on the Japanese for assistance, had nothing but praise for the Japanese squadron based in Malta that had escorted many British convoys across the Mediterranean Sea before it sailed for home. Winston Churchill voiced the general high opinion when he said that he "did not think that the Japanese [squadron] had ever done a foolish thing." The governor of Malta, Lord Methuen, who reviewed Japanese warships there in March 1919, also lauded the Japanese navy for "its splendid work in European waters" and expressed this hope: "God grant our alliance, cemented in blood, may it long endure." The Japanese warships' performance in the Mediterranean certainly merited high praise. Japanese destroyers' ratio of time at sea to time in port was the highest of any allied warships during the war: Japanese warships were under way 72 percent of the time. The British record was 60 percent, the Greek and French only 45 percent. British officers credited the Japanese warships with excellent performance—at least, they added, when all went according to plan. Postwar British criticisms that the Japanese "acted inferior to our men when unforeseen situations cropped up" reflected British prejudices expressed during the war—prejudices not supported by the actual record. That record clearly demonstrates instead how seriously Japanese naval officers took their duty. The commanders of several Japanese warships are reported to have committed hara-kiri (ritual suicide) when ships they were convoying were lost.[3]

Despite the cooperative manner in which the Japanese extended their wartime responsibilities, U.S. resentment of dependence upon the Japanese throughout the war and of Japanese gains in Micronesia closely paralleled that seen in British quarters. The Japanese returned this antagonism after 1917, when the view took root among naval officers that differences between the two powers were irreconcilable short of war. Japanese expansion into Siberia in 1918, seen by some Japanese as preempting U.S. containment on all sides, was to add to the antipathy between the two nations. By 1917, even while acting as an ally, the Imperial Japanese Navy had officially designated the United States its "most likely enemy" in any future conflict.[4]

Returning to Gillis' duties in China at this point, one of his first activities was helping protect the Kiangnan Naval Dockyard and Arsenal at Shanghai from a Japanese takeover. Kiangnan was founded in 1865 as one of the first industrial efforts undertaken in China and enjoyed an excellent reputation as a center for commercial shipbuilding and repair. It had long been managed by the British, but most of the engineers and technicians were Chinese. In April 1917 a U.S. firm, the Pacific Mail Steamship Company, had negotiated an agreement with the Chinese government by which the company and its "allied interests" were to manage the Kiangnan Naval Dockyard for twenty-five years and receive 62 percent of the net proceeds. Probably through one of his many informants, Gillis learned that Pacific Mail also had promised to loan $5 million to the Chinese, which was to be used for the purchase of submarines from a U.S. company that was a rival to his recent employer, Electric Boat. Gillis promptly notified Electric Boat's president, G. C. Davidson, and word did not take long to get to the U.S. State Department.

After some time, Japan learned of the deal, and Japanese agents harassed the manager of Pacific Mail, J. H. Rosseter, by clandestinely searching his baggage and confronting him in his hotel room on a trip to New York. The British protested the agreement and favored a counterplan that involved the British armaments firm Vickers and Japanese capitalists. The wrangling between the United States, Great Britain, and Japan continued until July 1918, when the U.S. Shipping Board intervened by signing a lucrative contract with the Kiangnan Naval Dockyard for four 10,000-ton commercial vessels with an option on eight more. Japan could not protest because its own booming industries were reliant upon American steel exports. For Gillis, the action by the Shipping Board was satisfactory because it precluded both the Pacific Mail and Vickers-Japanese proposals as well as saving the Kiangnan shipyard for the Chinese.[5]

During this period the Chinese navy succeeded in gaining quiet approval to send a mission to the United States. It was headed by Admiral Li Ting-Hsin, a friend and confidant of Gillis'. Gillis took the opportunity to urge the Navy Department to assist the Chinese mission. He believed that it was critical to help China acquire munitions in order to prevent Japanese efforts to control the Chinese navy. No sooner had the Chinese naval mission left for the United States when Secretary of State Robert Lansing and Viscount Ishii, the special Japanese ambassador, concluded their bilateral agreement on 2 November 1917, mentioned earlier, in which the United States recognized Japan's "special interests" in China, while Japan emphasized it respected the Open Door Policy and Chinese territorial integrity.

Unfortunately, there was an immediate misunderstanding among Japan, China, and the United States following the signing of the Lansing-Ishii accord and its subsequent release to the press on 6 November 1917. The Chinese translated the word "special" as "paramount," resulting in confusion and resentment in Peking. The Japanese also believed that the agreement centered on U.S. recognition of their potential control over China. The United States, however, believed that it had only recognized certain economic rights for Japan in China. In the end the Lansing-Ishii accord did little to allay tensions between the United States and Japan in the Pacific. Indeed, as events unfolded in the waning months of World War I, their rivalry was only heightened.[6] It did result in a serious blow to the Chinese naval mission, however. Its effort to gain training for officers and enlisted men in the United States and to acquire submarines again was rebuffed. Navy Secretary Daniels in April 1918 also emphatically denounced the old Taft-Knox Dollar Diplomacy by declaring to Lansing that he opposed "the use of any naval officer of his position to favor the procurement of contracts by a private company." Nearly simultaneously, Electric Boat proceeded to close its offices in China. Gillis, however, had one final card to play. He won from Admiral Li an agreement to negotiate with Electric Boat should China desire to buy submarines at some time in the future.[7]

Meanwhile in the intelligence game, the ONI's wartime operations in Europe—or the Far East—never approached the size or efficiency of its domestic intelligence work. Throughout World War I, Section B, responsible for foreign matters, contained only one-quarter of the personnel employed by Section A's domestic intelligence desks. Allied intelligence already blanketed the European field, and Captain Roger Welles, the new director of the ONI as of 16 April 1917, concentrated on strengthening the naval attaché network rather than on inaugurating a tardy espionage system. But the task of selecting attachés and their assistants confounded the DNI. "My experience in the Office of Naval Intelligence during the war showed one thing very plainly," Welles wrote Captain Ernest J. King in retrospect on 17 December 1919, "and that was the difficulty of selecting officers for the duties of Naval Attachés." Despite careful screening, many lacked training in diplomacy, international law, and foreign languages.[8]

Troubles with Captain William Dugald MacDougall, the U.S. naval attaché in London, exemplified Welles' concern: "About all we have received from MacDougall has been stuff about materiel and little or nothing of military value," the director complained. He wanted the attaché to penetrate O.B. 40, the old Admiralty building, which housed British naval intelligence headquarters under Admiral Hall. The office contained a most brilliant collection of intelligence experts in every field of espionage and communications. "At the British Admiralty," Rear Admiral William Sowden Sims, Commander, U.S. Naval Forces Operating in European Waters (COMUSNAVFOREUR), marveled, "they have a corps of grey-haired Oxford professors, Egyptologists, Cuneiform Inscription Readers, etc., who break ciphers with great facility, and, I may add, have broken practically every cipher that they have been put up against."[9]

With Britain now an ally, Welles expected to learn everything from Hall's team. "I am particularly anxious to get their lists of enemy suspects in the United States," he wrote Sims, "and I am sure such lists exist in their office." But Hall was not anxious to share his secrets with inexperienced and talkative Americans, and even at this stage he probably considered the United States a potential postwar rival. Hall's suspicions affronted Welles. "I think you can assure the Admiralty that they need not fear leaks from this Office," he wired Sims. Welles dispatched a personal representative, Lieutenant Commander John H. Roys, to London to smooth relations.[10]

At the same time in Asia, Lieutenant Commander Frederick Horne, the U.S. naval attaché in Tokyo, hoped to establish a secret information service in Japan. Assisted by Lieutenant Colonel William L. Redles, Horne proceeded cautiously. Ensign Robert G. Payne, a Japanese-language expert, arrived under the cover of a clerk assigned to count merchant ships in Japanese waters. However, growing Japanese suspicions limited Horne's effectiveness, and many of his wartime reports dealt in vague generalities.[11]

Information from Gillis in China was more provocative. The experienced agent bombarded the ONI with ominous reports of Japanese plots to conquer China, Manchuria, and Siberia. "Unless checked, Japan's aggressive policy in the Far East will bring war either with us or the British (or perhaps both) sooner or later," he warned, "and it is with the object of doing all in our power to prevent this deplorable event that I suggest our using every effort to obtain publicity."[12] His sense of urgency increased with each new request for money. Gillis asked for $10,000 to cover investigations in the East Indies and another $5,000 to check Japanese intrigue in Siberia. But apparently the latter sum was not well spent, since the U.S. naval attaché in Peking claimed that his sources reported that the Bolsheviks were mere terrorists and their ranks run by "Jews and former convicts."[13]

Gillis also demanded the dispatch of more agents to East Asia, including code experts and operatives to tap cables and intercept Japanese messages. "I am even not so sure but what it might be well for you to be in a position to lay your hand on a skilled 'cracksman' so that he could be available at short notice if it ever became desirable or necessary to resort to such extreme measures as breaking into a safe to get information of an incriminating character," he wrote to Captain Edward McCauley Jr., Welles' assistant, on 19 October 1917.[14] After he had assumed the duties of naval attaché in April 1917, Gillis had written a letter to the DNI that was forwarded by the DNI to the chief of naval operations and the chief of the Bureau of Navigation on 13 September 1917. In his letter Gillis urged that in the event his prediction of war between Japan and the United States were to come to pass "in the next few years," the Navy, in order to better be prepared, should take steps to have more officers and men obtain a working knowledge of the Japanese language. He suggested that the ability to read the language need not be a priority, but he noted that most Japanese officers were taught to speak English. In the same letter, Gillis suggested that "trustworthy Americans" be recruited as agents at once in Japan and China to constantly report on what was going on. Gillis' proposal included paying each recruit a lump sum of $3,000 in gold to act as a confidential agent for five years, with possible extension to ten years, as well as a yearly salary of $1,000. He also recommended that each agent be required to pass a comprehensive examination and take an oath of allegiance. He pointed out that now that the United States was at war and had compulsory military service, it was time to train officers and civilians in the Japanese language.[15]

Captain McCauley responded to Gillis on 18 September about the suggestion for agents in China and Japan. He explained that "the Authorities" were not as concerned with the Far East at that time as they might be (presumably they were preoccupied with Europe) but that "the service" (the Navy) recognized the need to keep Gillis' initial agent service going as well as the necessity for a "complete service" (we assume this refers to the SIS), for which Gillis had "well laid the foundation." McCauley went on to say he agreed with Gillis that the "Attaché Office" should handle anything in the way of naval interests and also went into a lengthy discourse on the subject of codes. The Navy had hastily produced a set of codes for use overseas, including one called the "Small code" and a "B book for 00" (not explained in the letter), but now a new and complete code called the "F" code would be transmitted shortly "by proper channels." This new code would resolve the difficulties with the "Int. Lar." code (also unexplained) that could render passages incomprehensible; he described it as "an utterly useless and extravagant expense." McCauley went on to note that he had been trying to get orders to go to sea duty and that now "Knox" (Lieutenant Commander Dudley Wright Knox, USN) was to relieve him.[16]

Gillis pursued his quest for an extensive secret service in a letter to DNI on 19 October in which he stated that such a service would have to be on an adequate scale and commensurate with the "seriousness of the situation," to be established "in the same manner we are going at the destroyer building program and the aeroplane construction." He said it would require a large number of thoroughly competent men to cover a large field of Japanese activities and went on to say, in conclusion, "If I am not very much mistaken, if all was known of what the Japanese have been doing, there would be an exposure of a condition of affairs which would put the Luxburg affair and the Swedish sending of German telegrams in the infant class."[17] Gillis' attachment to that same letter, in further justification for enlarging his secret service, indicated his belief that Japan's policies in China over the previous two years were proof "of disloyalty to the cause for which the United States and the allies are fighting." He renewed his suspicion (of 1916) that it would not take much to bring about a change of sides on the part of Japan and noted that "this probably explains her unwillingness to send her troops to Europe to fight against the Central Powers. Japan's attention at the present time is centered upon China, and her every effort directed towards consolidating herself there while the world powers are engaged in a life-and-death struggle in Europe."[18]

Naval intelligence did not rush a safecracker to Peking but did raise this issue in a letter from the assistant director of naval intelligence (ADNI) to the Office of the State Department Counselor on 2 January

1918, which forwarded Gillis' 19 October proposal, including a list of the districts in China to be covered and an indication of the order of their relative importance.[19] State quickly replied on 8 January, requesting Captain McCauley's views on the matter and a short statement of the extent of the service in the Far East in operation at the time under the ONI's direction.[20] McCauley responded with a lengthy letter that repeated many of Gillis' arguments and concluded with a recommendation that the regions where the Japanese were most active, such as Manchuria, Shantung, and Fukien Province, should "be covered with the least possible delay" and that his office had taken measures already to that effect.[21]

The ONI displayed unusual ingenuity in covering the Far Eastern agents it did acquire with clever cloaks. A female employee of Bonwit Teller & Company toured Asia on a clothes-buying trip while collecting information for the ONI. Another traveler used by the director worked as a salesman for the Nicholson File Company of Rhode Island and mailed information to the ONI from the Far East through his home office. For Southeast Asia, the intelligence agency came up with a forestry adviser who visited the area under the pretense of studying local supplies of timber.[22]

According to Jeffery Dorwart in his book on the ONI:

> Providing agents to follow Japanese activities in the Pacific Islands seized from Germany during the war proved far more difficult than finding good operatives for China. Welles informed the U.S. Naval Governor of Guam that he urgently required intelligence from the Marshalls, Carolines, and Marianas. Several missionaries reported observing Japanese fortifications on Truk and a wireless station and military garrison on Yap. Welles wanted verification and suggested that the Navy Department send a private schooner filled with ONI undercover personnel to the Marshalls and the Carolines, but Admiral [William S.] Benson [the chief of naval operations] vetoed the plan, warning the DNI never again to raise this sensitive question.[23]

Dorwart went on to relate:

> Information about Japanese escapades closer to the United States became more voluminous. Indeed, [William Clarkson] Van Antwerp [a U.S. Naval Academy graduate forced to resign early

in his career due to a glut of officers at the time but subsequently became a very successful investor] uncovered what he believed was a major Japanese plan to take over Lower California. He discovered that a mysterious Japanese agent named Kondo owned the Mexican Industrial Development Company and the Lower California Fisheries Company, and held concessions for coastal fishing off the Pacific coast of Mexico. The local intelligence director learned further that Kondo's firm planned to construct a chain of packing houses and wharves from Guaymas to Turtle Bay. "This will give this Japanese Company stations at practically every big point on the Lower California peninsula, as well as the West Coast, and will keep them in close touch with conditions at Magdalena Harbor," he complained.[24]

One of Gillis' next actions was to begin identifying Americans in China who could provide information on economic conditions, military preparations, and any activity inimical to American interests or movements. Over the next five years, Gillis worked extremely hard to create an effective intelligence network in China. Correspondence from Hutchins in late 1921 would describe Gillis' efforts as follows: "During the World War, Commander Gillis enlarged the scope of this office and made such good Chinese and foreign connections that when I arrived and took over [about September 1919] I found a government office that was fully independent of other US Government offices in China and was itself able to get accurate information from reliable Chinese and foreign sources and thereby keep ONI well informed, as well as to successfully cooperate with the Legation."

Review of the correspondence at the time shows that as tensions with Japan grew throughout this period, the mission of the Naval Information Service in China took on a more operational and proactive tone, especially by the end of Gillis' tenure. Shortly after he returned to China following the end of World War I, Hutchins described the American informants that Gillis had recruited as men who "could be depended upon to do any sort of work requiring skill and nerve." He goes on to state: "In case of a war between Japan and the United States, it would be of the utmost importance to cripple all of Japan's industries in China and the men mentioned in this report are ones who could be depended upon to carry out such work."[25] Most of the men selected by Gillis were fluent in Chinese and had been in China for a long time. The largest numbers of informants were either missionaries or businesspeople, who represented about one-third each the total of fifty-five individuals identified. The rest were engineers, journalists, doctors, lawyers, teachers, and bankers.

Of particular interest, Welles recruited Roy Chapman Andrews, the famous Mongolian explorer, a resident of Peking, and the curator of mammals at the American Museum of Natural History, as an operative for China during one of his visits to the United States in the spring of 1918.[26] The office supplied him with $4 a day and instructions to transmit messages to Gillis in invisible ink. Andrews would make frequent forays through Manchuria into the Gobi Desert. A letter to Gillis from Captain Welles dated 10 June 1918 states: "This will serve to vouch for the bearer of it, Roy Chapman Andrews, whom I believe you have already met. He will act under your orders. It is hoped that good use can be made of his abilities and cover."[27]

Andrews' tenure as an undercover agent was temporarily halted, however, when in December 1918 the ONI intercepted a letter from his wife, Yvette, to family in the United States that indicated her husband was "on a secret mission for the Government." She also adds in the letter that "there seems to be a little movement on foot to get rid of the Chinese President and set up the Empire again. It won't be anti foreign but there may be some shots flying around and it may be quite some fun." The ONI told Gillis to "Order Reynolds [Andrews' code name] home to report to the Office."[28] Nevertheless, several years later Andrews was apparently back in good grace because he was included on the 1921 "List of Reliable American Residents in China." The entry for him on that list indicates that he was "well qualified to undertake a risky job."

In other matters, on 27 October 1917 Gillis had suggested to DNI that while it was "in a way none of my business," he was sure that "should certain untoward events take place" (war between the United States and Japan) the naval attaché in Japan would find it difficult to transfer his archives and records to China—just when they would be most needed. He noted that he had written also to Lieutenant Commander Horne, the naval attaché in Tokyo, recommending that he forward his important papers—either copies to retain or the original for Gillis to copy by "Rectigraph" and then return to Japan. Gillis had purchased this then-state-of-the-art, camera-based photocopying machine that the U.S. government had been using since 1910. In the same letter Gillis followed up with more specific recommendations to increase intelligence gathering in China "to cope with Japanese schemes of territorial aggrandizement." He suggested the employment of special agents for Shantung, Manchuria, and Fukien, where he believed "Japanese activities are most pronounced." He recommended that three trustworthy Americans be engaged to cover these regions and that they each be paid a salary of $3,600 per year, along with the usual expenses.[29] Gillis did not wait for the ONI to reply and sent off yet another letter to McCauley on 27 October that outlined his intention to create "the volunteer intelligence service" and that he would "use great discretion in picking my men." He went on to advise McCauley that once he recruited his volunteers he would forward a list from time to time to the ONI.[30]

Captain Welles replied on 4 December, approving the recommendation regarding archives and records from Japan.[31] That same day he notified the naval attaché in Tokyo of his decision, directing him to "take up this matter with the Naval Attaché, Peking [Gillis]," to determine the best way to handle the records.[32]

Meanwhile, Gillis wrote to the DNI on 19 November 1917 that as a result of the Lansing-Ishii agreement, the Japanese were "conducting their usual press propaganda throughout the Far East," indicating that the United States would withdraw all men-of-war from Pacific waters, leaving American interests in the care of Japan, thereby creating a "very bad impression, especially amongst the Chinese." He urged that these assertions not be allowed to go uncontradicted. In this regard he requested that he be kept fully informed and suggested the need for a government gazette in the Far East—more so than for one in Washington—with supplements in both Chinese and Japanese and possible publication in Shanghai.[33] ADNI McCauley passed this request on to George Creel, the chairman of the Committee on Public Information, on 2 January 1918 for his consideration.[34] Captain Welles finally responded to Gillis on 14 January that the ONI had been told that it would not be possible to publish a government gazette for the Far East but that arrangements were being made for a wireless service of one thousand words a day at Shanghai and that Gillis would be advised as soon as it was placed in operation.[35]

Gillis strayed a bit from his usual pursuits in a second letter to Welles dated 19 November in which he invited the director's attention to Japan's vulnerability to attack from the sea by "aeroplane." Gillis explained that he was certain that the Imperial Japanese Army was not unaware of this threat and the danger from a military standpoint to Japan's wooden cities. He posited that a group of large, high-speed cruisers "built for the special purpose" of carrying a large number of assembled and disassembled airplanes would "make things very unpleasant for the large Japanese cities, and it would not be very difficult to wipe out such places as Tokyo, Yokohama, Osaka, Kobe, etc., with a few well-placed incendiary bombs or shells." (Gillis must have experienced grim satisfaction twenty-seven years later, during 1944–1945, when his prediction was proved to be right on the mark.) He concluded with a recommendation that "in view of the uncertainties of the world situation, both now and when the European War is over, it would seem that it might be well to proceed with the design and construction of such craft at the present time."[36] The DNI passed this letter on to the operations branch of the Navy Department on 26 December 1917 (there were no long holidays during the war).

The nineteenth of November must have been a particularly active day for Gillis because he sent yet another letter to the DNI with that date. In it he reinforced a suggestion he apparently had made earlier that it was desirable to place the planned cable office in Shanghai under the naval attaché at Peking. He explained that while it was not desirable to establish censorship, he wanted to be in "closer touch with it [the cable office], for it is quite possible that apparently harmless messages, when viewed from the receiving end, might very well have marked indications of quite the opposite character when looked at from this end. The personality of the sender, or even the subject matter, might indicate something to a person thoroughly acquainted with the local situation."[37] No reference has been found to indicate if this ever came about.

In a telegram marked "Very Confidential" to Gillis on 12 April 1918, the ONI announced that it was very important that it receive advance information of all suspects leaving the Far East for the United States and asked Gillis if he could arrange that.[38] No record of Gillis' reply has been found, but the request seems to have been a formidable one. Another telegram, this time from Gillis, advised the ONI that his ambassador had designated the naval attaché to take charge of all matters relative to personnel in connection with enemy trade, as had already been done in Tokyo. Gillis asked the ONI to approach the War Trade Board for additional office space, personnel, and funds for the job, noting that there were "excellent local men" available at once to do the work.[39] Gillis sent a second telegram in July, advising the DNI that he had "nothing to date" and that it would be impossible to do the War Trade Board work without assistance as he had earlier requested.[40] Rear Admiral Welles reminded the War Trade Board of Gillis' request in a letter dated 30 July. The chairman of the War Trade Board, Herman Oliphant, replied on 23 August that "owing to certain questions which have arisen regarding the whole question of Enemy Trade in China" it would be "well to hold this matter in abeyance until you hear from me further."[41] Perhaps the board realized the war was finally winding down at that point.

Gillis wrote a fourth letter to the DNI on 19 November 1917, this one about his concerns over the Lansing-Ishii accord. When he first learned of the Lansing-Ishii agreement and how it was being played in the press, Gillis was greatly agitated. For example, on 6 November the *New York Times* reported that the United States had apparently "recognized the application of a "Japanese Monroe Doctrine" to China.[42] On 8 November 1917 Gillis cabled Welles that the effect of the Lansing-Ishii accord "would without question result in immediate and marked increase in Japanese aggressive actions toward China."[43] He followed up on 19 November with the confidential letter to Welles bearing this warning:

> I wish to emphasize most emphatically the point that the Lansing-Ishii agreement has but resulted in the pouring of oil on the fire and we should be prepared for the worst. Japan and the government and people of that country have lost their heads completely over the China situation, and their desire to consolidate their position here while the powers are occupied elsewhere is leading them along a dangerous path. Don't misunderstand me, I am not so lacking in common sense as not to realize that the signing of the agreement was forced upon the United States, but I feel it my duty to let you know what its effect is now and what it probably will be. Japan has thrown all restraint to the winds and is bent on a course of seeing just how far she can go, and where it is to end except in trouble I fail to see.[44]

Gillis was not alone in his condemnation of the Lansing-Ishii accord. The U.S. Legation's minister in Peking, Paul Reinsch, had never been consulted by Secretary Lansing on the negotiations during the writing of the agreement. Instead, Reinsch states in the final chapter of his book *An American Diplomat in China* that he first learned of the Lansing-

Ishii note from the Japanese minister to Peking, Baron Hayashi.[45] His bitterness over this matter was felt keenly, and he resigned some seven months later. In his resignation letter of 7 June 1919 to President Wilson, Reinsch stated flatly that the situation in China was reaching extremes. He advised Wilson as follows:

> But in fact, the situation requires that the American people should be made to realize what is at stake here for us in order that they may give the necessary backing to the Government for support in any action which the developments here may require. Unless the American people realize this and the Government feels strong enough to take adequate action, the fruits of one hundred and forty years of American work in China will inevitably be lost. Our people will be permitted to exist here only at the sufferance of others, and the great opportunity which has been held out to us by the Chinese people to assist in the development of education and free institutions will be gone beyond recall. In its stead there will come a sinister situation dominated by the unscrupulous methods of the reactionary military regime centered in Tokyo, absolutist in tendency, cynical of the principles of free government and human progress. If this force, with all the methods it is accustomed to apply, remains unopposed there will be created in the Far East the greatest engine of military oppression and dominance that the world has yet seen, nor can we avoid the conclusion that the brunt of evil results will fall on the United States, as is already foreshadowed by the bitter hostility and abnormal vituperativeness of the Japanese press with regard to America.[46]

There must have been a close relationship between Reinsch and Gillis; Reinsch likely depended heavily on Gillis and his volunteer informants. This was alluded to several years later by Captain Arthur St. Clair Smith upon assuming the duty of naval attaché in Peking. On 4 January 1923 he wrote:

> One thing that has struck me as a newcomer here. The naval attaché seems to have a great deal more information about all sorts of things than any other individual. It seems I am very frequently furnishing the minister with the latest and best informa-

tion he has. This is natural enough in some ways for we have all sorts of information coming in from ships and various ports of China. The military attaché has little of this sort of thing. But, also Hutchins built himself a very good information service. He was in touch with the right kind of people who get about.[47]

Despite their vigorous reporting and analyses about conditions in China, neither Gillis nor Reinsch was being heard. An armistice was signed between Germany and the Allies to end the war on 11 November 1918. Americans had been witness to the bloodiest conflict the world had ever seen and no one was in the mood to risk confrontation with Japan in the Far East. The first correspondence that Gillis received from Rear Admiral Welles following the signing of the armistice underscored that fact:

November 14, 1918

From: Director of Naval Intelligence.
To: Naval Attaché, Peking.
Subject: Reduction of your organization.

1.   In view of the signing of the armistice, and the fact that a resumption of hostilities is not to be expected, it is the desire of this Office to reduce expenses as rapidly as possible by a gradual decrease in the force now under your direction.

2.   It is believed, as a first step, that it will be practicable for you to dispense without delay with the services of most of the local agents and assistants you may have in your employ, only retaining those whom you may need for the purpose of closing investigations now yet completed.

3.   This Office realized that much work will remain to be done until the final conclusion of peace, and it is its intention to have you maintain, until further notice, an organization which will be adequate to efficiently carry on all such activities as may still require your attention.

4.   You are expected to use your best discretion in this regard, and a report is requested as to the measures you may take in conformity with the instructions herein contained with such sug-gestions and recommendations as you may deem appropriate.[48]

Continued close surveillance of Japan's activities in China, it would appear, was near an end.

The ONI cabled Gillis on 20 November 1918, asking if he thought, in view of changed conditions, whether the Shanghai office was necessary.[49] Gillis replied that while conditions might have changed in Europe, they had not in the Far East. He cited Japanese chagrin at "German unconcealment," probably due to Japan's "shady action" in China during the war. He stressed that it was more necessary than ever to maintain an intelligence organization, especially in Shantung, Fukien, Hunan, and Manchuria, and "by exposure (of the) Japanese activities prevent racial feeling against white people which Japanese are trying to foment." He also said that the Allies should show their naval force in the Far East at once, before the peace conference.[50] Gillis became more urgent in his telegram of 28 November, in which he forwarded Minister Reinsch's cablegram of 26 November. That cable reiterated that "conditions may have changed in Europe and America, but not in the Far East" and in his opinion "Allies should exhibit show of Naval Force Far East at once and before peace conference."[51] There is no evidence such a naval force was sent to the Far East.

The ONI asked Gillis, on 25 November, to compile a record of the development and work of his office during the war—"lessons learned" in today's Navy parlance—with such recommendations and comments his experience might suggest, including "the various branches of intelligence work covered by your Office" and other, more general topics, such as a list of the names of officer and enlisted personnel in his office and their qualifications and relative efficiency.[52]

FINAL RETIREMENT AND DISENGAGEMENT FROM THE NAVY: 1919

Gillis' final days as an active naval officer were not quite over. On 3 January 1919 Gillis reported back on the reduction efforts in his office. He advised that there was but one paid "special confidential agent" working in connection with his office, one resident paid agent in Shanghai, and a special mail courier "as arranged two years ago before we entered the war." Nevertheless, he went on, "if it is thought necessary or desirable to keep track of Japanese activities in China and the Far East inimical to the United States . . . then I would suggest (as I have done on many previous occasions) an organization sufficient to cover the wide field of Japanese activities." Gillis provided a proposed organization of the naval attaché office, including three assistant naval attachés who might be able to replace the resident agents.[53]

Several months later Roger Welles was replaced as director of naval intelligence. Prior to his leaving he wrote the following assessment of Gillis in his final report of fitness dated 31 January 1919:

> Commander Gillis did excellent work in China for the Office of Naval Intelligence. His reports on file . . . of conditions in China are most valuable and show an exceptional understanding of the people and government; that he had most reliable sources of informants; that he was in touch with all activities of the government and that he was untiring in efforts to obtain reliable information. His ability to read and speak the Chinese language placed him at a great advantage over those not so prepared.
>
> He was an unusually good Naval Attaché.[54]

There was also still the matter of his replacement. Orders were finally issued in early June to Commander Charles T. Hutchins Jr. to return to Peking to relieve Gillis. Several months passed before Hutchins was able to put his personal affairs in order and proceed to China.[55] In the interim Gillis continued to report on conditions in China and Japanese activities. A series of reports were sent to Welles in the winter and early spring of 1919 that reflected a relentless effort by Japan to enhance its position in various areas of China, including Manchuria, Shantung, the Pacific Islands, and Siberia.

Some six months prior to the armistice, President Wilson had authorized nearly 9,000 U.S. troops to proceed to Siberia to assist the anti-Bolshevik forces in resisting the Communist revolution then sweeping eastern Russia. He had also requested that other Allied troops be sent. The Japanese initially agreed to send 12,000 troops, but made it clear that they would not act under orders of an international coalition. Once the Imperial Japanese Army took control, however, the force grew to an alarming 70,000 troops, and by early 1919 they had occupied all ports and major towns in the Maritime Province of eastern Siberia.[56]

Concerning the Pacific Islands, Braisted wrote that Gillis had notified the ONI in November that a German missionary from the Carolines had reported to someone in Shanghai that the Japanese on Truk, in the South Pacific, had been "pressing forward on large docks, coal piles, and apparently even steps to fortify the island." Braisted further asserted that even more ominous than Gillis' report was the "cloud of secrecy that had covered the islands occupied by Japan throughout the war."[57]

By the time Hutchins arrived, Gillis had released a final assessment entitled "Japan's Position Today and Her Attitude Towards the United States." The bottom-line assessment by Gillis states simply that "a war between the United States and Japan in the near future is inevitable; and also that Japan is preparing herself for this war and the United States is not."[58]

Sometime during this period Gillis received the award of the Navy Cross, the Navy's second-highest award for valor. The undated citation reads:

> For distinguished service in the line of his profession as Naval Attaché, Pekin, China, in which capacity his knowledge of the language enabled him to render special service in intelligence work and in obtaining information concerning various matters of great importance to the government.
>
> For the President,
> Secretary of the Navy[59]

Also during this period, in April, Gillis' first cousin, Dr. Ansel W. Gillis, a Presbyterian missionary in Korea, was arrested (along with others) by the Japanese authorities there. According to the *New York Times*, Korean officials asserted that the arrests were related to a "Japanese policy of repression and injustice" as the Korean officials, including Dr. Syngman Rhee, much later to become the first leader of South Korea, gathered for a three-day Korean Congress in Seoul. The article mentioned that the ultimate disposition of Dr. Gillis was not known.[60]

Shortly afterward I. V. Gillis' niece Helen Murray was a cosponsor at the launch of the USS *Gillis* (DD 260) on 29 May 1919 at the Bethlehem Shipbuilding Corporation in Quincy, Massachusetts. Irvin probably would have wanted to attend but was many miles away at the time. The *Gillis* was named after Irvin's father, Rear Admiral James H. Gillis, and another Gillis, possibly related, Commodore John P. Gillis (1803–1873),

USS *Gillis* (DD 260)
(U.S. Naval Institute Photo Archive)

who sailed with Commodore Perry's expedition to open Japan and participated in the Union Navy blockade during the Civil War. The USS *Gillis* was decommissioned in 1922, recommissioned as a seaplane tender destroyer (AVD 12) in 1941 after conversion, and participated in many actions during World War II from the Aleutians to Okinawa. After receiving two battle stars, the *Gillis* was decommissioned for the last time on 1 November 1945 and sold for scrapping.[61]

Meanwhile, nothing if not persistent and covering his bases as his Navy career drew to a close, Gillis had first reported to the ONI on 15 March that the Chinese and Japanese governments had exchanged notes regarding permission for foreign nations to establish, on the coast of Fukien Province, dockyards, coaling stations for military use, or naval bases—or to borrow foreign capital for setting up those establishments. The Chinese government replied that it had given no such permission, closing this chapter of Gillis' efforts on behalf of Bethlehem Steel.[62] Gillis also reopened negotiations with the Electric Boat Company about providing submarines to China. In his letter of 3 June 1919, responding to an

Electric Boat letter of 23 April, he said that the company's response was "most welcome." He proposed a new "arrangement" whereby he would receive an annual retainer of $1,500, to be paid each quarter and deposited to his account at Riggs National Bank in Washington, D.C. He also requested an initial $1,500 for 1918 (presumably back pay for his services that year) and $750 for the first half of 1919. Gillis also told Electric Boat that he expected his relief to be "along in the next few weeks."

In late August the White House announced Minister Paul Reinsch's resignation.[63] (The reasons were explained in detail in the previous section of this chapter.) On 23 September the *New York Times* reported that Reinsch received a large send-off when he departed Peking on 14 September, including American, British, and Chinese guards of honor; members of the Chinese cabinet; and a number of students just returned from the United States, who assembled on the train platform to "bid him Godspeed on his trip to the United States." A band attached to the U.S. armed forces played "Auld Lang Syne" as the train moved out. Also present were representatives from many other nations. Chinese newspapers announced that "this may be the inauguration of a new Anglo-American-Chinese alliance."[64] Sadly, that was not to be the case.

According to a report sent to the ONI on 23 September by Gillis' relief, the U.S. consul in Swatow, China, had observed the arrival of a Japanese cruiser, the *Akitsushima*, there on 10 December. Apparently the staff of the Japanese consulate in Swatow had specifically requested the services of the British pilot, not desiring the American pilot, a Captain Stocker, who had handled the ship in the past—evidence of growing anti-American feeling by the Japanese in China.[65]

Gillis finally received a reply from Electric Boat on his proposal regarding submarines for China and responded on 28 September. He advised that the Chinese Navy Board was willing to place a "good order" with Electric Boat assuming that financing could be arranged in the United States—with an advance to the Navy Board included within the construction loan. Gillis said that while he was not in favor of this arrangement, the Chinese quoted contracts they had made in the past with British firms such as Handley Page and Marconi, as well as Japanese companies, and they urged that he approach the U.S. authorities. He went on to describe his take on rumors that China had purchased six Italian submarines. For the Chinese to do this, they would have been in clear violation of the terms of their 9 January 1918 agreement with Electric Boat, a copy of which Gillis enclosed and which stated the Chinese would "give your firm the preference in making the arrangements" for submarine purchases.[66]

In related activity, the *New York Times* reported that as of 1 August Reinsch, the former U.S. minister, had been appointed as a counselor of the Chinese government at a salary of $20,000 a year.[67] Upon Reinsch's return to China on 9 October, he announced that Japan's pledge to restore the sovereignty of Shantung to the Chinese was "only a shell," urging the Japanese to treat Shantung on equal terms with the rest of the world. Reinsch explained that his new post was as a legal, not political, adviser and that U.S.-Chinese friendship was growing "despite the disappointment of our part in the Peace Conference."[68]

On 28 November Electric Boat responded to Gillis' letter of 3 June, stating that the company "could not possibly consider the financial arrangement suggested" and that the banking group in Chicago said that this was a risk it was not willing to take. The company also complained that Gillis did not provide sufficient details to enable Electric Boat to make any plans or estimates of cost. The letter closed with a statement that the company felt that its business was that of a shipbuilder and not of a banker. It was a very strong rejection.[69]

Closing this chapter of Gillis' life on a more personal note, an unpublished family history written by one of Irvin's nieces, Dr. Marjorie Murray Burtt, provides a unique insight into his character and his activities as they relate to the time he spent in China as naval attaché. Dr. Burtt noted that "in the Gillis family, the Navy was of great importance. I had the impression that Navy people were superior to Army folks" and that "it was taken for granted that Irvin should go to the Naval Academy." She wrote that "the only obstacle was that he did not measure up to the required height," but that he would probably grow up to the requirement before he graduated. She said that his nickname there, Splint, was related to the height question. "Someone said, 'He's a chip off the old block. 'Chip!' was the retort, [*sic*] 'He's only a splinter.'" Dr. Burtt surmised that his short stature "made him especially comfortable in China, where the average man is not tall by our standards."[70]

Dr. Burtt related having lunch with Irvin in his "very crowded cabin" when he commanded the torpedo boat *Winslow* during the celebrations in New York honoring Admiral Dewey following the Spanish-American War. She stated later that Gillis decided to retire early from the Navy in 1914 because a new ruling by the secretary of the Navy that black and white

sailors should eat together "shocked him," revealing his "strong conserva-
tive streak." She confirmed that he married a Chinese Buddhist lady named
Zhao Yubin, who the family somehow knew as the "Manchu Princess."
Dr. Burtt explained that they were married "after his home leave in 1909
and before 1920." Dr. Burtt said that she never saw the letter announc-
ing the marriage and also reported that her mother was shocked that "he,
a devout Christian, should have married a 'Heathen.'" According to Dr.
Burtt, Irvin and his wife had no children of their own, but they did adopt a
Chinese boy and girl who, not related by blood, later married one another,
since that appeared to be "acceptable in their culture."[71]

 We have not uncovered any further details regarding Gillis' marriage
or his adopted children other than several photographs of Irvin and Yubin
together.

CHAPTER 8

Gillis as a Civilian in China:
1919–1948

Editors' note: Bruce Swanson clearly indicated in his manuscript that he intended to focus upon Irvin Gillis' life and career only until he retired from the Navy; he did, however, leave a few paragraphs, and many reference materials, on the remaining portion of Gillis' life. We determined that Bruce planned to summarize that significant portion of Gillis' activities. We also noted that a great deal of this material has already been the subject of various authors' writings at Princeton University. Much of the material in this chapter, therefore, was prepared using an essay by Martin J. Heijdra, "The East Asian Library and the Gest Collection at Princeton University," which appeared in Peter Zhou's book on the topic of East Asian libraries. Also used were Bruce Swanson's numerous reference materials as well as original research by Don and Helen McDowell at Princeton's East Asian Library. It is intended that this chapter accommodate Bruce's wishes and appropriately summarize for the reader a significant period in Gillis' extraordinary life.

SETTLING INTO COLLECTING ANCIENT CHINESE BOOKS: THE CHAOTIC 1920s

Conditions in China before and during the 1920s

Manchus from northern China invaded Peking in 1644, established the Ch'ing dynasty, which ruled China until 1912, and incorporated many elements of Chinese culture during their long rule. As the Chinese population expanded faster than agricultural production in the late 1700s, the standard of living began to decline. Corruption and dishonesty emerged as increasing factors in the Ch'ing government.

After the Boxer Rebellion in 1900, the Manchus finally attempted a serious reform of the government and the economy, but the reforms were too late to save the dynasty. Following some years of turmoil, when the last Manchu emperor was but a six-year-old boy, the southern and central provinces declared their independence from Manchu rule in 1911. Dr. Sun Yat-sen was named provisional president of the Chinese Republic in 1912 in Nanking by the Kuomintang (KMT), or Chinese Nationalist Party, established by the revolutionaries.

The years between 1916 and 1928 are generally known as the warlord period. In the absence of a strong central government, each warlord of the various regions struggled to protect his own territory while attempting to devise a basis for national unity. Some aspired to the old "Mandate from Heaven" to rule all of China. During this era a new factor in Chinese politics emerged when the Chinese Communist Party (CCP) was founded in Shanghai in 1921. An agreement of cooperation was reached between the KMT and the CCP, as well as the Soviet Union, after Sun Yat-sen died in 1925. At the time of his death, Sun was no longer president, having been overwhelmed by support for the warlord Yuan Shih-k'ai soon after the revolution. After Yuan's death in 1916, many KMT leaders attempted to form a strong central Chinese government. Chiang Kai-shek, a graduate of a Japanese military school, was one who aspired to lead China. He became a member of the KMT Central Executive Committee in 1926 and soon became its most powerful leader by taking action against the Communists and arresting Russian advisers. In June 1926 Chiang was named commander in chief of the army and launched the Northern Expedition to unify China. By 1927 Chiang's forces had regained Chinese territory as far north as Shanghai and Nanking. That same year, having wrested control of considerable territory from many of the warlords, Chiang turned suddenly against the Communists, feeling they had become too revolutionary, and sent his troops into Shanghai to arrest and execute party members. With general chaos throughout China, many factions were competing both within political parties and between parties, with warlords, and with the Japanese, who had concessions in Manchuria that had been received following their war with Russia during 1904–1905.[1]

Gillis' Postretirement Life in China

Gillis had *ostensibly* fully retired from the Navy late in 1919. He continued his life in China and apparently never left that country again. He

I. V. Gillis and his wife, Zhao Yubin, in Peking garden (about 1920)

(Courtesy of the East Asian Library and the Gest Collection, Princeton University, Princeton, N.J.)

continued to work, attempting to develop business for several U.S. shipbuilders and other companies. However, the complexities of the political situation and the chaos in China were making the procurement of firm contracts by U.S. companies very difficult.

At various times Gillis also acted as adviser to entities of the Chinese government, including the Chinese Cabinet Office, the Ministry of the Navy, the Ministry of Communications, and the Coast Guard Administration. Gillis, at some point, had married Zhao Yubin, a woman eighteen years his junior, who was said to be a member of the former Manchu imperial clan. Existing records do not reveal the date of their marriage. It appears that using her family contacts, Gillis began to run a business as a book buyer.[2]

Thomas Sze, the distinguished engineer who was one of the first Chinese nationals to graduate from Cornell University (Class of 1905), wrote about Gillis in his unpublished memoirs. He stated that Gillis, with his considerable years in China, much of that time at the U.S. Legation in Peking as naval attaché, had become well known within the diplomatic and foreign communities and was a member of various social organizations in Peking. Accordingly, the legation used him regularly to escort distinguished visitors during their visits to Peking. He possessed excellent knowledge of the language and the culture and was a connoisseur of Chinese food.[3]

I. V. Gillis Meets G. M. Gest and Begins Book Collecting in Earnest

Gillis' book-collecting activities began when he met Guion Moore Gest, an engineer and businessman mentioned earlier in this narrative. Gest, who was troubled by failing eyesight, owned a company in New York City that had been involved in developing underground power works in China and other locations in Southeast Asia. This meeting resulted in an arrangement that is considered by many Chinese scholars to be one of the most important in Gillis' life in the nearly thirty years following his final retirement from the Navy.

Gillis suggested that Gest, later the founder of the Gest Chinese Research Library, try a traditional Chinese eye medicine. He assumed that it must work because the shop that sold the medicine was always crowded with customers buying it. He also noted that the eye medicine was shipped to many areas of the country. Gillis explained to Gest that there were unusual remedies in China, and many were unexplainable to Western medical practitioners. Much traditional knowledge of Chinese medicine was passed down through generations of people. Some of the remedies worked well over time, and they were customarily written down in books describing their precise contents or methods, accurately and in detail, in order to benefit future generations. Ting-Chow, in Chihli Province (currently Hebei Province), was the place of production for the eye medicine suggested for Gest, and the store that sold it was thought to be a century or more old. Gest decided to try the medicine, and it had a helpful result. Interested in what other traditional cures might have been handed down, Gest established a credit at the American Bank in Peking for the purpose of acquiring rare Chinese books on cures for human illnesses and to compensate Gillis for services rendered in that area.[4]

While medicine may have been the primary reason for Gest's interest in rare Chinese books, his long-standing interest in Buddhism probably was another of his principal motivations. Since there were other topics included in the initial purchases for the library, a broader view of Chinese civilization appears to have been behind the buying practices of Gest and Gillis. Gest intended all along to encourage a better understanding of China and a closer relationship between that country and the West through the study of Chinese literature.[5]

Gillis plunged into his new work as book collector and consultant for Gest with his usual thoroughness, discipline, and attention to every

I. V. Gillis in Peking, undated photograph

(Courtesy of the East Asian Library and the Gest Collection, Princeton University, Princeton, N.J.)

detail. He set up an office in his house and created a small staff of Chinese clerks working under his direction. When books came on the market, Gillis would consult with friends who were knowledgeable in the field and check the catalogs of the Capital Library (later to be known as the National Library of China) to determine their value. After this step, the negotiations for a sale would begin. The books were thoroughly reviewed to ascertain their condition and completeness, standard-form bookbinding was done on books needing such attention, and books were strengthened and resewn as required.

The Gest Chinese Research Library at McGill University

Gest's search for a location to house his collection of books and other items reached a point of urgency when Gillis advised him that a shipment of eight thousand volumes would arrive in October 1925. Gest settled upon McGill University in Montreal, Canada, to serve as the repository. He discussed the matter with Dr. Gerhard R. Lomer, the librarian there, and they came up with a plan of action for storage of the collection at McGill. Gest would provide the cataloging and administration, and McGill would provide the space and facilities. The Gest Chinese Research Library opened there on 13 February 1926. Gest, from the beginning, played a very active role in its running and wanted to see that it best fulfilled the requirements of a research library.[6]

Meanwhile, Gillis' interest in Chinese literature grew, and the collection expanded to encompass ancient books in additional subject areas. From these beginnings, the Gest Oriental Library eventually was established. This collection of ancient Chinese books has now become one of the core collections of the East Asian Library at Princeton University. In addition to Gest himself, the fame of the Gest Oriental Library is also in no small measure due to the exceptional knowledge and book-hunting skills of Gillis, his purchasing agent.[7] Open warfare between the various contending factions was occurring in many areas of China, and some of the battles were not too far from Peking. Gillis continued all the while to purchase books, which were becoming more available because of the conflict. Many people were forced to sell valuable collections or individual books as conditions generally worsened due to high inflation, outrageous prices, and difficult living conditions. Some families were selling books at a fraction of their value because of their urgent need for money.

Gillis apparently spent considerable time outside his house and its office in negotiating and buying these books. He was an expert on their value and was able to ascertain their authenticity, condition, and resale value.

When the library opened it had about 232 titles and 8,000 volumes. The library's initial curator was Dr. Robert de Resillac-Roese, a German who had moved to the United States. Gillis was less than satisfied with the work of de Resillac-Roese in cataloging and in his bibliographical skills, so Gillis began to do those tasks himself.[8] At the time, Gillis was very much focused on the actual content of a work as the primary interest of a research library rather than which edition a volume might be.

De Resillac-Roese provided a Report on Accessions and Activities of the Gest Chinese Research Library from 1 May 1928 to 1 May 1929. The library now held some 55,000 volumes in four classes: classics, history, philosophy, and belles lettres. The library was especially strong in dictionaries, history catalogs, medical works, and encyclopedias. He stated that the greatest treasure, just acquired, was a collection of 5,200 sutras that Gillis obtained from a Buddhist temple in the hills outside Peking. About 3,200 of these dated from the Yuan Dynasty (1280–1368). No other library in the world, he said, had such a collection. Dr. de Resillac-Roese further noted that Dr. Nancy Lee Swann, the former librarian of the Chinese Department at Columbia University, had been hired in June 1928. Swann and Gillis thus began their long and productive relationship involving Chinese literature.[9]

Swann subsequently became not only an important and key individual in regard to the library, but also to Gillis for about the next twenty years. After earning her bachelor's degree at the University of Texas in 1906, she moved to China in 1912. She returned to the United States to earn her master's degree in 1919. After living again in China for a time, she moved to New York and was awarded her PhD from Columbia University. As we shall see later, Gillis carried on an extensive correspondence with Swann, and he was a strong supporter of hers at the library.[10]

The respect Gillis commanded at this time from academics involved in Chinese history was clearly demonstrated by a request from de Resillac-Roese. He asked Gillis to comment directly to Sir Arthur W. Currie, principal and vice chancellor at McGill, on possible candidates for chair of Chinese literature at the university. Gillis recommended two individuals, provided most thoughtful and thorough comments in regard to those individuals, and supplied further possible contacts for additional background information.[11]

Gillis' knowledge of Chinese bibliography was widely admired by Chinese such as Hu Shih, a future curator of the Gest Oriental Library, and Wang Zhongmin, a rare book cataloger. In one letter Gillis stated that he had compiled a 40,000-card system with entries from many hundreds of different Chinese traditional bibliographies, which enabled him to do the work he did. Gillis explained that to be a successful book collector, one had to be knowledgeable, cautious, and secretive. There were other buyers on the market, including Chinese, Japanese, and Europeans. Gillis also made sure that Gest and others refrained from talking too much about the library in order not to raise prices or lose certain items altogether. The Gest Oriental Library contains a document, several pages long, with a list of all the secret Morse codes that Gillis and Gest used to communicate with each other: 88519, UNIF meant "Tuan blocks, but Ming period reprint," 88613 UWYL meant "do you think you can obtain better terms (by waiting or holding off)," and 88618 IJXYN meant "the collection

I. V. Gillis and his crew preparing rare Chinese books for shipment to Guion Gest, late 1920s

(Courtesy of the East Asian Library and the Gest Collection, Princeton University, Princeton, N.J.)

consists of about __ works bound in about __ ts'e, and the asking price is __ local currency."[12]

Whereas many sinologists in the early twentieth century considered it necessary to devise a new transcription system for Chinese, book collectors such as Gillis took it upon themselves to devise their own classification systems. Gillis—who was critical of Alfred Kaiming Chiu's scheme, developed at Harvard, as forcing Chinese civilization into a Western mold—employed a more traditional Chinese classification system. Gillis was the main cataloger, even with Nancy Lee Swann on board as curator, and sent his preliminary notes, catalogs, and corrections to Montreal. As his skills improved, the books he shipped were beautifully bound and had calligraphically superb Chinese characters.[13]

THE TURBULENT 1930s

In 1931 the Japanese used an incident in Manchuria to launch a full-blown invasion of that land. Japanese soldiers set off a bomb on the railroad track outside Mukden and seized the city. Before the end of the year the Japanese had driven the Chinese troops out of Manchuria and brought the entire region under their control. Some Chinese consider the "Manchurian incident" as the commencement of their War of Resistance against Japan and the actual beginning of World War II. In 1932 Japan declared Manchurian independence from China and established a state there called Manchukuo. The League of Nations formed a commission to investigate the invasion, giving Japan an excuse to withdraw from the organization. Japan then proceeded to expand further in northern China and establish a "Japanese-only" zone that Chinese troops could not enter without Japanese approval. In 1933 Japan pushed to bring all of northern China under its control and, in 1935, created a North China Autonomous Region consisting of five provinces.

In the meantime, Chiang Kai-shek continued his struggle against the Communists by mounting annual military campaigns. By 1934 the Communists, under constant Nationalist pressure, decided to escape by moving to the northwest on their famous Long March (1934–1935). In an odd incident in 1936, Chiang was captured by a group of Kuomintang and Chinese Communist Party members and, before his release, was persuaded to stop fighting the Communists and form a united front against the Japanese.

The Chinese position relative to Japan continued to deteriorate when Japanese troops engaged in a night maneuver in July 1937 at the Marco Polo Bridge outside Peking, using a minor skirmish as an excuse to initiate their ultimate takeover of the region. While Japanese troops quickly took control of areas around Peking, Chiang decided to attack Japanese troops in Shanghai. The Japanese responded by sending fifteen troop divisions to China, and the two sides began a full-scale war. In late 1937 the Japanese took Nanking and committed atrocities against hundreds of thousands of Chinese residents in what is now known as the "Rape of Nanking."[14] By the end of 1939 Japan controlled more than half of the territory and population of China.

The Gest Library in the Early 1930s

Difficulties also were on the horizon for the Gest Collection in the 1930s, as Martin Heijdra reports: "First, the Chinese Nationalist Party had placed an embargo on the export of nonreplaceable books. Announced by the Society for the Preservation of Cultural Relics, from 1931 onward books printed before 1851 were not to be exported." While the Gest Chinese Research Library was granted a very modest exception, books nevertheless rapidly began to accumulate in Peking. "Gillis became desperate; he wrote to Zhang Xueliang addressing the issue of the export of rare books, although he had previously criticized others for kowtowing to this warlord. The response was perfunctory and negative. A harrowing episode at Shanhaiguan ensued." During this incident, which is described in detail later in this chapter, a shipment was halted because the Japanese security police thought that the twenty-five boxes of books contained guns. Finally, after the Japanese occupation of Peking, the remaining 27,000 volumes in China could be shipped.[15]

In 1931 the Standard Press in "Peiping [Peking], China" published *The Characters Ch'ao and Hsi*, a scholarly book written by Gillis. *The Shuo Wen*, a Chinese book that dates to approximately AD 100, explains the meaning, form, and pronunciation of each Chinese character and has been recognized in China as the standard authority among scholars. Gillis, in his book, challenges the interpretation of two characters that are not included in *The Shuo Wen*. Gillis attempts to answer three difficult questions: "What does the character represent?" "What is its meaning?" "What is its composition?" Three hundred copies of Gillis' book were printed and beautifully bound.

In a September 1931 report, de Resillac-Roese, the curator in Montreal, reported that Gillis' purchases for the library between February and July 1931 numbered 169 works consisting of 12,234 volumes and 508 volumes of sutras dating from the Ming period.[16] A few years later, Gillis made an eloquent plea that a clear mission statement for the Gest Chinese Research Library should be developed so that all activities to support it could be drawn up. In regard to his indexing system, Gillis advised that he did not care a hang who chose to adopt or reject it and that he had no intention of being "muzzled" in order to make for some so-called harmony with any other library or institution: "If I see fit to criticize either them or any other individual, I shall certainly do so—harmony or no harmony."[17]

In 1932 Nancy Lee Swann was appointed full curator of the library. Her appointment was applauded by Gillis, who wrote Swann that he had told Gest: "I sincerely hope that when you do select and appoint the new Curator you will not allow the fact that he is a 'man' outweigh his sinological qualifications as set off against those of Miss Swann, for in full justice it must be acknowledged that hers are of no mean order."

Gillis remained supportive, and when Swann began to wonder whether she should start researching the Buddhist sutras in the Gest Collection, he had this to say to her: "I am in accord with Doctor Laufer [Berthold Laufer, a librarian at the Gest Chinese Research Library at McGill University] that your work in connection with the study of Chinese women in history is not only far more important, but of far more interest to students of Chinese culture and civilization."[18]

Similar correspondence between Gillis and Swann over the years concerned various technical points about library management, as well as the purchasing of particular books and the meaning of certain Chinese characters. There was much discussion about catalogs versus indexes and card content, size, paper, vertical or horizontal lines, and whether to put information on one or both sides. There were also discussions of other library systems, particularly those at the Harvard University Library and the Library of Congress. Gillis was shown to be a man of deep principle, with strong views regarding a number of the options discussed. He did not hold back on his views and opinions, but rather expressed them strongly and logically. He reasoned clearly and firmly, both on his own proposals and in comments on other proposals or systems. He also expressed strong views on events unfolding in China. He was most uncompromising in his view of matters ranging from rare Chinese books to the revolution in China.

Gillis wrote a long letter to Swann at the McGill Library in the summer of 1932 on the subject of index cards. In regard to the form of the index cards, he believed that the indexing system should meet the needs of the library in the best possible manner. He posed the question: "What is the mission of the Index cards?" He also asked, "Why do we make several classes of index cards, and to what use do we expect to put them?" This letter, perhaps more than any other, demonstrated Gillis' attention to detail, thoroughness, uncompromising spirit, and determination to do the best humanly possible when undertaking a task or project. It also demonstrated his logical and sound approach to issues and problems. He even showed a willingness to challenge the systems in place at the Chinese Library at Harvard University (Harvard-Yenching Library) and the Library of Congress, noting that instead of the catalogs (and indexing systems) being vehicles to facilitate the use of the books, the librarian in charge had simply considered the books as raw material put at his disposal to be worked up into an elaborate catalog and indexing system. Gillis asserted that an outstanding example of such folly was the Chinese section of the Harvard University Library, "with its supremely ridiculous classification system as devised by the Reverend William Hung." He noted that in many cases there had been a tendency to consider catalogs and indexes as an end in themselves and not as a means to an end.[19]

In March 1932 Gillis sent a lengthy letter to Swann that covered a number of subjects. Much of this letter discussed translations of a particular Chinese character, the pronunciation of others, and literary style. He noted that Swann had held the annual "tea party" at the Gest Chinese Research Library at McGill University on the Old Chinese New Year, but few Chinese had attended. The situation with the Japanese, Gillis agreed, probably kept them away. He reminded Swann that she should not forget that the Kuomintang had banned celebration of the Old Chinese New Year. Actions such as this, according to Gillis, were in keeping with the party's general policy of making the peasants and ordinary people as miserable and unhappy as possible. Gillis noted that some of the "Dynastic Histories" republished by the Commercial Press had been received. He stated that he had been waiting for the entire set before sending them on to Swann; however, since the Commercial Press had been destroyed, he would be sending on those he had received. Most of his time and that of his staff was spent on making book-notes and index cards, he observed. Gillis complimented Swann on her library work, particularly on her indexing efforts, and stated that his idea was to make the index comprehensive and not limited to his accessions only.[20]

In correspondence to Swann in April 1933, Gillis noted that the books he had purchased would all be packed for storage in a few days and that he would keep them in a safe place in the U.S. Legation's quarters during the uncertain and troubled times. He felt that trouble could come in Peking at any moment. He said that "the Nanking crowd has looted and gutted the Forbidden City, its museums, and the Summer Palace. Rumors are circulating that they intend to set the palaces on fire and destroy them if they are forced out of Peking and have to seek safety in flight towards the south." Gillis expressed the view that the Kuomintang "patriots" were quite capable of such actions. At the same time, they were the very people that posed as the preservers of China's "Cultural Monuments" and protectors against foreign vandals. Gillis said he was hopeful that he lived far enough away from the Forbidden City that a fire would not destroy his home and neighborhood. He also felt the palace moat's water barrier could help protect his neighborhood.[21]

Garden at Gillis' Peking home, May 1915; photograph by John Van Antwerp MacMurray

(Courtesy of the East Asian Library and the Gest Collection, Princeton University, Princeton, N.J.)

Gillis had deep feelings about the classification system then in use at the library. He did not like the system. He considered the qualifications of the originators of the system to be questionable. He considered the knowledge of one of the originators as limited to a smattering that had been picked up on travels in Asia. The second originator was a bookbinder brought over from the Government Printing Office in order to get the books in the Chinese collection in the best physical condition. The third individual, who claimed responsibility for the classification system, was employed at the Agricultural Department doing translating work. While born in China, he went abroad to the United States and Hong Kong, and most of his knowledge of Chinese literature would have been obtained while he was a youth. Their classification system had certain defects, but they did base the system on an acceptable previous classification scheme, and it was more sound than the system that was foisted off on Harvard University. Gillis felt that he and Swann had sufficient experience in classifying and indexing that they could take independent action.[22]

In July 1933 Gillis announced that no shipment of books was possible at that time. He believed that in the future, if the Kuomintang were to break up, or a more liberal and sensible attitude were shown by those in power, book shipments would then be feasible.[23]

Gillis became ill in September 1933 and entered a hospital, remaining there for a week. He wrote to Swann that he was exhausted from constant work, and his efforts to keep going had caused his digestive tract to practically stop working. He said he had not had a holiday for more than ten years and had been working at his desk for an average of nine to ten hours each day without relief.[24] Apparently he subsequently fully recovered.

In 1934 Gillis had arranged for the purchase of a copy of the Manchu Kanjur after more than three years of struggle, negotiations, and effort. The Manchu Kanjur, part of the Buddhist canon in Manchu translation, belongs to the rarest works of Manchu literature. For a long time it was even doubtful whether the huge work (108 volumes) had been translated into Manchu at all, and it was only because of detailed investigations that its existence was confirmed. A copy of the work taken to Tokyo perished during the earthquake of 1923. It had been reported that a further three copies of the work were extant in Chinese monasteries in 1930–1931. Parts of the printing blocks of the enormous work were discovered in Peking, and a complete copy turned up in the Potala Palace, the residence of the Dalai Lama in Lhasa, Tibet. At the last minute, however, it turned out there were no funds to pay for it. Unfortunately, Gillis had to release the owners from the purchase agreement to sell to him since they were trying to dispose of this unique and priceless work elsewhere. Later in the year Gillis advised Swann that the Manchu Kanjur would be sold to the Japanese because no Americans were interested enough to pay for these priceless and unique books. He was very disappointed.[25]

Gillis also expressed dismay when Swann wrote to him in late October 1934 and said among other things that a "numbered item" was missing. Gillis' comments on this item's loss demonstrate his deep feelings about Chinese literature and his personal sense of commitment to it. Gillis said that he looked up the item number and when he discovered which book was missing he nearly burst into tears. He wrote Swann, "How could your predecessor be so careless as to allow such a priceless work to lie around and result in its loss?" He said that he was so upset he hardly knew where he was and that the loss was so terrible to him that he was inclined to drop the library entirely for fear that his happiness would be destroyed by more such news and was absolutely beside himself at the loss. Gillis' deep feelings were further expressed when he stated that if the name of the thief were known he would "trace the book and recover it" and "do so even if he has to commit murder to get it back." His final words on the subject were "WE SIMPLY MUST GET IT BACK!!!"[26]

The Gest Library Departs McGill University

By the mid-1930s the Great Depression had put McGill, as well as Gest personally, under enormous financial strain. Gillis noted that Gest seemed to be ignoring his letters. Gillis was no longer buying for the Gest Chinese Research Library, and he wrote Gest in January 1935 to advise him that he was planning to close down and dismiss his staff if he had not heard from Gest by the end of April. He stressed that it had been well over half a year since he had last heard from Gest. Later Gillis wrote to Swann that if it were not for her, he would get no news about the library, and it seemed it was almost as if it did not exist as a working library but "just a collection of books on shelves for storage and safe keeping." Gillis commenced preparations for closing down his library operation at the end of June. During this period Gillis began to lose interest in the library, primarily due to the lack of communication from Gest, but also because of the lack of money. He confessed to Swann that his interest in the library was not what it used to be, that his work was no longer the pleasure it was in the past, and that he wanted to look forward to a few more years of quiet enjoyment of what life he had left. He further stated that he had not heard from Gest in six months, all of which made it very difficult for him to see the present unsatisfactory communications and financial conditions.[27]

At the same time, Gest was concluding that McGill was no longer the place for his collection and undertook plans to sell his library to a different university. Swann and Gillis had some inkling that Gest was trying to sell the library to a U.S. institution, but both were very skeptical about any success; it came as a surprise to them when Abraham Flexner, the first director of the Institute for Advanced Study at Princeton, decided to purchase the collection for $135,000 at $1 per volume.

Princeton announced its purchase on 1 July 1936. On 31 July the Gest Chinese Research Library was moved to temporary storage in Princeton at 20 Nassau Street until permanent quarters could be prepared. Renamed the Gest Oriental Library, the collection was to be fully under the administration of the Princeton Library as compensation for services the library performed for the members of the institute. Several problems arose during the preparations to open the Gest Oriental Library. Fire in a truck damaged some volumes, and Gillis was asked to replace these, which he managed, perhaps not wholeheartedly. He apparently was not happy with the move.[28]

By early November 1936 Gillis was still in limbo in regard to Gest. However, he felt that if the Japanese consolidated control over the region, he would be able to get books shipped. He cautioned Swann not to judge things in China by her former personal firsthand knowledge of it and advised her to forget all the good things she used to know about the country and its people, remembering only the bad. Gillis was seriously perturbed by the political events then transpiring in China.[29]

A Very Difficult Book Shipment

As mentioned earlier, one of Gillis' shipments encountered great difficulty in getting past the Japanese security police. In a letter to Gest in mid-January 1937, Gillis provided details regarding his attempt to ship the books he had acquired. The effort began in mid-December 1936 when Gillis visited an ex-official who was a friend of a friend and asked him for assistance in getting the books shipped. The plan was to transport the books by railroad through the China-Manchurian border station at

Shan-hai-kuan (about two hundred miles from Peking) to Mukden, and from there to Ta-lien, and then by ship to New York. The ex-official knew a "fixer" who was supposed to have a brother in the Chinese customs service at Shan-hai-kuan who could arrange for the cases of books to go through with nothing more than a brief examination on each side of the border. Before these actions could transpire, a couple of visits to Shan-hai-kuan by the fixer were required. Gillis wrote in his letter to Gest that he was suspicious of the fixer's actions and questioned if they really took place. Gillis continued to push matters as best he could, even though he was annoyed and perplexed by the delays. Finally Gillis went to the railway yard himself and watched the cases loaded on the car. With this completed, Gillis felt optimistic that the books would be on their way soon. However, this only began a week in which he did not have a single minute's peace of mind or freedom from anxiety, and at night, he wished for daylight to come.

To safeguard things and keep an eye on the fixer, whom he now felt was a knave and a rogue, he sent along a trusted foreign friend as his representative and his Chinese clerk to act as his interpreter. Gillis did not go himself because he decided he must be available to solve any problems that might come up. The trusted friend and the clerk set off at night for Shan-hai-kuan and reached there the next morning, while the railroad car with the books arrived in midafternoon. The next day it did not take his trusted representative and clerk long to see that all was not going according to plan. The fixer was busy but had not done anything useful and appeared not to be capable of doing anything to help expedite the shipment. At the same time, the Japanese military authorities were in full control at Shau-hai-kuan. The Chinese officials were doing only as the Japanese told them. The Japanese placed several detectives on the trail of Gillis' representative and clerk, and followed them closely. Gillis' clerk sent a telegraph to Gillis recommending that he bring the books back as soon as possible because the situation was fraught with dangers and pitfalls. A day later Gillis' trusted representative wrote to him along the same lines, saying that it was quite hopeless to get the books past customs. Gillis quickly ordered the books brought back; however, the Japanese military authorities decided at that time to take action. The representative and the clerk discovered that there was no railroad car available for the books. Tons and tons of goods smuggled in by the Japanese were piled up waiting for railroad cars, and it would probably be seven to ten days before one would be available. Gillis' representative cleverly managed to arrange for a loaded railway car in the yards to be unloaded under cover of darkness and then to bribe a shunting engineer to move it to where the books were stored.

With the books' return shipment apparently on track, Gillis' representative and his clerk boarded the train for the return to Peking. The Japanese detectives stepped on board, took them off the train, and put them under detention for being suspicious characters. Subsequently, the representative and the clerk were interrogated both together and separately, their bags were searched, all of their documents, papers, and letters were carefully examined, and explanations were demanded of them. Gillis had anticipated interference by Chinese customs authorities, and so had carefully prepared several letters and sworn out an affidavit at the U.S. Embassy attesting to the contents of the cases. This turned out to be a wise precaution. The documents and the straightforward cooperation of Gillis' representative convinced the Japanese authorities that this was not a case of gunrunning into Manchukuo (Manchuria), as they had suspected.

Gillis' clerk and his representative subsequently returned to Peking, arriving on a morning train. Gillis was still very troubled and worried about the books and whether they would be returned in proper condition. His clerk had a classmate in the railway freight office, so Gillis had him telegraph his friend asking if the books had actually left, as had been arranged. At last word was received that the railway car had arrived. Gillis arranged to have the books unloaded and placed in storage without delay, and finally got a call that all twenty-five cases were in safe storage. Only one case had been opened by the Japanese to assure themselves that the shipment was books and not arms. A check of the contents of the opened case showed the books to be intact, with none missing or damaged. Gillis wrote that he got his first night of unbroken sleep in about ten days. The stress brought Gillis to the verge of a nervous breakdown. [30]

Subsequently Gillis was offended by a statement by the Institute's Abraham Flexner to the effect that he could not understand why Gillis was delaying sending the remainder of the books—apparently disregarding Gillis' nerve-wracking Shan-hai-kuan episode. Gillis insisted that at that point, he only had a personal relationship with Gest and no longer a formal relationship with the library. Furthermore, Swann and Gillis had a suspicion that Gest was attempting to sell the library.

The library had told Gillis that there was no longer any money for his Peking operation, but an apologetic letter from Frank Aydelotte, the director of the Institute for Advanced Study, announced that in 1941, just before Japan's attack on Pearl Harbor, the institute had decided to underwrite the printing, binding, and distribution of Gillis' *Title Index to the Catalogue of the Gest Oriental Library*. This somewhat mollified the disappointed Gillis. Nevertheless, since around 1939 a purchasing agent was no longer considered necessary, Gillis was increasingly saddened that he was no longer buying for Gest, for, in the confusion resulting from the intensifying war in China, rare and valuable books were coming on the market in unprecedented quantities.[31]

GILLIS: PROBABLY STILL A U.S. GOVERNMENT INTELLIGENCE COLLECTOR AS WELL AS A MUNITIONS SALESMAN FOLLOWING HIS NAVY RETIREMENT

During the period between 1913 and 1917, Gillis began a long professional and personal relationship with John Van Antwerp MacMurray, diplomat and photographer, who was then stationed as secretary of the U.S. Legation in Peking. This relationship continued after MacMurray was reassigned to the position of consul at the U.S. Embassy in Tokyo between 1917 and 1919. MacMurray returned as minister to China between 1925 and 1929. In 1929 he left China after having conflicts with his superior and also left the Foreign Service to take up a position at the Walter Hines Page School of International Relations at Johns Hopkins University, in Baltimore. Returning to the Foreign Service in 1933, MacMurray served as ambassador to Turkey from 1936 to 1942.

From the correspondence between these two friends over a number of years, whether MacMurray was in Peking, Tokyo, Washington, or Baltimore, it is very apparent how much they trusted and respected each other. The topic of foreign affairs was a frequent subject of their exchanges. Early on, MacMurray described Gillis as a "delightful, downright, outspoken Navy-phile, who conceals a very sound brain under a perfectly irresponsible manner and says with the utmost cheerfulness the most pessimistic things about all creation."[32]

Early in 1921 MacMurray wrote Gillis from Washington requesting information for the State Department on how certain public funds had been expended by Gillis. Gillis took great exception to the request because it sounded to him that it came from some lower-level auditor in the State Department. Gillis noted that the account had been approved by the U.S. minister and chargé in Peking and that the matter took place some time ago. For these and other reasons Gillis was disinclined to take any further action because of the nature of confidential secret service funds. Gillis also noted that MacMurray already was familiar with how the funds were used and that another reason he did not want to comply was that there was a "working agreement with British authorities." Further, he advised MacMurray that when he undertook the work it was distinctly understood that he was not to submit detailed accounts of this activity, which was "in connection with certain investigations for our own and the British Governments." Gillis concluded that some accountant was behind the request and not the secretary of state, who would hardly bother with a $4,000 expenditure for a report that was confidential and actually for him. He planned no action on the Washington request.[33]

It would appear that this investigation might be related to secret intelligence activities; MacMurray could have been the conduit for certain intelligence being passed to the State Department and other recipients in Washington.

Gillis corresponded with his friend MacMurray aperiodically from 1921 through at least 1928. For example, Gillis included in a letter to MacMurray in 1925 an extract of an *Atlantic Monthly* article dated July of that year that described conditions in Spain that were analogous to the conditions in China at that time. While the article discussed the Spanish national character, it might also have been applicable to China in that there were two defects: first, the predominance of passion over will, so that one prefers imagination to common sense and takes the idea of doing a thing for having done it, thus becoming the land of "tomorrow"; second, the preference of friendship and affection over justice, so that a place could always be found for a friend in need of a favor at the cost of someone who was not a friend.[34]

In June 1927 Gillis suggested to MacMurray that he would be interested in taking up the position of archivist or permanent undersecretary to the diplomatic body in Peking. Gillis certainly was in a unique position in China with contacts in the State Department, business, and Chinese society. He further suggested that before MacMurray might mention the matter to the appropriate authority, he sound out certain other diplomats from other countries. If this were done, apparently, there could not be serious objections. No written response to Gillis' note has been discovered. However, a handwritten comment on Gillis' note by MacMurray, in his papers on file at Princeton, says that he discussed this with Gillis on 9 August 1927.[35]

Further fueling the suspicion that Gillis was continuing his intelligence collection activities was a report by John A. Logan, who accompanied the 1931–1932 Lamb Expedition to northern Tibet, that while Gillis dealt in books, he was still in the service of the U.S. government as chief of intelligence in the Far East. In 1954 Logan wrote: "As we were taking many photographs, I made a negative of each sketch and then destroyed the sketch. These negatives were mixed in with the hundreds of others we took and upon my return to Peking, I redrew them in large scale and turned them over to Capt. [sic] I. V. Gillis, our former Naval Attaché and who was then head of intelligence in Asia. He made two copies, one for the American Geographical Society and one for Intelligence and then destroyed the plates."[36]

Logan's unpublished article contains the most definitive information that has been found describing Gillis as involved in intelligence activities after 1919. Gillis also was listed in 1921 by the naval attaché in Peking as a "possible resource for information to benefit the United States," hinting at a continuation of his earlier clandestine work.[37]

Finally, when the Japanese invaded Peking in 1937, the occupying authorities indeed suspected that Gillis was a spy for the United States. A few years later, perhaps because of this suspicion, they decided he was to be sent to Shantung for internment.[38] As we shall see, he never made it there.

Still Pursuing Business Opportunities

In addition to his possible intelligence-related tasks and work for other companies, after 1919 Gillis also was working for E. I. Du Pont de Nemours. He wrote in January 1924 to his sponsor, K. K. V. Casey, the company's director of military sales, that two recent sales for gunpowder had gone to European companies. The sales involved a large amount of gunpowder, and Gillis complained that he could have had both sales except for the unilateral U.S. compliance with the ongoing arms embargo, proclaimed in 1922 by President Warren G. Harding in response to domestic violence in China.[39] The Chinese authorities actually had come to him first, but he could not comply. Gillis sent Casey a clipping from a newspaper that indicated little attention was being paid to the arms embargo by countries other than the United States.[40] No further information concerning Gillis' work for Du Pont has been uncovered.

WAR AND HOUSE ARREST IN THE 1940s

By the time war broke out in Europe in late 1939, the Chinese people were exhausted from fighting the Japanese, but the Japanese were spread too thin in China to press the war to victory. As a result, the two sides were stalemated.[41] After the Japanese navy bombed Pearl Harbor on 7 December 1941, the United States sent more military and financial help to China. Problems developed later in the war, however, when the United States wanted to supply military aid to all Chinese who were fighting against the Japanese, including the Communists. Chiang Kai-shek, of course, did not trust the Communists, and the KMT-CCP united effort began to break down.[42]

Continuing Work on Library Matters with Nancy Swann

All during 1940 Gillis continued to buy and collect books. While very interested in the Gest Oriental Library, he was not buying for it. By October 1940 Gillis indicated that conditions for shipping from China were very difficult; all sorts of restrictions were in force regarding parcel-post shipments. After many forms were completed and all the numerous requirements complied with, one would often be informed that export was not permitted, with no explanation provided.[43]

In early 1941 Swann advised Gillis that the first installment of his index for the Gest Collection had been received and that she envisioned many uses for it. She said that there was no need to send a copy to Gest because he was seriously ill. He was totally blind, among other things, and being cared for by his daughter and her husband. Two surgeries were recommended, but a consultation at Johns Hopkins Hospital, made possible by Dr. Flexner and Dr. Aydelotte, resulted in surgery being performed only on his eyes, which might have helped to some limited degree.[44]

Gillis continued to work on his index and catalog of the Gest Oriental Library for Swann personally, not for the library. Gillis made every effort to complete the compilation as soon as possible. He announced that he wanted to complete it "before President Roosevelt starts his planned war with Japan in assistance to China." But, Gillis wrote, "it is not China at all, but just a big gang of crooks as ever existed, busily engaged in exploiting the Chinese people and making fools out of our own country and people." Gillis crossed out "President" and wrote "Governor-General" before Roosevelt's name in his letter to Swann.[45] He was never one to mince words. He added that the next installment would make a total of about two-thirds of the entire index and warned that if war came (and he felt certain it would), he would be interned, and it would be up to Swann to complete the index. In his familiar, acerbic way, he asserted: "We lost our independence and have now returned to be a Dominion part of the British Empire. I presume that it is proper as one British subject to another. God Save the King!"[46]

By mid-April 1941 Gillis had completed some 70 percent of the indexing task, and the remaining 30 percent was in the hands of the printer. Gillis worked on this index, which contained about 40,000 items, for the better part of two years. Gillis advised Swann in late May 1941 that his fears of not completing the index had dissipated and that he felt he would be finished within two weeks, with a total page count of 1,484.

The cost of the index was expected to be between $7,000 and $8,000, and Gillis directed that only one hundred copies be printed at a cost of about $75 per copy. He considered this amount to be more than anybody, even a library, would be willing to pay. Accordingly, Gillis said he was willing to pay two-thirds of the expense himself, bringing the cost down to $25 per copy. If copies could be sold at this reduced price, Gillis would consider a free distribution by himself and write off the entire cost of compilation and publication.[47]

Praise for the New Index and Cataloging System

Gillis received a letter from Dr. Arthur W. Hummel Sr. of the Library of Congress that was very complimentary of the index, expressing his view of the value of the indexing system and noting that others also expressed admiration for the system. This compliment, from a close associate of William Hung, the adviser and sponsor of the system adopted by the Harvard-Yenching Library, is significant. Hummel noted that the Gillis System was the only index that gave consideration to the important difference between indexing single characters and the indexing of groups of characters.[48]

Preparations for the War Years

The North American Council of the College of Chinese Studies in Peking met 17 June 1941 in New York. A resolution was unanimously adopted for Gillis to become a member of the council and be designated as custodian of all the property of the college in Peking with full power to take any and all steps necessary and possible for the safety of the property and school during an emergency. Gillis accepted the position.[49]

In early July 1941 Gillis advised Swann that he had completed the supplement to the index, consisting of sixty-one pages, and was sending it to her, for all practical purposes completing the compilations except for a few odds and ends. He told Swann that it had been an arduous task, done with much haste due to his worry that hostilities would prevent completion of the undertaking. With the index completed, Gillis wrote, "One thing is certain; the worry as to the completion of this task has 'taught me a lesson' and with conditions as they are and are likely to remain for the rest of my life, I shall never again undertake any work of a continuing nature and from now on, I shall confine my activities to such tasks as can be completed in a short period of time, say a month at most."[50]

Gillis wrote to Swann in November a pessimistic letter in which he complained of being tired, worried, and not optimistic about the future. He congratulated Swann on obtaining the funds to purchase the index. Gillis also mentioned his concern that he might not be able to send any more copies of the index to her, for shipments seemed to present insurmountable difficulties. He closed by stating that if the war held off long enough, it was just barely possible that he might be able to send some more copies.[51]

Under House Arrest

By 1941 the Japanese were in full control in Peking. Sometime after U.S. entry into the war, the Japanese authorities ordered Gillis to move to Shantung Province, southeast of Peking. On the day of departure, Gillis collapsed in the rail station, however, and his Chinese friends used their connections to allow him to stay in Peking, under house arrest in the British Legation. Years later, on 28 February 1946, when Gillis could write freely again, he told Swann that the Japanese had taken his library, catalogs, records, and memoranda. By then he had lost interest and faith in his adopted country and slowly went back to business despite his deteriorating health.[52] The loss of his records and memoranda at the hands of the Japanese occupiers of his Peking home is a principal reason for Gillis' biographers' lack of personal material about his life. He does not appear to have transmitted any of this material to those family members who were available to be interviewed, and it is unlikely that civil records about a non-Chinese resident would still exist in view of the chaos in Peking that ensued over the following decades.

GILLIS' VIEWS ON PEOPLE AND ISSUES

As has been noted regarding his letters, Gillis reveals some of his personality traits and is shown to be quite opinionated about people in general and other librarians and modern Chinese intellectuals in particular. The Kuomintang and its representatives were favorite targets. As an example, the only thing Gillis ever refused Gest personally was to serve as an intermediary for Gest and H. H. Kung, the venal, wealthy banker, politician, and finance minister in the Kuomintang government.[53]

Another example is contained in a letter Gillis wrote to Swann in December 1932. In reference to the book embargo, he said that he was of the firm conviction that nothing would be gained by approaching the League of Nations. He went on to say that he found little that was praiseworthy in the organization. Gillis called it "a group of cackling hens and mischief-making busy bodies; and like all busy bodies, they have to justify their existence and interferences by making the most out of every incident and petty controversy that arises and magnify it out of all proportion." He further felt that "the conflagrations spread through the League's pernicious activities." He observed that the long-dormant ill feelings between Japan and the United States had reemerged and went on to state that "the League of Nations is about as fine an instrumentality for keeping the world stirred up as a man could have devised."[54]

His views on other people were no less strong. Gillis felt it necessary to study and know both the old and new China in order to understand and comprehend the country and its people. He believed, for example, that Pearl Buck had a one-sided view of China, asserting that her limitations were due to the environment in which she spent her life and to her limited circle of friends and associates among the Chinese. Her mature years had been lived since the original revolution in 1911, but what transpired since that time was not representative of the old China or the new China that was sure to come. Gillis believed Buck's viewpoint was "but froth and scum on the surface of the water, and the depths remain unseen and undisturbed." He further believed that Buck "has most skillfully portrayed the China of her time and place but such is ephemeral, and China and her people are not to be known and judged by such a standard." Gillis felt that Buck's fictional characters were no more representative of China than was the Kuomintang.[55]

In a letter to Swann in July 1934, Gillis was very critical of Dr. Arthur W. Hummel Sr., chief of the Orientalia Division at the Library of Congress at the time. Gillis wondered if Hummel "made any really serious study himself." Gillis said, as an American, he hated to see a national institution like the Library of Congress put itself in a position to be taken lightly by scholars. The issue to Gillis was a catalog of Chinese books in the Library of Congress that was influenced by Hummel, who may have been swayed by "a conceited youngster at Harvard." Gillis felt Hummel placed far too much confidence in his young Chinese assistants.[56]

Taking on his commander in chief, Gillis told Swann in November 1941: "If the war comes, and everything indicates that it will, then it is probable you will not see any more copies. War means the end of everything out here in China, including the lives of many of us Americans. We shall have that madman Roosevelt to thank for our deaths."[57] This was not his only negative comment about President Roosevelt, and it is an example of Gillis' tightly wound persona and strong views that appear throughout this narrative.

THE LIBRARY AFTER THE WAR YEARS

The first official information regarding Gillis after late 1941 is in a form letter dated 3 October 1945 from the U.S. Army to Marjorie Murray, Gillis' niece, indicating that he had been liberated from Japanese custody.[58] Gillis later noted having received a Red Cross letter from Murray and stated that he and his wife, Yubin, continued to live in the British Embassy compound very comfortably. With regard to their health, Gillis said that Yubin was in good condition, and he couldn't complain, but that he was told he looked his age—seventy-one. He further noted that he personally had not received bad treatment from the Japanese authorities,

I. V. Gillis, his wife, servants, and Captain Hines, USMC, inside the British Legation quarters in Peking following Gillis' release from Japanese captivity, October 1945

(Courtesy of the Mudd Library, Princeton University, Princeton, N.J.)

except that the three Japanese families living in his house had confiscated his valuable library of Chinese and foreign books that he had collected for thirty-plus years. Gillis said he had no expectation of seeing them again.

He noted that the Japanese families living in his house had not yet moved out because they were unable to obtain transportation back to Japan. Gillis explained: "Because Yubin was able to lease the house to respectable Japanese enabled us to retain the place intact and made it possible to avoid interference by Japanese authorities and military. However, it will take money to restore it to its former condition. Accordingly, we are in the British compound and expect to stay for some time to come."[59]

Swann, who was in her last year as full-time curator of the library, was looking forward to starting the distribution process for the indexes that had been agreed to before the start of the war. However, she planned to continue to be active in the library seven or eight months each year. Swann asked if Gillis would consider permitting the Institute for Advanced Study to acquire his small personal library in Peking. She anticipated that the library at Princeton would probably get permanent quarters within the next two years.[60]

Gillis told Swann that he and his wife were living in House Number Twenty in the British Embassy compound in Peking and that he had just received two letters from her that were dated August 1945. Gillis also said they would soon be able to move back to their old residence. In reference to his lost books, indexes, catalogs, and other items, the Japanese appeared to have taken almost everything. Additionally, he had no assistants or secretary to help him. Gillis was pessimistic and sounded depressed. He wrote that he realized that his life, in effect, had ended, and he had little to live for, except his wife. Most of his old friends were either dead or had left China. The country had never been in a worse state. Gillis said, with his usual candidness, "President Truman and Secretary Byrnes are pitiful ignoramuses as to China and are on par with President Roosevelt, the worst President we have ever had, and that fool Cordell Hull."[61]

Gillis was able to move back into his house in April 1946. Having found ten to twelve copies of the index for the Gest Oriental Library, he believed it might be possible that there were more copies among the chaos in his house. He advised Swann that he would ship them as soon as he could. He explained that he had no assistants and had to do everything

Photograph taken in 2007 of the front door to I. V. Gillis' home in K'ou Tai Hutung, Peking, not far from the Forbidden City

(Courtesy of Cao Shuwen, East Asian Library, Princeton University, Princeton, N.J.)

himself. The Japanese did no major damage to the house itself, and he had no trouble with the Chinese. Gillis reported that he had begun looking for a secretary and told Swann that his adopted son was dead. It appeared that his son had been his secretary at some time in the past. He also advised Swann to "never visit this God forsaken country again, for it is a nightmare and worse today" than at any time during his thirty-five years there. He said that China was fully back to the Boxer days of antiforeignism.[62] By June 1946 Gillis had found twenty-four copies of the Gest Oriental Library indexes and told Swann that he would ship twenty-two copies to her. He further noted that prices had become sky-high, including for printing and publishing.[63]

By the fall of that year Gillis was very discouraged, considered himself finished and at the end, and could no longer take any active part in life. He planned to drop all matters in connection with the Gest Oriental Library and the Institute for Advanced Study. Now seventy-two years of age, he had not been able to restore order to the turmoil and chaos in his house. He seemed to be on the edge of despair with no help from the supportive associates he had worked with before the war. Gillis tried to pass the days as best he could, but he seemed obsessed with the thought of the wreck that had been made in China by "those fools Roosevelt and Chamberlain, not to mention Cordell Hull and that ass Truman." With regard to payment for the Gest catalogs, he said that the matter would have to be taken up with his wife because he would have passed on within the next few months. However, he was not certain how interested she would be in the whole matter.[64]

In November 1946 Swann sent Gillis a draft for $1,500 related to the indexes. The money came from the Rockefeller Foundation to the Institute for Advanced Studies, now headed by Dr. Aydelotte, who had written that "if one thinks of the contribution which he [Gillis] made to Chinese scholarship in this country by his work in assembling the Gest Library and making the Index the payment is amply justified." Swann suggested that perhaps Gillis' wife could undertake the task of gathering whatever copies of the index she might find, whether bound or unbound. Swann also suggested that she could keep them until the library could find someone to call for them.[65]

Gillis did not respond to Swann until March 1947, when he wrote a very pessimistic letter to her. He explained that living in China was not at all what it used to be. "We are in a completely anti-foreign atmosphere," he said In addition, he had not as yet cashed the check from Princeton because he did not want to receive back the "Chinese money put out by Nanking which is not worth the paper it is printed upon." He even dropped his subscription to the *Peking Chronicle* because of the outrageous cost. Moreover, the corruption among Chinese officials, he observed, had never been worse in all his years in the country. As the days went by, however, and as he got more settled into his house, he began to feel normal again. He looked forward to the approaching spring, and he may have been heartened when his doctor told him that he would be all right for at least a year. He had six clerks before the war, but, still without help, he felt that if he could get some assistance, he would go back to work on the Gest indexes when the weather was warmer. Coal was too costly, and he had to economize in heating, as did many others.[66]

Swann told Gillis in June that the library would like as many copies of the indexes as he could find and announced that Dr. Aydelotte was retiring. The new director of the Institute for Advanced Study was to be Dr. J. Robert Oppenheimer, a physicist and the wartime director of the Manhattan Project. While he was rather young for the job at forty-two years old, Swann understood that Oppenheimer was interested in humanities as well as science. She hoped he would consider setting up the library to be a center for a school for Chinese studies, which was what they had talked and dreamed about for years. She sought an opportunity to talk to and convince "Oppy" about this matter.[67]

By 11 June 1947 Gillis had hired a secretary and was concentrating on the indexes. His health had improved, and he was working hard—which he enjoyed. After he located some thirty-five to forty copies of the indexes, he asked Swann to let him know at once if the copies were wanted, estimating the cost for preparation and shipping at about $2 per copy. He warned that there might be a certain amount of difficulty, for the Chinese had become very antiforeign and took every opportunity to make trouble in any way they could. However, Gillis believed he could "wangle" it.[68]

Gillis wrote to Swann again in August. According to him, the thirty-five to forty unbound copies of the index were in lots and not numbered. He stated that his secretary was no longer with him and, since he did not feel particularly well at age seventy-three, he was not able to tackle the job of pagination. He decided to hire a couple of young Chinese he knew to take on the work. The Chinese were librarians at the Peking Club, spoke English, and were both sons of two of his servants. He had known the young men as children and had practically brought them up as youths. Thus, Gillis stated, they had confidence in each other.[69]

As a final accolade concerning Gillis' decades of book purchasing and collecting acumen for the Gest Oriental Library, perhaps Wang Zhongmin (the rare book cataloger) and Hu Shih (the curator of the Gest Oriental Library from 1950 to 1952) sum up his accomplishments best. Wang Zhongmin commented: "Among all the (Chinese) collections which I have ever examined, I think that the Gest collection is a very important one. I have examined 1,500 items at the Library of Congress and also 2,700 items which have been on deposit (during the war) in this country by the National Library of Peiping, yet I have found that of Gest's A section (Classics) seventy per cent are not duplicated either in the Library of Congress 'Orientalia' section, or in the National Library of Peiping's rare book section. Of the D section (literary writings) I found that fifty percent are not duplicated. This suffices to prove the value of the Gest collection."[70]

Hu Shih did a survey of books in the Gest Oriental Library and suggested that about 41,195 of the more than 100,000 volumes should be considered rare books.[71] In addition to the collecting of books, another major Gillis contribution was his specially designed and unique index system for the effective retrieval of books from a large collection.

THE PASSING OF A "PLAIN SAILOR-MAN": 1948

The death of Irvin Van Gorder Gillis at the age of seventy-three was documented in a copy of the roster of members of the International Lodge, Free Mason, Peking, China, of 31 August 1948, which listed the fact that "Irvin Van Gorder Gillis, Capt, 1 K'ou Tai Hutung, North City, Peking, died 1 September, 1948."[72] Gillis' passing was also noted in the 1894 class year section of *Shipmate*, the Naval Academy's alumni magazine, published by the Retired Naval Officer's Club, Annapolis, Maryland: "Irvin Van Gorder Gillis, (Cdr. USN-Ret. Deceased). We are sorry to report the death of Cdr. Gillis, who died on September 2, 1948, at Peiping, China."[73]

EPILOGUE

Since there was no cause of death noted in the available records, we may assume that Gillis' long-standing heart problems resulted in his demise.

Peking gravesite of I. V Gillis (precise location unknown)
(Courtesy of the East Asian Library and the Gest Collection, Princeton University, Princeton, N.J.)

He, of course, will be remembered among those who will discover and admire his many adventures and achievements during the first forty-five years of his life: high achiever at the U.S. Naval Academy; brilliant junior naval officer who contributed to improving the Navy's signal book and to better naval-engineering practices; daring hero of the Spanish-American War; successful service in, and command of, many U.S. Navy warships in both war and peace; diplomat as a naval attaché in Tokyo during the Russo-Japanese War and several tours of duty at the U.S. Legation in Peking over a twelve-year period during one of the most tumultuous and significant times in Chinese history; foreign military salesman in China for Bethlehem Steel and Electric Boat, and perhaps for others as well, such as Du Pont; leader of naval, and possibly broader, intelligence collection in China for many years; linguist and student of Chinese culture; and recipient of the nation's second-highest award for valor, the Navy Cross, for his contribution to the nation's security.

But Irvin Gillis' most lasting legacy securely resides for the use of scholars around the world at Princeton University's East Asian Library.

The tens of thousands of rare or unique original Chinese literary documents there, collected over a period of thirty-five years, are a treasure that is beyond measure and represent an extraordinary effort, conducted with so much skill and determination over so many years on Gillis' part. This collection is a fitting tribute to the "plain sailor-man" who was anything but.

APPENDIX A

I. V. Gillis, Alfred Thayer Mahan, and the Age of Navalism

Gillis' commissioning came near the midpoint of the 1890s, which saw dramatic changes in the U.S Navy as it completed the transition from wood and sail to steel and steam. His father's Navy had consisted of a century-old conglomeration of commerce-raider and coastal-defense vessels. No better description of the Navy's obsolescence can be found than the devastating statistic presented by U.S. secretary of the Navy Benjamin F. Tracy in his annual report of 1889. Tracy estimated that the U.S. fleet, with a mere forty-four ships, ranked twelfth in the world. By comparison, Great Britain, the number one naval power, possessed 367 warships.

Soon after Tracy's gloomy pronouncement, a book appeared that had a profound impact on all the leading maritime nations of the world, nearly all of which were grappling with the challenges of empire. It was, of course, Captain Alfred Thayer Mahan's *The Influence of Sea Power upon History, 1660–1783,* published in May 1890. Mahan eschewed *guerre de course,* arguing that a navy should be primarily an offensive force that could be concentrated at a decisive point in order to destroy or master an enemy fleet. The operative word was "concentration," for Mahan preached that under no circumstances should a fleet divide or disperse. All this was much in the manner of Admiral Nelson at the Battle of Trafalgar. In eloquent prose the essence of Mahan's thesis was as follows:

- Every world power possessed a large, efficient merchant fleet enabling them to carry on projectable trade around the globe.

- The same powers possessed strong navies, allowing them to extend and maintain their influence throughout the world.

- Britain's control over key straits and the Suez Canal provided it with overwhelming military and commercial advantage.

- The possession of key sites about the world offered strategic naval advantage in the form of maintenance and coaling facilities.

Understandably, then, a major force in young Gillis' "apprentice" years was *The Influence of Sea Power Upon History, 1660–1783*. Mahan was a contemporary of Gillis' father and, like the elder Gillis, endured duty on board the Navy's increasingly obsolete ships. He was also finally advanced to captain in 1885, after spending thirteen years as a commander. Unlike James H. Gillis, Mahan did not possess a ready aptitude for ships. In fact, over the years he had been in involved in a number of ship collisions. However, Mahan was recognized for his intellectual abilities and, following his promotion in 1885, had received orders to the newly organized Naval War College in Newport, Rhode Island, as a lecturer on naval history and tactics. Mahan thrived at Newport and developed his ideas regarding the influence of sea power. The Naval War College sponsored a series of lectures the following year given by Captain Mahan that led to the publication in 1890 of his famous work. In 1887 Mahan met Theodore Roosevelt, a young guest lecturer at the War College, and the two became fast friends. Mahan did not rest his case on just the one book, however. Throughout the 1890s and well into the twentieth century, he churned out more books and dozens of articles in support of his basic sea-power philosophy.

To understand Gillis during this period and the remainder of his naval career, it is necessary to provide some degree of information about Mahan and his influence, which would shape Gillis' thoughts and actions. While young Gillis was taking his entrance examination for the Naval Academy, Captain Mahan published his book. Mahan observed in an eloquent style that a nation's greatness was directly related to its naval strength. For Mahan, sea power consisted not only of a modern "fleet-in-being" but also called for the development of an economic infrastructure, which he interpreted as domestic production, foreign commercial trade, a national shipping industry, and colonies—the latter to include the acquisition of strategic bases. In Mahan's analysis "navalism" and imperialism formed the bedrock upon which any national growth, prosperity, and destiny rested. He also drew another conclusion, positing that American geostrategic interests were best served by maintaining superiority in the Caribbean, demanding fair treatment and cooperation regarding U.S. interests in the Pacific, and by remaining interested in, but aloof from, the rivalries of the European powers when they engaged in purely continental disputes. Mahan's book was an instant sensation both in the United States and abroad.

Mahan offered a vision for achieving empire. Drawing upon the British experience a century earlier, Mahan proclaimed his sea-power doctrine: "It is not the taking of individual ships or convoys, be they few or many, that strikes down the money power of a nation; it is the possession of that overbearing power on the sea which drives the enemy flag from it, or allows it to appear only as a fugitive; and which by controlling the great common, closes the highways by which commerce moves to and from the enemy's shores. This overbearing power can only be exercised by great navies." Mahan did not stop enunciating the historically well-known lesson of the Royal Navy's ability to command the sea. He argued that a strong navy was but one ingredient that ensured Britain's success. The others were industry, markets, a strong merchant marine, and overseas colonies. In Mahan's new thesis sea power and mercantile imperialism were patriotic imperatives that when properly exercised guaranteed national prosperity and greatness.

The timing of Mahan's sea-power tour de force could not have been more propitious for, beginning with the Chilean episode in 1891–1892, nearly each year leading up to the Spanish-American War in 1898 presented a diplomatic and naval challenge for the United States. In 1893 Hawaii was declared a protectorate, and several units of the U.S. fleet in the Pacific, including the flagship USS *Boston*, were sent to Honolulu to help overthrow the Hawaiian queen, Liliuokalani. The South Atlantic Squadron was ordered to Rio de Janeiro to back a rebel blockade of the city. Then, during 1895–1896, the United States became concerned about a British government dispute with Venezuela over British Guiana. When the Royal Navy showed up in force, it was readily apparent that the U.S. Navy could not pose a determined challenge. Also in 1895, Americans became enraged over Spanish brutality in Cuba, and serious planning for a possible confrontation began. Mahan, in fact, urged that in such a confrontation, the U.S. Asiatic Fleet must strike in the Far East so that the Spanish fleet there could not be used to augment units at Cuba.

Japan presented a new challenge in the Far East as well with the stunning news of its resounding naval victory in 1894 over a larger, more heavily armored Chinese fleet, assuring its convincing naval mastery of China. The Japanese, who had translated and widely circulated Mahan's book, had been concerned about China's growing naval power, embodied in seven armor-clad ships, including two battleships displacing 7,500 tons each. In reaction the Japanese in the first several years of the 1890s began adding ships from abroad, particularly from England. While they awaited the ships' commissioning, Japanese naval schools began teaching theoretical maneuvering exercises. By early 1894 Japan had acquired a fleet of fast, lightly armored cruisers, and a war with China was imminent. In September a decisive engagement between the fleets took place near the mouth of the Yalu River in the northern Yellow Sea. In short order the Japanese, using superior speed and tactics, destroyed the larger, more heavily armored Chinese fleet. In a lengthy, five-column description of the battle in the *New York Times*, the Japanese naval attaché to the United States, Lieutenant Naoki Myakka, credited Mahan's theories for Japan's success. He wrote: "We Japanese naval men are students of those important lessons which Capt. Mahan's able writings inculcate, and I think that what our Navy has done in this vein furnishes a very interesting illustration of what he terms the decisive influence of sea power in history."

The United States, not yet fully engaged in Asia, soon joined the worried ranks of the European powers when Japanese workers' migration to Hawaii threatened to absorb the islands into Japan's orbit of influence. American alarm was heightened when a Japanese warship visited Honolulu in early 1897 in apparent protest of the all-white Hawaiian government's prohibition against further Japanese immigration. Roosevelt wrote to Mahan in May 1897: "If I had my way, we would annex those islands tomorrow . . . I believe we should build the Nicaraguan canal at once and . . . build a dozen new battleships, half of them on the Pacific Coast; . . . I am fully alive to the danger from Japan." Indeed, all major nations took immediate notice when Japan's naval achievement resulted in the Treaty of Shimonoseki, whereby Korea essentially became a Japanese protectorate, and China was forced to cede to the victorious Japanese not only Taiwan (Formosa), but also the Pescadores and the Liao-tung Peninsula. The latter contained the important commercial port of Ta-lien (Dalian) and the strategic ice-free naval base at Port Arthur (Lüshun).

Closer to home, Spain's control of Cuba and Puerto Rico meant that the southern flank of the United States lay exposed to attack from the Spanish navy, which had ready access to depots and arsenals at Havana and San Juan. The Naval War College and the Office of Naval Intelligence undertook studies to develop plans on how best to fight Spain should the occasion arise. There also was the continuing suspicion of Great Britain and its mighty Royal Navy. A boundary dispute between England and Venezuela arose in 1895, and when the British put troops ashore along the border between British Guiana and Venezuela, the United States protested that the action represented a clear violation of the Monroe Doctrine. Roosevelt warned the British: "Let the fight come if it must. I rather hope that the fight will come soon. The clamor of the peace faction had convinced me that this country needs a war." The statement represented a clear echo of the word "jingoism," which had been coined in the late 1870s to describe Britain's foreign policy. It caught the fancy of the U.S. press and came to be defined as aggressive, bellicose patriotism. A war scare quickly developed but just as quickly dissipated. However, the incident only served to further highlight American naval deficiencies, as many in the U.S. Navy continued to harbor deep concern about British naval power, while at the same time confirming Mahan's thesis.

It was immediately obvious to even the most casual observer that no "overbearing power" existed in the U.S. naval inventory, and even the forces that did exist were too few, too obsolete, and too dispersed about the world's oceans to be of much value against a modern naval fleet. Mahan's work stimulated reform in the Navy, and a movement rapidly gained momentum pushed along by a chorus of influential supporters. The United States, indeed, was quick to respond. Beginning in 1890 and continuing to the end of the century, successive administrations supported bigger and grander naval building programs. For example, from 1890 to 1896 both the Harrison and the Cleveland administrations approved new ship construction projects, and the total number of vessels in commission leaped from forty-four to one hundred ten. Included in these numbers were twenty-seven cruisers and eight battleships, of which the *Texas* and the *Maine* were the lead ships, having been commissioned in 1895. By 1896 Mahan's ideas had gained increasing popularity among a number of influential politicians and naval officers, and before year's end one more battleship and an armored cruiser had been added to the U.S. Navy's order of battle, along with assorted destroyers, gunboats, and monitors. Additionally a fleet of fifteen experimental torpedo boats were placed in commission, as well as the fleet's first developmental submarine. The McKinley administration maintained the pace into 1897. As reported in the 13 November edition of the *New York Times*, Theodore Roosevelt, McKinley's new assistant secretary of the Navy, commented at a dinner of the Society of Naval Architects that "we have a Navy which, ship for ship, need not fear comparison with any navy in the world." He also warned that it would be a "cruel disaster" if the United States did not maintain the expertise it had gained in recent years by permitting "the plants they have built up and the experts they have trained to be scattered." By the time war came with Spain in 1898, the U.S. Navy had made a dramatic leap forward: The total number of ships in commission had tripled since 1890. In the end an overwhelmed Spain was soundly defeated, and the United States, led by the Navy, began to flex its newly developed imperial muscles.

Mahan at this point continued to publish books and articles that were all variations on his main theme urging the United States to press ahead with naval modernization. His argument received significant reinforcement from the seemingly annual events or mini crises that required naval action. As mentioned previously, one of Mahan's earliest disciples was Theodore Roosevelt, who had met Mahan some years earlier at the newly established Naval War College at Newport, Rhode Island. Soon after the book appeared, Roosevelt dashed off a note to Mahan in which he enthused: "During the last two days, I have spent half my time, busy as I am, in reading your book. That I found it interesting is shown by the fact that having taken it up, I have gone straight through and finished it. It is a very good book—admirable; and I am greatly in error if it does not become a naval classic."

Roosevelt had not erred. Mahan's book quickly gained world acclaim, and the British, the French, and the Germans were soon praising Mahan and inviting him to lecture. The book first of all resonated technologically with numerous twentieth-century companies, such as Friedrich Krupp AG, Vickers, Armstrong Whitworth, and Bethlehem Steel, which had become synonymous with state-of-the-art naval equipment. A second audience was a pool of trained and proficient officers and enlisted men. Nearly all the leading naval powers were under constant strain to keep up with the demand for trained crews by bigger, more technologically advanced ships. For example, in 1895, the complement for the U.S. Navy's first battleship, the *Texas*, was 396 officers and men. By 1914 the newer "super dreadnought" battleship of the *Pennsylvania* class required almost 1,100 crewmen, a threefold increase. The third essential element concerned bases for refueling and maintenance. The naval race set in motion a rapid search for the reliable support outposts required for efficient movement of a nation's naval forces. The end result was a dizzying rearrangement of territorial ownership as the strong preyed upon the weak.

In presenting his elements of sea power, Mahan first proposed that naval warfare and victory at sea would be decided only by battle-fleet engagement. Thus:

- Commerce raiding was out.
- Coastal defense was out.
- Capital ships were essential.
- Fleet engagements were key.
- Command of the seas was the objective.
- Fleets should be concentrated and not divided.

Mahan also encouraged the application of modern technology and tactics. He advocated the construction of a "fleet-in-being," composed of armored cruisers and battleships organized into fleets and squadrons. It required learning how to maneuver these new ships in concert as a single, effective fighting force. The first step was taken with the newly formed Squadron of Evolution in early 1890 under the command of one of Commodore Gillis' old nemeses, John G. Walker, organized so that its ships could be rapidly concentrated into a single cohesive force whose principal purpose was to fight a grand, conclusive battle at sea. Also, Mahan believed the Atlantic Ocean, and by extension the Caribbean, should be the main locus of U.S. naval might.

By the time war with Spain came in 1898, Mahan had readjusted slightly. He became obsessed with the U.S. need to annex Hawaii, which finally was accomplished in July 1898. He also strongly advocated building a canal across the Central American isthmus. A canal, he asserted, would provide the United States with both economic and military benefits such as accrued to Britain with the opening of the Suez Canal several decades earlier. Going a step further, he lent emphatic support to the idea of acquiring or possessing key sites around the world that offered a strategic naval advantage in the form of bases and coaling facilities. The idea did not originate with Mahan, but in identifying the concept as an important adjunct to U.S. sea power, he gained converts, including Theodore Roosevelt, who ultimately was the catalyst to the building of the Panama Canal.

There were several essential requirements for successful execution of Mahan's principles. The first, and probably the most important, was to have a strong industrial and shipbuilding base. By 1890 the United States had most of the wounds of the Civil War behind it and had achieved coast-to-coast continental expansion with the final conquest of the native Indian tribes in the West. It had also embarked on its own industrial revolution and, on the eve of World War I, possessed nearly a dozen modern shipbuilding yards extending from Bath, Maine, to Newport News, Virginia, on the East Coast and several in the San Francisco Bay area. Augmenting these facilities were various companies specializing in propulsion systems, guns, and armor plate. American shipbuilding and technical know-how progressed so rapidly that most companies gained a worldwide reputation for excellence and garnered contracts to build warships for other nations. It was a cutthroat business, and bribery or special side arrangements were common. Many companies had consultants who took up residence in a country to respond rapidly to even the most tepid contract inquiries. As a result, representatives of companies such as Armstrong Whitworth, Vickers, Krupp, Blohm & Voss, Mitsubishi, and Bethlehem Steel haunted the various naval ministries looking for deals. One of the most active companies seeking overseas contracts was Bethlehem Steel, whose officers frequently heaped praise on Mahan. One observer gushed in 1897 that Captain Mahan was "as much in evidence those days through his discussion of naval matters as was ever [Oliver Hazard] Perry or John Paul Jones through [their] naval victories."

A chorus of influential supporters joined in singing the praises of the Mahan sea-power doctrine. The most prominent was Theodore Roosevelt, who, as assistant secretary of the Navy, declared in June 1897: "It is certain that we need a first-class navy, not merely a navy for defense." Another Mahan proponent was Henry Cabot Lodge, the venerable and influential senator from Massachusetts, who, as a devoted disciple, unhesitatingly threw his considerable support behind larger and larger naval spending programs over the three decades he served in the Senate. Mahan himself also kept up the drumbeat, as he continuously wrote articles and books designed to shape American opinion. When distilled, they provided a new geostrategic blueprint. Later, when Roosevelt became president, he often sought Mahan's advice on all manner of naval topics, and the two exchanged extensive correspondence right up to Mahan's death in 1914.

In 1890 the two greatest navies belonged to Britain and France, but the world soon saw three more nations enter the naval game: Germany, Japan, and the United States. During the decade of the 1890s, most of the world's maritime nations signed on to Mahan's sea-power thesis and moved rapidly ahead with naval modernization that emphasized bigger ships and bigger guns. The British did not need any coaxing, of course, but nevertheless their admirals cheered his book. Kaiser Wilhelm had it translated and began Germany's inexorable building of its navy in the image of Mahan's vision. The French navy, too, moved ahead in its usual individual manner. The best example, however, was Japan. Over the next three decades the naval poker game that ensued was for high stakes as these five nations, driven by imperial ambitions, jockeyed for power. At the same time, commercial imperialism continued spreading like a fever among the powers as they maneuvered for colonial advantage around the globe.

In large part, however, Mahan's work was intended to stimulate reform at home, in the U.S. Navy, and it succeeded admirably. A movement for a more modern Navy rapidly gained momentum and did not diminish until after World War I. The big-gun battleship became the Navy's primary mainstay, the principal prowess of which was direct fleet combat. Mahan drew wide support within the Navy, both from senior and junior officers alike, as his articles appeared in more than a dozen magazines. The message was clear and offered a blueprint for action. According to one Mahan biographer, William E. Livezey, it could "be summarized as dominance in the Caribbean, equality and co-operation in the Pacific, and interested abstention from the strictly Continental rivalries of the European powers." Livezey went on to state that fulfillment of the Mahan vision also "demanded the acquisition of strategic bases and the construction of a modern navy, supplemented by adequate coast defenses and prosperous national shipping."

There can be little doubt that for most junior officers it was an exciting time to be in the Navy, and few doubted that promotion and command opportunities would continue to be bright. As for I. V. Gillis, once he gained his commission in July 1896, he found himself on the cutting edge of the United States' effort to achieve Mahan's vision. Gillis' entry into the Naval Academy and his own subsequent naval career would span the years 1890 to 1919, coinciding almost exactly with the so-called Age of Navalism. It was during those three decades that the quest for, and the successful achievement of, empire rested with a nation's ability to field powerful fleets. The naval contest that ensued was for high stakes, with winners usually adding to their territorial holdings and losers forever weakened by the imposition of humiliating indemnities. The "game" proved to be quite addictive, and once in it, winners could not easily drop out, lest it be perceived as a sign of weakness. Gillis must have received early exposure to Mahan's ideas and, as his career progressed, become a willing and eager proselyte.

In four years, starting in 1896, as a young ensign, he served on board the first U.S. battleship, the 308-foot *Texas*. Commissioned in August 1895, it had taken six years to build at a cost of $2.5 million. The 6,300-ton reciprocating engines delivered 8,600 horsepower with a maximum speed of seventeen knots. The *Texas*' main battery of two 12-inch guns had a major design flaw, however. The forward turret was mounted to port while the aft turret was to starboard, thus preventing the guns from being fired in broadside. The fighting distance was line of sight at about 4,000 yards. The ship's operating radius was limited to 2,900 miles because of its small coal capacity of 850 tons. Thirteen years later, Gillis reported on board the brand-new battleship *Michigan*, and the contrast was quite apparent. The cost to build the *Michigan*, which was the first "all-big-gun" battleship, was $7 million, and it had taken only three years to place the ship in commission after first being laid down. It displaced 16,000 tons, was 452 feet long, and required a crew of nearly 900 officers and men. The engines were still steam reciprocators but were oil-fired. They were rated at 16,000 horsepower with a capability of driving the ship at twenty-one knots maximum speed. The biggest difference from the *Texas* was the ship's main battery. The *Michigan* mounted 12-inch breech-loading rifled guns that could accurately deliver sixteen 350-pound projectiles each minute at an effective range up to seven miles.

Gillis then fought in the Spanish-American War in the waters off Cuba in an experimental torpedo boat, the USS *Porter*, and received praise for his heroism. At the end of the decade, he was named commanding officer of the *Porter*, a rare honor for an officer only twenty-four years old. All of his reports of fitness indicated he was among the Navy's best and brightest. The reports also highlighted the fact that he possessed an unusual flair for engineering; in fact, though he was an accomplished line officer, he did not mind serving in the grimy, hot engine rooms inhabited by sailors known as "greasers." In his first and second decades of service Gillis displayed a keen aptitude for the new emerging naval technologies, especially propulsion systems. Most line officers shied away from engine room assignments, preferring to relegate the duty to others and the troubleshooting to senior enlisted men. Gillis was different. He did not mind rolling up his sleeves and taking on the challenge of fixing a piece of cranky machinery. He felt right at home analyzing engineering blueprints and was quite capable at tearing down and rebuilding all sorts of machinery. He seemed to relish mechanical problem solving; on numerous occasions his superiors gave him high marks for his technical skills, and they also turned to him to troubleshoot and correct engineering problems, even in ships other than his own.

Gillis' second decade of service took a different turn, highlighted by his introduction to the Far East. He served with distinction on board five ships, performing as navigator, chief engineer, and commanding officer of various vessels, including the flagship of the Asiatic Fleet's Third Squadron. In between sea duty tours, by way of contrast, Gillis performed as an attaché, first in Tokyo during the Russo-Japanese War and then during 1907–1908 as the first naval attaché to China. A survey of Gillis' reports of fitness also highlights the fact that he was attracted to foreign affairs. He had studied French at the Naval Academy; he apparently became quite fluent in the language and continued to study it throughout his naval career. Most of his superiors commented on his language skills and also noted that he had more than a passing knowledge of Spanish as well. From the moment he took up residency in Peking in 1914, Gillis immersed himself in the study of Chinese writing and began to master Mandarin Chinese.

Gillis' third decade was his most challenging. He returned to China as part of a team representing the Bethlehem Steel Company in its efforts to sell naval ships and hardware to the Chinese navy. The collapse of the Manchu Dynasty and subsequent political upheaval stifled the Dollar Diplomacy effort of Bethlehem Steel, but Gillis had undergone a career-changing experience. In 1914 he briefly returned to the United States and retired from the Navy. Within several months he was back in Peking, where he resided for the rest of his life as an American expatriate on retainer to several U.S. shipbuilding companies, including Bethlehem Steel and the Electric Boat Company of Connecticut. Despite the political instability in China, Gillis continued to try to sell warships to the Chinese. The excitement surrounding the outbreak of World War I in 1914 quickly attracted Gillis, and the U.S. Office of Naval Intelligence recruited him to run a Chinese information service to keep track of Japanese activities in Asia. Several years later, when the United States entered the war, it became necessary to recall Gillis to active duty once again, as naval attaché to

Peking. During this period Gillis carefully observed Japanese encroachments in China and Manchuria, Russian reactions to these threats, and other Western powers' incursions into Shanghai and up the Yangtze River valley. He recognized the implications of the failure of the United States to do much about Japan's depredations in China, and when he finally retired from the Navy for the last time in late 1919, he warned his superiors that in the not-too-distant future a war would break out in Asia between the United States and Japan. During these latter tours he put to use and refined his practical knowledge of Mahan's thesis in a broader political-military context of big-power maneuverings. His Navy career markedly exemplified the application of the principles of navalism.

Sources

Apt, Benjamin L. "Mahan's Forebears: The Debate over Maritime Strategy, 1868–1883." *Naval War College Review* 50, no. 3, sequence 359 (Summer 1997).

Livezey, William E. *Mahan on Sea Power*. Norman: University of Oklahoma Press, 1981.

Mahan, Alfred Thayer. *The Influence of Sea Power upon History, 1660–1783*. Boston: Little, Brown, 1890.

Mattox, Henry. "Two If by Sea." *American Diplomacy* 5, no. 2 (2001). CIAO. http://www.ciaonet.org (accessed 21 November 2011).

"Roosevelt on the Navy." *New York Times*, 13 November 1897.

Seager, Robert. *Alfred Thayer Mahan: The Man and His Letters*. Annapolis, Md.: Naval Institute Press, 1977.

"Secretary Long's Report." *New York Times*, 17 November 1907.

APPENDIX B

I. V. Gillis' Record of Naval Service

1890–1894	U.S. Naval Academy, Annapolis, Maryland: naval cadet
1894–1896	USS *New York* (ACR 2): midshipman
1 July 1896	Promoted to ensign
1896–1897	USS *Texas* (second-class battleship; no hull number assigned): signal officer
1897–1898	USS *Porter* (TB 6): executive officer and navigator
1898–1899	USS *Texas*: deck officer
1899–1900	USS *Porter*: commanding officer
27 February 1900	Promoted to lieutenant (junior grade)
1900–1902	USS *Annapolis* (PG 10): chief navigator and chief engineer
20 July 1901	Promoted to (full) lieutenant
1902–1903	USS *Monadnock* (BM 3): chief engineer
1903–1904	USS *Kentucky* (BB 6): deck officer
1904–1905	Assistant U.S. naval attaché, Tokyo, Japan
1905–1906	Reserve Torpedo Flotilla, Norfolk, Virginia: commanding officer
1905	Additional duty: USS *Atlanta* (protected cruiser/barracks ship, in reserve): commanding officer
1907–1908	U.S. naval attaché, Peking, China
1 July 1907	Promoted to lieutenant commander
1908	USS *Rainbow* (AS 7): commanding officer
1908	USS *Ohio* (BB 12): chief navigator
1909	USS *Michigan* (BB 27): chief navigator and senior engineer

1910	Temporary duty: escort to Chinese Naval Commission
1911–1914	Assistant U.S. naval attaché, Peking, China
7 May 1914	Promoted to commander
30 June 1914	Retired to the Naval Reserve
1915–1917	Recalled to special duty: chief intelligence officer, China*
1917–1919	U.S. naval attaché, Peking, China
31 January 1919	Retired from the U.S. Navy

Total sea service: 13 years, 3 months (1894–1914 and 1917–1920)
Total shore duty: 8 years, 5 months

---

*Not counted as naval service.

APPENDIX C

Gillis Family Tree

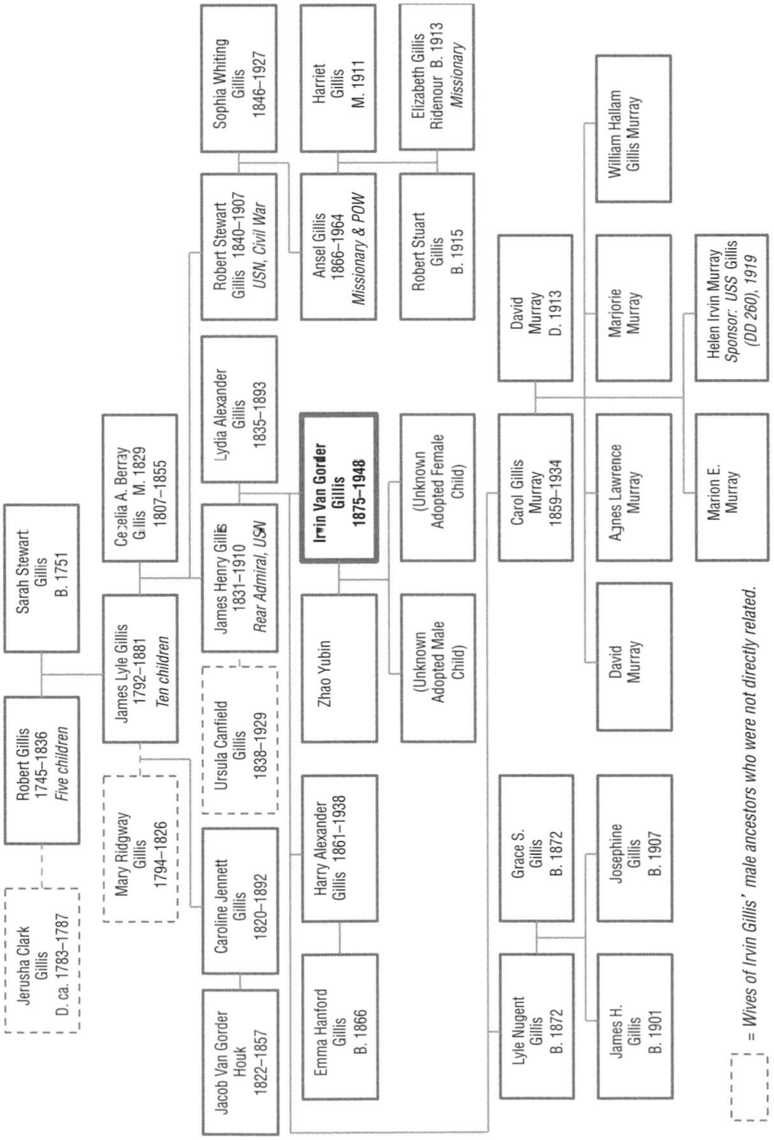
Jerusha Clark Gillis D. ca. 1783–1787
Robert Gillis 1745–1836 Five children
Sarah Stewart Gillis B. 1751
Mary Ridgway Gillis 1794–1826
James Lyle Gillis 1792–1881 Ten children
Celelia A. Berray Gillis M. 1829 1807–1855
Jacob Van Gorder Houk 1822–1857
Caroline Jennett Gillis 1820–1892
Ursula Canfield Gillis 1838–1929
James Henry Gillis 1831–1910 Rear Admiral, USN
Lydia Alexander Gillis 1835–1893
Robert Stewart Gillis 1840–1907 USN, Civil War
Sophia Whiting Gillis 1846–1927
Emma Hanford Gillis B. 1866
Harry Alexander Gillis 1861–1938
Zhao Yubin
Irvin Van Gorder Gillis 1875–1948
Ansel Gillis 1866–1964 Missionary & POW
Harriet Gillis M. 1911
(Unknown Adopted Male Child)
(Unknown Adopted Female Child)
Robert Stuart Gillis B. 1915
Elizabeth Gillis Ridenour B. 1913 Missionary
Lyle Nugent Gillis B. 1872
Grace S. Gillis B. 1872
Carol Gillis Murray 1859–1934
David Murray D. 1913
James H. Gillis B. 1901
Josephine Gillis B. 1907
David Murray
Agnes Lawrence Murray
Marjorie Murray
William Hallam Gillis Murray
Marion E. Murray
Helen Irvin Murray Sponsor: USS Gillis (DD 260), 1919
= Wives of Irvin Gillis' male ancestors who were not directly related.

APPENDIX D

U.S. Naval Academy Course of Instruction, ca. 1895

The following are examples of courses taken by Midshipman I. V. Gillis. This sample is taken from the 1895 *U.S. Naval Academy Course of Instruction.*

FIRST YEAR—FOURTH CLASS—*Continued*
Second Term

Department	Number of recitations per week	Number of months	Subjects	Text Books
Mathematics	3	4	ALGEBRA: Course for first term continued. Development of algebraic functions by means of indeterminate coefficients and the binomial theorem; permutations and combinations; theory of probability; summation of series; continued fractions; logarithms; exponential equations; theory of equations, including the solution of numerical equations; determinants.	Hall and Knight's Higher Algebra
	2	4	GEOMETRY: Course for first term continued. Spherical geometry; the cone and of the cylinder; mensuration of rectilinear figures, and of the sphere, cone and cylinder; application of algebra to determinate geometry.	Wentworth's Geometry

FIRST YEAR—FOURTH CLASS—*Continued*
Second Term

Department	Number of recitations per week	Number of months	Subjects	Text Books
English Studies, History and Law	2	4	ENGLISH: Rhetoric and composition; choice and use of words; kinds of composition; narration and description; argumentative composition; exercises in the composition of letters and telegrams. Themes	A.S. Hill's Rhetoric. Ayres's Orthoepist. Ayres's Verbalist.
	3	4	HISTORY: Progress of colonial development in America and the history of the United States; important points in the naval history of the United States by notes or lectures.	Eliot's History of the United States. Mitchell's Atlas.
Modern Languages	5	4	FRENCH: "Natural Method."	Bercy's La Langue Francaise 1ᵉ partie. Bellow's Dictionary.
			SPANISH: (Given as an advanced course.) "Natural Method."	Worman's First Spanish Book. Seoane's Dictionary.
			GERMAN: (Given as an advanced course.) "Natural Method."	Dreyspring's Cumulative Method and German Verb Drill. Whitney's Dictionary.

SECOND YEAR—THIRD CLASS
First Term

Department	Number of recitations per week	Number of months	Subjects	Text Books
Mathematics	1	4	DESCRIPTIVE GEOMETRY: Orthographic projections, representation of points, lines and planes; problems relating to the right line and the plane; representations of surfaces of the second order; projections of the sphere.	Church's Descriptive Geometry. Hendrickson-Dressel's Stereographic projection.
	4	4	TRIGONOMETRY: Measures of arcs and angles; trigonometric functions; an analytical investigation of trigonometric formulas, with their application to all the cases of planes and spherical triangles; construction and use of trigonometric tables; inverse trigonometric functions; De Moivre's theorem; solution of trigonometric equations; practical applications of trigonometry to the solution of plane and spherical triangles; the astronomical triangle and the measurements of heights and distances.	Rittenhouse's Exercises in Descriptive Geometry Drawing. Chauvenet's Trigonometry. Levett and Davison's Plane Trigonometry. Bowditch's Useful Tables.

SECOND YEAR—THIRD CLASS—*Continued*
First Term

Department	Number of recitations per week	Number of months	Subjects	Text Books
English Studies, History and Law	2	4	ENGLISH: Classification of words; definition of words by usage and by derivation; synonyms; laws of change in the meaning of words; faults in diction and their remedies; selection and arrangement; elementary principles of reasoning; principles of composition; exercises in the composition of official dispatches, letters, and telegrams. Themes.	Abbott and Seeley's English Lessons for English People. Webster's Dictionary.
			LAW: The Constitution of the United States.	Andrew's Manual of the Constitution.
Modern Languages	3	4	FRENCH: "Natural Method."	Bocher's Series of French Plays. Bercy's La Langue Francaise 2ᵉ partie. Bellow's Dictionary.
			SPANISH: (Given as an advanced course.) "Natural Method."	Knapp's Spanish Grammar
			GERMAN: (Given as an advanced course.) "Natural Method."	Dreyspring's Cumulative Method and German Verb Drill. Whitney's Dictionary.

APPENDIX E

Chinese Names (Systems of Romanization)

Chinese names are written in this narrative in the roman alphabet (instead of Chinese characters). Today, the common system for romanizing Chinese words is called Pinyin. It was developed by the People's Republic of China (PRC) and is that country's current official system of romanization. In mainland China before the advent of the PRC in 1949, the system of romanization introduced by Westerners and in wide use for many years was called Wade-Giles. It is also the system used in Taiwan today. While quite different from their Pinyin versions, printed words using Wade-Giles are often more familiar to Western readers due to their usage for many decades. For that reason, and because that is what appeared in the documents we cited from that era, most Chinese words and names in this book are written in Wade-Giles, the system in use when Irvin Gillis lived and worked in China.

Other romanization systems also were developed by Western scholars. One of these was the Chinese Postal Map Romanization System. In the map system the word for the current Chinese capital, Beijing, was spelled in Gillis' time as "Peking," which is the spelling we use in this text. It was also occasionally spelled "Pekin." We recognized that using Wade-Giles or other older systems, however, raises some difficulties in pronouncing Chinese words properly.

It should be noted that while the spelling appears differently, *the written words are spoken by Chinese speakers exactly the same way in the various systems.* "Peking" was, and is, *always* pronounced in China as "Bay-jing." Other common words suffer from the same mispronunciation by Western readers and speakers.

A summary of the unique use of certain roman letters in Pinyin, the more modern system, may help those wishing to pronounce some of the Chinese words they encounter that are written in that system.

Consonants

C is pronounced like the *ts* in *tsetse fly*.
Q is pronounced like the *ch* in *cheek*.
X is pronounced like the *sh* in *shed*.
ZH is pronounced like the *j* in *joint*.

Vowels

E is pronounced like the *e* in *moment*.
E before *ng* is pronounced like the *u* in *sung*.
O is pronounced like the *aw* in *paw*.
OU is pronounced like the *o* in *so*.
O before *ng* also is pronounced like the *o* in *so*.

A short list of common words in both older romanization systems and Pinyin serves as an example.

Older systems	Pinyin (modern, official usage)
Peking	Beijing
Ts'ingtao	Qingdao
Chungking	Chongqing
Fukien	Fujian
Foochow	Fuzhou
Hankow	Hangzhou
Kwangtung	Guangdong
Nanking	Nanjing
Shantung	Shandong
Szechwan	Sichuan
Tientsin	Tianjin
Sian	Xi'an

As the short review using the pronunciation guidelines for Pinyin reveals, that system comes much closer to enabling non-Chinese to say the Chinese words more accurately. Just as with "Peking," "Foochow" was *never* pronounced the way it is spelled in Wade-Giles; "Fuzhou" in Pinyin is a much closer approximation ("Foo-joe").

We just thought the reader might like to know.

NOTES

CHAPTER 1.
Education, Sea Duty in the Atlantic, and Trial by Fire: 1875–1900

1. U.S. Navy, *Record of Officers*, James Henry Gillis, NARA, RG 24.
2. "Cutters on the Lakes," *New York Times*, 13 February 1899, p. 9.
3. "Brooklyn Navy Yard," Officer's Row Project, http://officersrow. org.history.htm (accessed 15 August 2007); "The National Navy Yards," *New York Times*, 12 April 1885.
4. "Boys in the Naval Service," *New York Times*, 8 December 1882.
5. Russell H. Bastert, "A New Approach to the Origins of Blaine's Pan American Policy," *Hispanic American Historical Review* 39, no. 3 (August 1959): 375–412; Commodore [James H.] Gillis, "My First Cruise," *Morning Oregonian* (Portland), 30 July 1893, p. 12; U.S. Navy, *Record of Officers*, James Henry Gillis, NARA, RG 24; Lewis R. Hamersly, ed., *The Records of Living Officers of the U.S. Navy and Marine Corps*, 4th ed. (Philadelphia: L. R. Hamersly, 1890), 69–70; "Obituary of Rear Admiral James H. Gillis," *Army and Navy Journal*, 11 December 1910; "Obituary of Commodore James H. Gillis," *New York Times*, 8 December 1910; Lewis R. Hamersly, ed., *Who's Who in Pennsylvania* (New York: L. R. Hamersly, 1904), 263; John McIntosh Kell, *Recollections of a Naval Life* (Washington, D.C.: Neale, 1900), 97–98, 102, 108.
6. [Henry Souther], "The Late James L. Gillis, the Patriarch of Elk County," *Pittsburg Daily Post*, 30 July 1881, and *Philadelphia Times*, 29 July 1881; W. J. McKnight, *A Pioneer Outline History of Northwestern Pennsylvania, 1780–1850* (Philadelphia: Lippincott, 1905), 497–508, 718–723; *History of the Counties of McKean, Elk, Cameron, and Potter, Penna., with Biographical Sketches* (Chicago: J. H. Beers, 1890), 727; *Portrait and Biographical Album, Henry County, Iowa* (Chicago: Acme Publishing, 1888), 202–205.

7. Ginger Doyel, "Plebe Summer 1904," *Shipmate,* July–August 2004, 32–35.

8. "Selecting Naval Candidates," *New York Times,* 19 October 1890; "Train Naval Cadets," *New York Times,* 18 September 1892.

9. Walter G. Richardson, "Life and Study at the Naval Academy," *New England Magazine* 14, no. 3 (May 1893): 305.

10. J. D. Jerrald Kelly, "The United States Naval Academy," *Harper's New Monthly Magazine,* July 1888, 173.

11. *The Lucky Bag* (Annapolis, Md.: U.S. Naval Academy, 1894), 146.

12. Records of the U.S. Naval Academy, RG 405, Conduct Record for the Class of 1894, SCNL.

13. *Lucky Bag,* 66–68.

14. Records of the U.S. Naval Academy, RG 405, Conduct Record for the Class Appointed in 1890, SCNL; Richardson, "Life and Study at the Naval Academy," 312.

15. "Commodore Gillis's Wife Critically Ill," *Washington Post,* 2 August 1893; "Mrs. Gillis Is Dead," *Washington Post,* 3 August 1893.

16. U.S. Navy, *Record of Officers,* James Henry Gillis, NARA, RG 24.

17. Records of the U.S. Naval Academy, RG 405, Conduct Record for the Class Appointed in 1890; "Class of '94, Naval Academy: About the Men Who Are to Be Graduated," *New York Times,* 4 June 1894.

18. Gerald E. Wheeler, *Admiral William Veazie Pratt, U.S. Navy* (Washington, D.C.: Naval History Division, Department of the Navy, 1974), 12.

19. Robley D. Evans, *A Sailor's Log* (New York: D. Appleton, 1908), chap. 21–23.

20. Ibid., 102.

21. Ibid., 385.

22. Ibid.; Robley D. Evans, *An Admiral's Log: Being Continued Recollections of Naval Life* (New York: D. Appleton, 1910).

23. Wheeler, *Admiral William Veazie Pratt,* 15.

24. Evans, *Sailor's Log,* 391–392.

25. Ibid., chap. 30.

26. Ibid., 384–386.

27. U.S. Navy, *Record of Officers, 1829–1924*, SCNL, roll 7, vols. 12 and 13, Irvin Van Gorder Gillis; Kenneth J. Hagan, *The People's Navy* (New York: Free Press, 1991), 209.

28. Alfred Thayer Mahan, *The Influence of Sea Power upon History, 1660–1783* (Boston: Little, Brown, 1890).

29. New York Police Commissioner Theodore Roosevelt to U.S. Senator (New York) Henry Cabot Lodge, December 1895, quoted in *The Martial Spirit: A Study of Our War with Spain*, by Walter Millis (Boston: Houghton Mifflin, 1931), 38.

30. U.S. Navy, "Report on the Fitness of Officers," Lieut. Irvin V. Gillis, 1 January 1897–31 March 1897, NARA, RG 24.

31. *Annual Report of the Secretary of the Navy for the Year 1888* (Washington, D.C.: Government Printing Office, 1888), 20.

32. I. V. Gillis, "A Report on Ship Signaling Prepared by Officers of the Battle Ship *Texas*," 1896, and "Updated Instructions for the Care of 'Double Bottoms,'" n.d., New-York Historical Society Manuscript Collection, Miscellaneous Manuscripts, I. V. Gillis.

33. "Repairs to the Texas; Twenty of Her Crew Deserted When She was in Dry Dock," *New York Times*, 30 September 1897.

34. U.S. Navy, "Report on the Fitness of Officers," Lieut. I. V. Gillis, [ca. August] 1897, NARA, RG 24.

35. Richard V. Simpson, *Building the Mosquito Fleet: The U.S. Navy's First Torpedo Boats* (Charleston, S.C.: Arcadia, 2001), 62–73, 90–92, 88–107, 134.

36. U.S. Navy, "Report on the Fitness of Officers," Lieut. I. V. Gillis, 23 September 1897–31 December 1897, NARA, RG 24.

37. [Sylvester H. Scovel], "Brave World Correspondent May Be Killed or Captured," *New York World*, 28 April 1898.

38. John C. Fremont Jr., "Torpedo-Boat Service," *Harper's New Monthly Magazine*, November 1898, 832.

39. Ibid., 830–832.

40. "Log of the U.S. Torpedo Boat *Porter*," J. C. Fremont, Lieut., USN, Commanding, Saturday, 4 June 1898, signed by Lt. I. V. Gillis, NARA, RG 24, ARC ID 58128.

41. Fremont, "Torpedo-Boat Service," 837.

42. W. B. Northrop, "Capturing a Plunging Torpedo," illus. by F. W. Burton, *English Illustrated Magazine* 47 (February 1907): 533–534.

43. James Rankin Young and J. Hampton Moore, *History of Our War with Spain* (Philadelphia: National Publishing, 1898), 598–599.

44. "The Porter at the Navy Yard: She Comes Here for Overhauling and Repairs—Ensign Gillis Talks of Her Experiences," *New York Times*, 20 July 1898.

45. Above quotation from Rudyard Kipling, "M'Andrew's Hymn," *Rudyard Kipling's Verse, Inclusive Edition, 1885–1919* (Garden City, N.Y.: Doubleday, Page, 1919), 137.

46. "Texas Tars Our Guests," *New York Times*, 2 August 1898.

47. "Engineers in the Navy; Admiral Melville Says They Are Decreasing in Number—Changes Needed," *New York Times*, 18 October 1901.

48. U.S. Navy, "Report on the Fitness of Officers," Lieutenant Junior Grade Irvin V. Gillis, 1 July–22 August 1899, NARA, RG 24.

49. Above quotation from Unattributed, "Our Hero," *Poems of Dewey and the Philippines*, quoted in *Admiral Dewey at Manila and the Complete Story of the Philippines: Life and Glorious Deeds of Admiral George Dewey*, by Joseph L. Stickney (Chicago: Imperial Publishing, 1899), 373.

50. "The Dewey Naval Parade: Greatest Marine Pageant in the History of the City to Take Place," *New York Times*, 30 August 1899.

51. "Log of the U.S. Torpedo Boat 'Porter,'" Lieut. I. V. Gillis, USN, Commanding, 10 October 1899, NARA, RG 24, ARC ID 581208.

52. "Log of the U.S. Torpedo Boat 'Porter,'" Lieut. I. V. Gillis, USN, Commanding, 17 August 1900, NARA, RG 24, ARC ID 581208.

53. "Log of the U.S. Torpedo Boat 'Porter,'" Lieut. I. V. Gillis, USN, Commanding, 2 July 1900, NARA, RG 24, ARC ID 581208.

54. "The News of Newport," *New York Times*, 29 June 1900.

55. "Log of the U.S. Torpedo Boat 'Porter,'" Lieut. I. V. Gillis, USN, Commanding, 5 September 1900, NARA, RG 24, ARC ID 581208.

56. U.S. Navy, "Report on the Fitness of Officers," Lieut. I. V. Gillis, 3 May–30 June 1900, NARA, RG 24.

57. "Naval Attack on Newport," *New York Times*, 25 September 1900; "Naval Manoeuvres End," *New York Times*, 26 September 1900; "The Newport Manoeuvres," *New York Times*, 27 September 1900.

58. U.S. Navy, "Report on the Fitness of Officers," Lieut. Irvin V. Gillis, 1 July–29 September 1900, NARA, RG 24.

CHAPTER 2.
Sea Duty in the Pacific (I): 1900–1904

1. "USS Annapolis (PG-10)," Answers.com, http://www.answers.com/topic/uss-annapolis-pg-10 (accessed 6 December 2011).

2. "USS Annapolis: The Wardroom and Crew Mess," *Naval Engineers Journal* 115, no. 1 (Winter 2003).

3. "The Philippine-American War (1899–1902)," filipino-americans.com, http://www.filipino-americans.com/filamwar.html (accessed 17 February 2006), 2.

4. "Guimaras Island," Heritage Site of the Visayan Island in the Philippines, http://www.admu.edu.ph/offices/mirlab/panublion/r6_guimaras.html (accessed 17 February 2006).

5. "The United Service," *New York Times*, 24 January 1902.

6. "Philippine-American War (1899–1902)," 11.

7. Victor Nebrida, *The Balangiga Massacre: Getting Even* (Los Angeles: Philippine History Group, 1977), 6–7.

8. "Philippine-American War (1899–1902)," 10.

9. "Insurrection in the Philippines," U-S-History.com, http://www.u-s-history.com/pages/h830.html (accessed 16 February 2006), 2.

10. U.S. Navy ship's log, USS *Annapolis*, 10 August 1902, NARA, RG 24.

11. "Engineers in the Navy," *New York Times*, 19 October 1901.

12. "The Naval Promotion Plan," *New York Times*, 7 December 1897.

13. U.S. Navy ship's log, USS *Annapolis*, 25 November 1902, NARA, RG 24.

14. William R. Braisted, *The United States Navy in the Pacific, 1897–1909* (Austin: University of Texas Press, 1958), 117.

15. Robley D. Evans, *An Admiral's Log: Being Continued Recollections of Naval Life* (New York: D. Appleton, 1910), 195.

16. "The United Service," *New York Times*, 29 November 1902.

17. Evans, *Admiral's Log*, 196.

18. Ibid.

19. Ibid.

20. U.S. Navy ship's log, USS *Monadnock,* 19 November 1902, NARA, RG 24.

21. Evans, *Admiral's Log*, 199.

22. Ibid., 205.

23. "USS Monadnock," NavSource.org, http://www.navsource.org/archives/01/monadnock.htm (accessed 3 February 2006).

24. Evans, *Admiral's Log*, 199.

25. Kemp Tolley, *Yangtze Patrol: The U.S. Navy in China* (Annapolis, Md.: Naval Institute Press, 1971), 58–59.

26. Ibid., 59.

27. Ibid., 80.

28. "Open Door," Answers.com, http://www.answers.com/topic/open-door-policy-1 (accessed 9 January 2007).

29. "Foreign Affairs, 1899," U-S-History.com, http://www.u-s-history.com/pages/h908.html (accessed 9 January 2007).

30. Jeffery M. Dorwart, *The Office of Naval Intelligence: The Birth of America's First Intelligence Agency, 1865–1918* (Annapolis, Md.: Naval Institute Press, 1979), 71.

31. Braisted, *United States Navy in the Pacific, 1897–1909*, 116.

32. Ibid., 126.

33. Ibid., 125.

34. Ibid., 126.

35. Ibid., 138, 143, 146.

36. Ibid., 144.

37. Evans, *Admiral's Log*, 268.

38. Ibid., 269.

39. Ibid., 280.

40. U.S. Navy ship's log, USS *Monadnock,* 25 August 1903, NARA, RG 24.

41. U.S. Navy Department, W. H. Moody, Secretary of the Navy, to I. V. Gillis, U.S. Navy, 20 July 1903, NARA, RG 38.

42. "BB-6 USS KENTUCKY 1896–1904," NavSourceOnline, http://www.navsource.org/archives/01/06a.htm/encyclopedia/u/uss_kentucky_(bb 6).htm (accessed 30 June 2006).

43. U.S. Navy ship's log, USS *Kentucky,* 26 August 1903, NARA, RG 24.

44. Evans, *Admiral's Log*, 263, 269.

45. U.S. Navy ship's log, USS *Kentucky,* 19 October 1903, NARA, RG 24.

46. Evans, *Admiral's Log*, 269.

47. Braisted, *United States Navy in the Pacific, 1897–1909*, 141.

48. Evans, *Admiral's Log*, 84, 180.

49. Ibid., 268.

50. Braisted, *United States Navy in the Pacific, 1897–1909*, 145.

51. Evans, *Admiral's Log*, 279.

52. Ibid., 280.

53. Ibid., 281–282.

54. Braisted, *United States Navy in the Pacific, 1897–1909*, 148.

55. Evans, *Admiral's Log*, 282.

56. U.S. Navy ship's log, USS *Kentucky*, 5 December 1903, NARA, RG 24.

57. Evans, *Admiral's Log*, 293.

58. Braisted, *United States Navy in the Pacific, 1897–1909*, 151.

59. Evans, *Admiral's Log*, 299.

60. Ibid., 302.

61. Braisted, *United States Navy in the Pacific, 1897–1909*, 152.

62. U.S. Navy Department, CDR Mahan (SOPA Shanghai) to Commanding Officer, *USS Vicksburg*, 25 December 1903, NARA, RG 45.

63. Rear Admiral Uriu, IJN, to SOPA U.S. Navy Chemulpo, 9 February 1904, Library of Congress.

64. Dorwart, *Office of Naval Intelligence*, 80.

65. U.S. Navy ship's log, USS *Kentucky*, 20 January 1904, NARA, RG 24.

66. "The Great Game: The Struggle for Empire in Central Asia," Simon Fraser University, School of Computing Science (SFU Online), http://cs.sfu.ca/nanoop/weblog/archives/000090.html (accessed 14 November 2011).

CHAPTER 3.
The Lure of Naval Intelligence: Ashore in Asia and Back to the Atlantic, 1904–1907

1. "General Order No. 292 (23 March 1882)," Naval History and Heritage Command, Navy Department Library, www.history.navy.mil/library/online/ndl_order292.htm (accessed 14 November 2011); Wyman H. Packard, *A Century of Naval Intelligence* (Washington, D.C.: Office of Naval Intelligence and Naval History Center, 1996), 9.

2. Packard, *Century of Naval Intelligence*, 10, 11.

3. Ibid., 39, 40.

4. Ibid., 40.

5. Ibid., 59, 60.

6. Jeffery M. Dorwart, *The Office of Naval Intelligence: The Birth of America's First Intelligence Agency, 1865–1918* (Annapolis, Md.: Naval Institute Press, 1979), 45.

7. Jack L. Hammersmith, *Spoilsmen in a Flowery Fairyland: The Development of the U.S. Legation in Japan, 1859–1906* (Kent, Ohio: Kent State University Press, 1941), 232, 269.

8. Ibid., 234.

9. Geoffrey Miller, *The Millstone: British Policy in the Mediterranean, 1900–1904* (Yorkshire, U.K.: Manor House, 1999), 1.

10. Yoji Koda, "The Russo-Japanese War: Primary Causes of Japanese Success," *Naval War College Review* 58 (Spring 2005): 1–8.

11. Ibid., 12.

12. Hammersmith, *Spoilsmen*, 241.

13. Packard, *Century of Naval Intelligence*, 60, 61.

14. Hammersmith, *Spoilsmen*, 241.

15. Herbert Croly, *Willard Straight* (New York: Macmillan, 1924), 126.

16. Hammersmith, *Spoilsmen*, 242.

17. Packard, *Century of Naval Intelligence*, 61.

18. Miller, *Millstone*, 1.

19. Edward Morris, *Theodore Rex* (New York: Random House, 2001), 397.

20. Hammersmith, *Spoilsmen*, 240.

21. Dorwart, *Office of Naval Intelligence*, 74.

22. Ibid., 138.

23. Ibid., 36.

24. Ibid., 81.

25. Ibid., 82.

26. Robley D. Evans, *An Admiral's Log: Being Continued Recollections of Naval Life* (New York: D. Appleton, 1910), 180.

27. Ibid., 283.

28. Ibid., 176.

29. Ibid., 303.

30. Hammersmith, *Spoilsmen*, 242.

31. F. M. Huntington-Wilson, *Memoirs of an Ex-Diplomat* (Boston: B. Humphries, 1945), 123.

32. Ibid., 236.

33. Richard Harding Davis, *Three Gringos in Venezuela and Central America* (New York: Harper & Bros., 1896).

34. Croly, *Willard Straight*, 126–136.

35. William R. Braisted, *The United States Navy in the Pacific, 1897–1909* (Austin: University of Texas Press, 1958), 161.

36. Peter Slattery, *Reporting the Russo-Japanese War, 1904–1905* (Kent, U.K.: Global Oriental, 2004), 20–27.

37. Koda, "Russo-Japanese War," 1–8.

38. Dorwart, *Office of Naval Intelligence*, 82.

39. Hammersmith, *Spoilsmen*, 247.

40. "Togo Lost but Three Boats," *New York Times*, 1 June 1905.

41. "Orders to Naval Officers," *Washington Post*, 4 February 1905.

42. Hammersmith, *Spoilsmen*, 247.

43. Ralph Elden Minger, *William Howard Taft and U.S. Foreign Policy: The Apprenticeship Years, 1900–1908* (Urbana: University of Illinois Press, 1975), 142.

44. Braisted, *United States Navy in the Pacific, 1897–1909*, 181.

45. Minger, *William Howard Taft*, 142, 148.

46. Ibid., 150.

47. U.S. Navy, "Report on the Fitness of Officers," Irvin V. Gillis, 3 June–30 June 1905.

48. "USS Atlanta," Navy history.com, http://www.historycentral.com/NAVY/cruiser/Atlanta.html (accessed 6 May 2006).

49. Evans, *Admiral's Log*, 387.

50. "Obituary Notes," *New York Times*, 16 June 1913.

51. Secretary of the Navy to Gillis, 14 February 1907, NARA, RG 38.

52. "Naval Examining Board Proceedings," re: LT I. V. Gillis, 15 April 1907, NARA, RG 24.

53. Invitation to the Ensign Worth Bagley Statue Unveiling Ceremony, 17 May 1907, Manuscript Department, New-York Historical Society, New York.

54. M. Hill Goodspeed, *U.S. Navy: A Complete History* (Washington, D.C.: Naval History Foundation, 2003), 276.

55. Seaton Schroeder, "Gleanings from the Sea of Japan," *Proceedings* (Annapolis. Md., U.S. Naval Institute) 32/1/119 (March 1906).
56. Braisted, *United States Navy in the Pacific, 1897–1909*, 193.
57. Ibid., 204, 205.
58. Packard, *Century of Naval Intelligence*, 11.
59. "Raymond Rodgers, Rear Admiral Dies," *New York Times*, 29 December 1925.
60. Dorwart, *Office of Naval Intelligence*, 83.
61. Braisted, *United States Navy in the Pacific, 1897–1909*, 199–201.
62. Ibid., 196.
63. Ibid., 198, 199.
64. Ibid., 203–205.
65. Ibid., 209.
66. Evans, *Admiral's Log*, 178–194.
67. Bruce Swanson, *Eighth Voyage of the Dragon* (Annapolis, Md.: Naval Institute Press, 1982), 119.
68. Director of Naval Intelligence (DNI) Rodgers to U.S. Naval Attaché to Tokyo, Dougherty, 25 June 1907, NARA, RG 38.
69. Secretary of State Root to Gillis, 23 May 1907, NARA, RG 59.
70. DNI Rodgers to Gillis, 31 May 1907, NARA, RG 38.

CHAPTER 4.
China Naval Attaché and Rocks and Shoals: 1907–1908

1. "Orders to Naval Officers," *Washington Post*, 6 June 1907.
2. Navy Department, DNI, to Chief, Bureau of Navigation, 18 June 1907, NARA RG 45.
3. DNI to President, Fore River Shipbuilding Company, 3 June 1907, NARA, RG 45.
4. Secretary of the Navy to Gillis, 25 June 1907, NARA, RG 38.
5. Secretary of the Navy to Secretary of State, 1 July 1907, NARA, RG 45.
6. "Distinguished Men Sail," *New York Times*, 26 July 1907.
7. Dougherty to DNI Rodgers, 24 August 1907, NARA, RG 38.
8. Gillis to DNI and Secretary of the Navy, 21 September 1907, NARA, RG 38.
9. "Will Inspect Consulates," *Washington Post*, 2 October 1907.

10. "U.S. Consular Officials in China (Shanghai)," and "U.S. Diplomatic Chiefs of Mission to China," China page, Political Graveyard, http://www.politicalgraveyard.com/geo/ZZ/CH.html (accessed 31 May 2006).

11. Kenneth Wimmel, *William Woodville Rockhill, Scholar-Diplomat of the Tibetan Highlands* (Bangkok: Orchid Press, 2003), 39.

12. "Taft at Shanghai," *Washington Post*, 9 October 1907.

13. "Taft's Significant Shanghai Speech," *New York Times*, 24 November 1907.

14. F. M. Huntington-Wilson, *Memoirs of an Ex-Diplomat* (Boston: B. Humphries, 1945), 141.

15. Bruce Swanson, *Eighth Voyage of the Dragon* (Annapolis, Md.: Naval Institute Press, 1982), 116–118.

16. Gillis to DNI Rodgers, 8 January 1908, NARA, RG 38.

17. U.S. Navy, "Report on the Fitness of Officers," Irvin V. Gillis, 16 September–31 December 1907, NARA, RG 24.

18. Navy Department Instruction No. 7850–26 of 19 March 1907, NARA, RG 45.

19. DNI Rodgers to Gillis, 3 June 1907, NARA, RG 38.

20. DNI Rodgers to Gillis, 9 July 1907, NARA, RG 38.

21. Bureau of Navigation to Gillis, 10 July 1907, NARA, RG 38.

22. DNI Rodgers to Gillis, 18 November 1907, NARA, RG 38.

23. Gillis' Intelligence Report No. 10, "Organization of the Navy, etc.," 9 December 1907, NARA, RG 38.

24. Gillis to DNI Rodgers, 8 January 1908, NARA, RG 38.

25. Gillis to DNI Rodgers, 16 January 1908, NARA, RG 38.

26. U.S. Ambassador to Berlin Tower to Secretary of State Root, 16 September 1907, NARA, RG 59.

27. Gillis to DNI Rodgers, 16 January 1908, NARA, RG 38.

28. Gillis to DNI Rodgers, 20 January 1908, NARA, RG 38.

29. DNI Rodgers to Gillis, 12 February 1908, NARA, RG 38.

30. Wimmel, *Rockhill*, 141.

31. Ibid., 8–138.

32. "E. T. Williams, 89, Diplomat, Teacher," obituary, *New York Times*, 29 January 1944.

33. "Colonel Leonard Dead; Lawyer, Soldier," obituary, *Washington Post*, 10 April 1945.

34. Secretary of the Navy to Gillis, 5 March 1908, NARA, RG 38.
35. Gillis to DNI Rodgers, 30 April 1908, NARA, RG 38.
36. Gillis to Secretary of the Navy, 2 May 1908, NARA, RG 38.
37. Gillis to DNI Rodgers, 21 August 1908, NARA, RG 38.
38. Secretary of the Navy to Secretary of State, 17 June 1908, NARA, RG 45.
39. DNI Rodgers to Gillis, 17 June 1908, NARA, RG 38.
40. DNI Rodgers to Gillis, 18 June 1908 (formal letter), NARA, RG 38.
41. DNI Rodgers to Gillis, 18 June 1908, NARA, RG 38.
42. Gillis to ONI, 16 July 1908, NARA, RG 38.
43. Gillis to DNI Rodgers, 21 August 1908, NARA, RG 38.
44. Preceding Croly quotes from Herbert Croly, *Willard Straight* (New York: Macmillan, 1924) 261–265.
45. Ibid., 232.
46. Ibid., 266.
47. Ibid., 250.
48. Wimmel, *Rockhill*, 169.
49. All preceding quotes from Gillis to Rodgers taken from Gillis to DNI Rodgers, 21 August 1908, NARA, RG 38.
50. Wimmel, *Rockhill*, 166.
51. Gillis to DNI Rodgers, 21 August 1908, NARA, RG 38.

CHAPTER 5.
Sea Duty in the Pacific (II), Then Dollar Diplomacy in China: 1908–1914

1. U.S. Navy, "Report on the Fitness of Officers," I. V. Gillis, 21 August–26 November 1908, NARA, RG 24.
2. Kemp Tolley, *Yangtze Patrol: The U.S. Navy in China* (Annapolis, Md.: Naval Institute Press, 1971), 61.
3. "Admiral Harber at Peking," *New York Times*, 4 September 1908.
4. "China Fleet Will Remain Away," *New York Times*, 3 May 1908; "Rockhill Advises Change," *New York Times*, 3 May 1908.
5. William R. Braisted, *The United States Navy in the Pacific, 1897–1909* (Austin: University of Texas Press, 1958), 229.
6. Ibid., 231, 232.
7. "Fine Shooting at Sea," *New York Times*, 28 October 1908.

8. Secretary of the Navy to Gillis, 16 March 1909, NARA, RG 38.

9. Secretary of the Navy to Gillis, 14 April 1909, NARA, RG 38.

10. Chief, Bureau of Navigation, to Gillis, 4 October 1909, NARA, RG 38.

11. "Knox Chooses New Aide," *New York Times*, 10 February 1909.

12. "George Von Lengerke Meyer," 1911 Classic Encyclopedia, www.1911 encyclopedia.org/George_Von_Lengerke_Meyer (accessed 7 February 2007).

13. "Myers and Straight in Russia," *New York Times*, 30 July 1910.

14. "Calhoun to Go to China," *New York Times*, 6 December 1909.

15. "Calhoun Reaches Peking," *New York Times*, 17 April 1910.

16. Herbert Croly, *Willard Straight* (New York: Macmillan, 1924), 283–285.

17. Ibid., 325, 326.

18. William R. Braisted, *The United States Navy in the Pacific, 1909–1922* (Austin: University of Texas Press, 1971), 79, 80.

19. Bruce Swanson, *Eighth Voyage of the Dragon* (Annapolis, Md.: Naval Institute Press, 1982), 120.

20. Braisted, *United States Navy in the Pacific, 1909–1922*, 81.

21. U.S. Navy, "Report on the Fitness of Officers," I. V. Gillis, 17 May–30 June 1909, NARA, RG 24.

22. "USS Michigan (BB 27)," Navy.mil, http://www.chinfo.navy.mil/navpalib/ships/battleships/michigan/bb27-mich.html (accessed 4 February 2007).

23. "Chinese Prince to Visit the U.S.," *Washington Post*, 20 March 1910.

24. "Mr. Taft Dinner Host for Prince Tsai Tao," *Washington Post*, 20 April 1910.

25. "China Looks Westward," *Washington Post*, 2 August 1910.

26. "Mr. Taft Gives a Dinner for Prince Suun of China," *Washington Post*, 28 September 1910.

27. Braisted, *United States Navy in the Pacific, 1909–1922*, 83, 84.

28. Ibid., 83.

29. Swanson, *Eighth Voyage*, 121.

30. "China Will Build Navy," *Washington Post*, 4 December 1910.

31. Acting Secretary of the Navy to Secretary of State, No. 6320/142, 18 October 1910, NARA, RG 59.

32. U.S. Navy, "Report on the Fitness of Officers," I. V. Gillis: 26 November–31 December 1908 (the *Ohio*), 1 July–1 September 1909 (the *Michigan* and the Office of Inspection of Machinery), and 1 April–30 September 1910 (the *Michigan*), NARA, RG 24.

33. "Uncle Sam's Pawnshop Victims," *Washington Post*, 8 August 1909; "Kings' Gifts to the Fleet," *New York Times*, 21 March 1910.

34. Braisted, *The United States Navy in the Pacific, 1909–1922*, 85.

35. "Com. Gillis Buried at Arlington Cemetery," *Washington Post*, 10 December 1910.

36. "Frank B. Upham," absolute astronomy.com, www.absolutehistory. com/reference/frank_b_upham (accessed 2 February 2006).

37. Braisted, *United States Navy in the Pacific, 1909–1922*, 88.

38. "To Build Chinese Ship," *Washington Post*, 13 January 1911.

39. "China and the Bethlehem Steel Co.," *Business History Review* 42, no. 1 (Spring 1968): 53.

40. Swanson, *Eighth Voyage*, 122.

41. Braisted, *United States Navy in the Pacific, 1909–1922*, 88.

42. U.S. Navy, "Report on the Fitness of Officers," I. V. Gillis, 1 April– 30 September 1912, NARA, RG 24.

43. Braisted, *United States Navy in the Pacific, 1909–1922*, 87, 88.

44. "Naval Bill Stirs War Talk in House," *New York Times*, 21 February 1911.

45. "Mikado's Naval Attaché Ridicules Hobson's War Talk," *New York Times*, 26 February 1911.

46. Braisted, *United States Navy in the Pacific, 1909–1922*, 51, 52.

47. Edward S. Miller, *War Plan Orange* (Annapolis, Md.: Naval Institute Press, 1991), 1–3, 24, 25.

48. Braisted, *United States Navy in the Pacific, 1909–1922*, 52.

49. Ibid., 89–92.

50. "Chinese Warship Coming," *Washington Post*, 21 June 1911.

51. Swanson, *Eighth Voyage*, 123–125.

52. Braisted, *United States Navy in the Pacific, 1909–1922*, 91.

53. Frederica M. Bunge and Rinn-Sup Shinn, *China: A Country Study* (Washington, D.C.: Government Printing Office, 1981), 23.

54. Braisted, *United States Navy in the Pacific, 1909–1922*, 92.

55. Wyman H. Packard, *A Century of Naval Intelligence* (Washington, D.C.: Office of Naval Intelligence and Naval History Center, 1996),

11; Jeffery M. Dorwart, *The Office of Naval Intelligence: The Birth of America's First Intelligence Agency, 1865–1918* (Annapolis, Md.: Naval Institute Press, 1979), 93.

56. Braisted, *United States Navy in the Pacific, 1909–1922*, 263–267.
57. Ibid., 125, 126.
58. Ibid., 132, 133.
59. Ibid., 138.
60. Ibid., 264.
61. Ibid.
62. U.S. Navy, "Report on the Fitness of Officers," I. V. Gillis, 1 April–30 September 1913, NARA, RG 24.
63. U.S. Navy, "Report on the Fitness of Officers," I. V. Gillis, 1 October–15 December 1913, NARA, RG 24.
64. Braisted, *United States Navy in the Pacific, 1909–1922*, 265, 266.
65. Lois MacMurray Starkey, "J. V. A. MacMurray: Diplomat and Photographer in China, 1913–1929" (master's thesis, Harvard University, 1990), 61, 62.
66. Braisted, *United States Navy in the Pacific, 1909–1922*, 275–278.
67. Ibid., 273.
68. "Naval Examining Board Proceedings," re: I. V. Gillis, 4 May 1914, NARA, RG 24.
69. Assistant Secretary of the Navy Franklin D. Roosevelt to the President, 7 May 1914, NARA, RG 45.
70. Braisted, *United States Navy in the Pacific, 1909–1922*, 282.

CHAPTER 6.
Career Decision: Gillis Retires and Returns to China, 1914–1917

1. William R. Braisted, *The United States Navy in the Pacific, 1909–1922* (Austin: University of Texas Press, 1971), 282, 283.
2. "British Help for Foreign Navies," Professional Notes, *Proceedings* (Annapolis, Md., U.S. Naval Institute) 40, no. 2 (May–June 1914): 847–848.
3. Braisted, *United States Navy in the Pacific, 1909–1922*, 273.
4. Ibid., 275.
5. Frederica M. Bunge and Rinn-Sup Shinn, *China: A Country Study* (Washington, D.C.: Government Printing Office, 1981), 23.

6. Braisted, *United States Navy in the Pacific, 1909–1922*, 155.

7. Ibid., 158, 159.

8. "Thomas Holcomb, General, USMC," Arlington National Cemetery, http://www.arlingtoncemetery.net/tholcomb.htm (accessed 17 July 2006).

9. "A China Marine's Story," Wehrmacht-Awards.com, http://www.wehrmacht-awards.com/forums/showthread.php?t=83135, chap. 3 (accessed 21 November 2006); "History of the 353rd Infantry Regiment—Col. James H. Reeves," Kansas Collection of Books, http://www.kancoll.org/books/dienst/353-pix-x.html (accessed 16 March 2007).

10. "Captain Charles Thomas Hutchins, USN, Ret., Class of 1901," U.S. Naval Academy Alumni Association and Foundation, http://www.usna.com/Alumni Only (accessed 26 May 2007).

11. "Hutchins-Anglin," *New York Times*, 12 July 1910.

12. "USS Taylor (DD-94)," Answers.com, http://www.answers.com/topic/USS-Taylor (accessed 15 November 2011).

13. "Naval Orders," *New York Times*, 13 June 1919.

14. Alexander Ramsay, *The Peking Who's Who, 1922* (Peking: Tientsin Press, 1922).

15. "S. C. Thomas Sze Remembered through Sibley Endowment," Cornell Chronicle, http://www.news.cornell.edu/Chronicle (accessed 6 September 2006).

16. Thomas Sze, "Captain I. V. Gillis, Founder of the Gest Oriental Library," chapter from the unpublished memoirs of Thomas Sze, undated, GCPU.

17. "Trade with China as a Great Prize—Discussed at a Luncheon Given to the Business Envoys of the Eastern Republic," *New York Times*, 3 June 1915.

18. Braisted, *United States Navy in the Pacific, 1909–1922*, 275.

19. Hu Shih, "The Gest Oriental Library at Princeton University," *Princeton University Library Chronicle* 15, no. 3 (Spring 1954): 113.

20. Paul S. Reinsch, *An American Diplomat in China* (New York: Doubleday, Page, 1922), 90, 91.

21. Ibid., 101–105.

22. Braisted, *United States Navy in the Pacific, 1909–1922*, 282–285.

23. "The Twenty-One Demands," FirstWorldWar.Com, http://firstworld war.com/atoz/21demands.html (accessed 3 April 2007).

24. Braisted, *United States Navy in the Pacific, 1909–1922*, 278, 279.

25. Ibid., 280.

26. Ibid., 280–281.

27. Ibid., 282.

28. Ibid., 283, 284.

29. William R. Braisted, "China, the United States Navy, and the Bethlehem Steel Corporation, 1909–1929," *Business History Review* 42 (Spring 1968): 60–61.

30. Jeffery M. Dorwart, *The Office of Naval Intelligence: The Birth of America's First Intelligence Agency, 1865–1918* (Annapolis, Md.: Naval Institute Press, 1979), 96.

31. Wyman H. Packard, *A Century of Naval Intelligence* (Washington, D.C.: Office of Naval Intelligence and Naval History Center, 1996), 11, 12, 41, 42.

32. DNI Oliver to Gillis, 15 November 1915, NARA, RG 38.

33. DNI (Confidential) to Hutchins, 18 November 1915, NARA, RG 38.

34. DNI to Horne, 19 November 1915, NARA, RG 38.

35. Secretary of the Navy Daniels to Horne, 17 November 1915, NARA, RG 38.

36. DNI to Hutchins, 21 February 1916, NARA, RG 38.

CHAPTER 7.

World War I and Recall to Active Duty: Naval Attaché in Peking, 1917–1919

1. William R. Braisted, *The United States Navy in the Pacific, 1909–1922* (Austin: University of Texas Press, 1971), 292–294.

2. Ibid., 332–335.

3. Timothy D. Saxon, "Anglo-Japanese Naval Cooperation, 1914–1918," *Naval War College Review* 53, no. 1, sequence 369 (Winter 2000): 13.

4. Ibid., 4.

5. Braisted, *United States Navy in the Pacific, 1909–1922*, 319–322.

6. "World Affairs—Lansing-Ishii Agreement, November 2, 1917," u-s-history.com, http://www.u-s-history.com/pages/h1351.html (accessed 26 May 2007).

7. Braisted, *United States Navy in the Pacific, 1909–1922*, 323, 324.

8. Wyman H. Packard, *A Century of Naval Intelligence* (Washington, D.C.: Office of Naval Intelligence and Naval History Center, 1996), 66.

9. Jeffery M. Dorwart, *The Office of Naval Intelligence: The Birth of America's First Intelligence Agency, 1865–1918* (Annapolis, Md.: Naval Institute Press, 1979), 123; William Sowden Sims, *The Victory at Sea* (New York: Doubleday, Page, 1920), 241.

10. Dorwart, *Office of Naval Intelligence*, 123–124.

11. Ibid., 137, 138.

12. Gillis to DNI, 19 November 1917, NARA, RG 38.

13. Dorwart, *Office of Naval Intelligence*, 138.

14. Gillis to ADNI McCauley, 19 October 1917, NARA, RG 38.

15. DNI to Chief of Naval Operations, 13 September 1917, NARA, RG 45.

16. ADNI to Gillis, 18 September 1917, NARA, RG 38.

17. The German minister in Argentina, Graf K. L. Luxburg, with the assistance of the Swedish Embassy there, had transmitted a message to Berlin suggesting that ships carrying supplies for the Entente (countries allied against Germany and its allies) be spared or sunk without trace. The message was intercepted by the Entente and made public by Secretary of State Lansing. The Entente countries levied much criticism against Sweden, resulting in Prime Minister Hjalmar Hammarskjöld's resignation.

18. Gillis to DNI, 19 October 1917, NARA, RG 38.

19. ADNI to Department of State, 2 January 1918, NARA, RG 45.

20. Department of State to ADNI, 8 January 1918, NARA, RG 59.

21. ADNI to Department of State, 14 January 1918, NARA, RG 45.

22. Dorwart, *Office of Naval Intelligence*, 138.

23. Ibid., 138–139.

24. Ibid., 139.

25. Hutchins (U.S. naval attaché, Peking) to DNI, 9 November 1921, NARA, RG 38.

26. L. Lanier Winslow to Acting DNI George Williams, 10 January 1919, NARA, RG 45.

27. DNI Roger Welles Jr. to Gillis, 10 June 1918, NARA, RG 38.

28. NAVINTEL to Gillis, 24 January 1919, NARA, RG 38.

29. Gillis to DNI, 27 October 1917, NARA, RG 38.

30. Gillis to ADNI McCauley, 27 October 1917, NARA, RG 38.

31. DNI to Gillis, 4 December 1917, NARA, RG 38.

32. DNI to Horne, 4 December 1917, NARA, RG 38.

33. Gillis to DNI, 19 November 1917, NARA, RG 38.

34. ADNI to Chairman, Committee on Public Information, 2 January 1918, NARA, RG 45.

35. DNI to Gillis, 14 January 1918, NARA, RG 38.

36. Gillis to DNI (second letter), 19 November 1917, NARA, RG 38.

37. Gillis to DNI (third letter), 19 November 1917, NARA, RG 38.

38. ONI to Gillis, 12 April 1918, NARA, RG 38.

39. Gillis to DNI, 27 May 1918, NARA, RG 38.

40. Gillis to DNI, 29 July 1918, NARA, RG 38.

41. Chairman, War Trade Board, to DNI, 23 August 1918, NARA, RG 45.

42. "We Agree with Japan on China," *New York Times*, 6 November 1917.

43. Braisted, *United States Navy in the Pacific, 1909–1922*, 337.

44. Gillis to DNI (fourth letter), 19 November 1917, NARA, RG 38.

45. Paul S. Reinsch, *An American Diplomat in China* (New York: Doubleday, Page, 1922), 307.

46. Ibid., 364–365.

47. Naval Attaché to Peking Arthur St. Clair Smith to DNI, 4 January 1923, NARA, RG 38.

48. DNI to Gillis, 14 November 1918, NARA, RG 38.

49. ONI to Gillis, 20 November 1918, NARA, RG 38.

50. Gillis to ONI, 22 November 1918, NARA, RG 38.

51. Gillis to ONI, 28 November 1918, NARA, RG 38.

52. DNI to Gillis, 25 November 1918, NARA, RG 38.

53. Gillis to DNI, 3 January 1919, NARA, RG 38.

54. U.S. Navy, "Report on the Fitness of Officers," I. V. Gillis, 1 October 1918–31 January 1919, NARA, RG 24.

55. "Naval Orders," *New York Times*, 12 June 1919.

56. Braisted, *United States Navy in the Pacific, 1909–1922*, 383.

57. Ibid., 444.

58. "Japan's Position Today and Her Attitude Towards the United States," Gillis's report to ONI, 25 September 1919, NARA, RG 38.

59. "Full Text Citations for Award of the Navy Cross to Members of the U.S. Navy, World War I," Home of Heroes, http://www.home ofheroes.com/verify/1_Citations/nc_02_WWI_Navy-ADM.html (accessed 4 August 2004).

60. "Japanese Arrest Americans in Korea," *New York Times*, 14 April 1919.

61. "USS Gillis (AVD-12, DD-260)," 1996–2011 NavSource Naval History, http://www.navsource.org/archives/09/56/56612/htm (accessed 20 November 2011).

62. "Exchange of Notes Respecting the Fukien Question," *Peking Leader*, 15 March 1919.

63. "Reinsch Resigns His Post in Peking," *New York Times*, 28 August 1919.

64. "Farewell to Reinsch," *New York Times*, 23 September 1919.

65. "Swatow, China; Re visit of Japanese Cruiser AKITSUSHIMA and failure to take American pilot," ONI report from "K," 23 September 1919, NARA, RG 38.

66. Gillis to Electric Boat Company, 28 September 1919, photocopy in author's possession.

67. "China Pays Reinsch $20,000 a Year," *New York Times*, 6 October 1919.

68. "Reinsch Expects Japan to Restore Shantung," *New York Times*, 10 October 1919.

69. Electric Boat Company to Gillis, 28 November 1919, photocopy in author's possession.

70. Marjorie Murray Burtt, "Murray Myths and Legends," unpublished family history, 30, e-mail communication from Martha Gates Mawson to Vance Morrison, 1 January 2010.

71. Ibid., 32.

CHAPTER 8.
Gillis as a Civilian in China: 1919–1948

1. "The Early Rule of the Manchus—Civil War," *The World Book Encyclopedia*, vol. 3 (Chicago: World Book, 2008), 502–504.

2. Martin J. Heijdra, "The East Asian Library and the Gest Collection at Princeton University," in *Collecting East Asia: East Asian Libraries in North America, 1868–2008*, ed. Peter X. Zhou (Ann Arbor, Mich.: Association for Asian Studies, 2010), 122.

3. Ibid., 122–123; Thomas Sze, "Captain I. V. Gillis, Founder of the Gest Oriental Library," chapter from the unpublished memoirs of Thomas Sze, undated, GCPU.

4. Su Chen and Juming Zhao, "The Gest Chinese Research Library at McGill University, 1926–1936," *East Asian Library Journal* 11, no. 2 (Autumn 2004): 53.

5. Heijdra, "East Asian Library," 122.

6. Su and Juming, "Gest Chinese Research Library," 53.

7. Heijdra, "East Asian Library," 122.

8. Ibid., 124.

9. Dr. de Resillac-Roese Report on Gest Chinese Research Library, 30 May 1929, GCPU.

10. Heijdra, "East Asian Library," 124.

11. Gillis to Currie, 28 October 1929, GCPU.

12. Heijdra, "East Asian Library," 123.

13. Ibid., 124.

14. Dorothy Perkins, "The War of Resistance against Japan (1937–1945)," *Encyclopedia of China: The Essential Reference to China—Its History and Culture* (Warwick, N.Y.: Roundtable, 1999), 555.

15. Heijdra, "East Asian Library," 125.

16. Dr. de Resillac-Roese Report on Gest Chinese Research Library, July–September 1931, GCPU.

17. Gillis to Swann, 9 January 1937, GCPU.

18. Heijdra, "East Asian Library," 125.

19. Gillis to Swann, 10 July 1932, GCPU.

20. Gillis to Swann, 12 March 1932, GCPU.

21. Gillis to Swann, 4 April 1933, GCPU.

22. Gillis to Swann, 1 October 1933, GCPU.

23. Gillis to Swann, 5 October 1937, GCPU.

24. Gillis to Swann, 28 September 1933, GCPU.

25. Gillis to Swann, 2 August 1934, GCPU.

26. Gillis to Swann, 4 December 1934, GCPU.

27. Gillis to Swann, 10 February 1935, GCPU.

28. Heijdra, "East Asian Library," 125–126.

29. Gillis to Swann, 5 November 1936, GCPU.

30. Gillis to Gest, 14 January 1937, GCPU.

31. Heijdra, "East Asian Library," 126–127.

32. Lois MacMurray Starkey, "J. V. A. MacMurray: Diplomat and Photographer in China, 1913–1929" (master's thesis, Harvard University, 1990).

33. Gillis to MacMurray 3 May 1921, GCPU.

34. Gillis to MacMurray, 19 July 1925, GCPU.

35. MacMurray papers, EALPU.

36. John A. Logan, "'Ta Wha' (Big Talk)," 1954, 4–5, unpublished manuscript, EALPU.

37. Naval Attaché, China, to Office of Naval Intelligence, 7 July 1921, NARA, RG 38.

38. Heijdra, "East Asian Library," 135.

39. "President Harding's Proclamation on Embargo on Shipment of Arms to China," *China Review* 2, no. 1 (January 1922): 163.

40. Gillis to Casey, 25 February 1924, GCPU.

41. Perkins, "War of Resistance," 555.

42. Ibid., 171.

43. Gillis to Swann, 16 October 1940, GCPU.

44. Swann to Gillis, 20 February 1941, GCPU.

45. Gillis to Swann, 2 March 1941, GCPU.

46. Gillis to Swann, 17 April 1941, GCPU.

47. Gillis to Swann, 30 May 1941 GCPU.

48. Ibid.

49. Edward H. Hume, Chairman, North American Council of Chinese Studies, to Gillis, 20 June 1941, GCPU.

50. Gillis to Swann, 9 July 1941, GCPU.

51. Gillis to Swann, 12 November 1941, GCPU.

52. Heijdra, "East Asian Library," 123.

53. Gillis to Swann, 28 February 1946, GCPU.

54. Gillis to Swann, 19 December 1932, GCPU.

55. Gillis to Swann, 26 February 1933, GCPU.

56. Gillis to Swann, 22 July 1934, GCPU.

57. Gillis to Swann, 12 November 1941, GCPU.

58. Provost Marshal to Murray, 3 October 1945, GCPU.

59. Gillis to Murray, 19 October 1945, GCPU.

60. Swann to Gillis, 8 February 1946, GCPU.

61. Gillis to Swann, 28 February 1946, GCPU.

62. Gillis to Swan, 17 April 1946, GCPU.

63. Gillis to Swann, 12 June 1946, GCPU.

64. Gillis to Swann, 15 October 1946, GCPU.

65. Swann to Gillis, November 1946, GCPU.

66. Gillis to Swann, 6 March 1947, GCPU.

67. Swann to Gillis, 2 June 1947, GCPU.

68. Gillis to Swann, 8 July 1947, GCPU.

69. Gillis to Swann, 13 August 1947, GCPU.

70. Hu Shih, "The Gest Oriental Library at Princeton University," *Princeton University Library Chronicle* 15, no. 3 (Spring 1954): 116.

71. Ibid., 120–121.

72. International Lodge Roster of Members, 31 August 1948, Honnold/ Mudd Library, Claremont, Calif.

73. "Class Year of 1894," *Shipmate,* December 1948, 28.

BIBLIOGRAPHY

Archival Sources

The names and citations of archival sources used in the notes have been abbreviated as follows:

EALPU   East Asian Library, Princeton University, Princeton, N.J.

GCPU   Gest Collection, Princeton University, Princeton, N.J.

NARA   National Archives and Records Administration, Washington, D.C.

    RG 24   Record Group 24 (ship's deck logs and personnel records)

    RG 38   Record Group 38 (naval attaché communications)

    RG 45   Record Group 45 (chief of naval operations and classified documents)

    RG 59   Record Group 59 (State Department communications)

SCNL   Special Collections, Nimitz Library, U.S. Naval Academy, Annapolis, Md.

Books, Magazine and Journal Articles, and Unpublished Manuscripts

Annual Report of the Secretary of the Navy for the Year 1888. Washington, D.C.: Government Printing Office, 1888.

Bastert, Russell H. "A New Approach to the Origins of Blaine's Pan American Policy." *Hispanic American Historical Review* 39, no. 3 (August 1959).

Braisted, William R. "China, the United States Navy, and the Bethlehem Steel Corporation, 1909–1929." *Business History Review* 42 (Spring 1968).

———. *The United States Navy in the Pacific, 1897–1909.* Austin: University of Texas Press, 1958.

———. *The United States Navy in the Pacific, 1909–1922.* Austin: University of Texas Press, 1971.

Bunge, Frederica M., and Rinn-Sup Shinn. *China: A Country Study.* Washington, D.C.: Government Printing Office, 1981.

Chen, Su, and Juming Zhao. "The Gest Chinese Research Library at McGill University, 1926–1936." *East Asian Library Journal* 11, no. 2 (Autumn 2004).

"Class Year of 1894." *Shipmate,* December 1948.

Croly, Herbert. *Willard Straight.* New York: Macmillan, 1924.

Davis, Richard Harding. *Three Gringos in Venezuela and Central America.* New York: Harper & Bros., 1896.

Dorwart, Jeffery M. *The Office of Naval Intelligence: The Birth of America's First Intelligence Agency, 1865–1918.* Annapolis, Md.: Naval Institute Press, 1979.

Doyel, Ginger. "Plebe Summer 1904." *Shipmate,* July–August 2004.

Evans, Robley D. *An Admiral's Log: Being Continued Recollections of Naval Life.* New York: D. Appleton, 1910.

———. *A Sailor's Log.* New York: D. Appleton, 1908.

Fremont, John C., Jr. "Torpedo-Boat Service." *Harper's New Monthly Magazine,* November 1898.

Goodspeed, M. Hill. *U.S. Navy: A Complete History.* Washington, D.C.: Naval History Foundation, 2003.

Hagan, Kenneth J. *The People's Navy.* New York: Free Press, 1991.

Hamersly, Lewis R., ed. *The Records of Living Officers of the U.S. Navy and Marine Corps.* 4th ed. Philadelphia: L. R. Hamersly, 1890.

———. *Who's Who in Pennsylvania.* New York: L. R. Hamersly, 1904.

Hammersmith, Jack L. *Spoilsmen in a Flowery Fairyland: The Development of the U.S. Legation in Japan, 1859–1906.* Kent, Ohio: Kent State University Press, 1941.

Heijdra, Martin J. "The East Asian Library and the Gest Collection at Princeton University." In *Collecting East Asia: East Asian Libraries in North America, 1868–2008,* ed. Peter X. Zhou. Ann Arbor, Mich.: Association for Asian Studies, 2010.

History of the Counties of McKean, Elk, Cameron, and Potter, Penna., with Biographical Sketches. Chicago: J. H. Beers, 1890.

Huntington-Wilson, F. M. *Memoirs of an Ex-Diplomat.* Boston: B. Humphries, 1945.

Kell, John McIntosh. *Recollections of a Naval Life*. Washington, D.C.: Neale, 1900.

Kelly, J. D. Jerrald. "The United States Naval Academy." *Harper's New Monthly Magazine*, July 1888.

Kipling, Rudyard. *Rudyard Kipling's Verse, Inclusive Edition, 1885–1919*. Garden City, N.Y.: Doubleday, Page, 1919.

Koda, Yoji. "The Russo-Japanese War: Primary Causes of Japanese Success." *Naval War College Review* 58 (Spring 2005).

The Lucky Bag. Annapolis, Md.: U.S. Naval Academy, 1894.

Mahan, Alfred Thayer. *The Influence of Sea Power upon History, 1660–1783*. Boston: Little, Brown, 1890.

McKnight, W. J. *A Pioneer Outline History of Northwestern Pennsylvania, 1780–1850*. Philadelphia: Lippincott, 1905.

Miller, Edward S. *War Plan Orange*. Annapolis, Md.: Naval Institute Press, 1991.

Miller, Geoffrey. *The Millstone: British Policy in the Mediterranean*. Yorkshire, U.K.: Manor House, 1999.

Millis, Walter. *The Martial Spirit: A Study of Our War with Spain*. Boston: Houghton Mifflin, 1931.

Minger, Ralph Elden. *William Howard Taft and U.S. Foreign Policy: The Apprenticeship Years, 1900–1908*. Urbana: University of Illinois Press, 1975.

Morris, Edward. *Theodore Rex*. New York: Random House, 2001.

Nebrida, Victor. *The Balangiga Massacre: Getting Even*. Los Angeles: Philippine History Group, 1977.

Northrop, W. B. "Capturing a Plunging Torpedo." Illus. by F. W. Burton. *English Illustrated Magazine* 47 (February 1907).

Packard, Wyman H. *A Century of Naval Intelligence*. Washington, D.C.: Office of Naval Intelligence and Naval History Center, 1996.

Perkins, Dorothy. "The War of Resistance against Japan (1937–1945)." *Encyclopedia of China: The Essential Reference to China—Its History and Culture*. Warwick, N.Y.: Roundtable, 1999.

Portrait and Biographical Album, Henry County, Iowa. Chicago: Acme Publishing, 1888.

"President Harding's Proclamation on Embargo on Shipment of Arms to China." *China Review* 2, no. 1 (January 1922).

Ramsay, Alexander. *The Peking Who's Who, 1922*. Peking: Tientsin Press, 1922.

Reinsch, Paul S. *An American Diplomat in China*. New York: Doubleday, Page, 1922.

Richardson, Walter G. "Life and Study at the Naval Academy." *New England Magazine* 14, no. 3 (May 1893).

Saxon, Timothy D. "Anglo-Japanese Naval Cooperation, 1914–1918." *Naval War College Review* 53, no. 1, sequence 369 (Winter 2000).

Schroeder, Seaton. "Gleanings from the Sea of Japan." *Proceedings* (Annapolis, Md.: U.S. Naval Institute) 32/1/119 (March 1906).

Shih, Hu. "The Gest Oriental Library at Princeton University." *Princeton University Library Chronicle* 15, no. 3 (Spring 1954).

Simpson, Richard V. *Building the Mosquito Fleet: The U.S. Navy's First Torpedo Boats*. Charleston, S.C.: Arcadia, 2001.

Sims, William Sowden. *The Victory at Sea*. New York: Doubleday, Page, 1920.

Slattery, Peter. *Reporting the Russo-Japanese War, 1904–1905*. Kent, U.K.: Global Oriental, 2004.

Starkey, Lois MacMurray. "J. V. A. MacMurray: Diplomat and Photographer in China, 1913–1929." Master's thesis, Harvard University, 1990.

Stickney, Joseph L. *Admiral Dewey at Manila and the Complete Story of the Philippines: Life and Glorious Deeds of Admiral George Dewey*. Chicago: Imperial Publishing, 1899.

Swanson, Bruce. *Eighth Voyage of the Dragon*. Annapolis, Md.: Naval Institute Press, 1982.

Sze, Thomas. "Captain I. V. Gillis, Founder of the Gest Oriental Library." Chapter from the unpublished memoirs of Thomas Sze, undated, GCPU.

Tolley, Kemp. *Yangtze Patrol: The U.S. Navy in China*. Annapolis, Md.: Naval Institute Press, 1971.

Unattributed. "Our Hero." *Poems of Dewey and the Philippines*. Quoted in *Admiral Dewey at Manila and the Complete Story of the Philippines: Life and Glorious Deeds of Admiral George Dewey*, by Joseph L. Stickney. Chicago: Imperial Publishing, 1899.

"USS Annapolis: The Wardroom and Crew Mess." *Naval Engineers Journal* 115, no. 1 (Winter 2003).

Wheeler, Gerald E. *Admiral William Veazie Pratt, U.S. Navy*. Washington, D.C.: Naval History Division, Department of the Navy, 1974.

Wimmel, Kenneth. *William Woodville Rockhill, Scholar-Diplomat of the Tibetan Highlands*. Bangkok: Orchid Press, 2003.

Young, James Rankin, and J. Hampton Moore. *History of Our War with Spain*. Philadelphia: National Publishing, 1898.

INDEX

About the Author

BRUCE SWANSON was a China specialist for forty-three years. Fluent in Chinese Mandarin, he held an MS in the subject from Georgetown University and then earned an MBA from Loyola College in Baltimore, Maryland. As a U.S. naval officer he served in Asia for six years and traveled extensively in that region.

A well-known authority on Chinese maritime affairs, Swanson lectured at the U.S. Naval Academy and the Naval Postgraduate School in Monterey, California. His many articles on the Chinese navy and his frequent participation in conferences related to the maritime environment in Asia earned him international respect.

After retirement from the Navy, Swanson was employed as a strategy analyst at the Center for Naval Analyses in Alexandria, Virginia, and then as a defense contractor in Marietta, Georgia, where he lived with his wife, RoseAnn, his four children, and their families. Swanson died suddenly in late 2007, but just prior to his passing, requested that his nearly finished draft about I. V. Gillis be completed and published.

Following Swanson's untimely death, his manuscript was completed by Captain Vance Morrison, U.S. Navy (Ret.), former U.S. and acting defense attaché to the People's Republic of China; Rear Admiral Don McDowell, U.S. Navy (Ret.), former commander Naval Security Group Command; and Dr. Nancy Tomasko, former editor of the *East Asian Library Journal*, Princeton University.